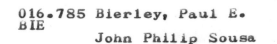

016.785 Bierley, Paul E.
BIE
        John Philip Sousa

                                749476

DATE			

MUSIC IN AMERICAN LIFE

Books in the series:

Only a Miner: Studies in Recorded Coal-Mining Songs
ARCHIE GREEN

Great Day Coming: Folk Music and the American Left
R. SERGE DENISOFF

JOHN PHILIP SOUSA
A Descriptive Catalog
of His Works

PAUL E. BIERLEY

JOHN PHILIP SOUSA

A
DESCRIPTIVE CATALOG
OF HIS WORKS

UNIVERSITY OF ILLINOIS PRESS
Urbana   Chicago   London

To my wife Pauline,
whose patience made
it possible.

FOREWORD

In his recently published *Theme and Variations*, violinist-philosopher Yehudi Menuhin claims that "national ambitions and technological progress go hand in hand with the tonic-dominant harmonies of the Sousa march!" This seems a curious oversimplification; I doubt, for one thing, that a statistical count would show tonic-dominant harmonies to be proportionately any more numerous in Sousa marches than they are in Beethoven symphonies — an amendment Mr. Menuhin might accept, since in his book he is contrasting Western technology and the harmonic system with Indian culture and the greater tonal sophistication of its music. Yet it remains that Mr. Menuhin equated Sousa with technological progress, and so I find it amusing to observe that the first substantial book on Sousa has been written not by a professional musical scholar but by a musician who is by profession an engineer.

Yehudi Menuhin is among the small though growing number of American musicians who have been attracted toward the esoteric East. Other musicians and scholars have started to look closer to home for their esoterica, as with Gottschalk and Scott Joplin. The musicology factories have at last turned their attention to American music, but they have not yet worked their way forward to post–Civil War developments. Paul Bierley, on the other hand, has for years been amassing enormous amounts of information about the composer who I think more than any other represents the mainstream of American music in the general public consciousness, here and abroad. This book, a compendium of information about Sousa's works, is one result; another is to be a biography, separately published.

Paul Bierley is not the only or even the first person to have undertaken a "life and works of John Philip Sousa." I have lost count of those who, over the years, have announced in one way or another that they were writing "the" book on Sousa, only to fade away as the enormity of the research problem became plain. Only Paul Bierley, with the help of his patient Pauline, spent weeks combing the record books in the Copyright Office to compile the copyright data which form an important contribution of this book. Only Paul Bierley, so far as I am aware, gained access to the trunkloads of manuscript materials that were long stored in the Sousa family's Long Island home. Only Paul Bierley has methodically worked the mines, not only at the Library of Congress but at the University of Illinois and Stetson University and the Marine Band and the Sousa Band's fraternal organization and goodness knows where else (my Sousa memory, unlike Paul's, is finite). Not until all these sources were exhausted and the contents sifted and collated could this extraordinary catalog of the works of John Philip Sousa be published.

I say "catalog" because, being a music reference librarian, I find that aspect of the book most delights me. Yet it is a pleasure to point out that for once we reference librarians will also have an easy means of answering the kind of question we often get and often cannot answer: "What is the story behind the piece?" Who, for instance, could ever guess that the "Resumption

March" (1879) was so named in honor of the return to the use of gold and silver coins after the inflation and depression following the Civil War? (And will we have another of the same title in 1979?) It is not merely the marches that are thus explained, and documented, with locations of the manuscripts and copyright data, with anecdotes and frequent comments on musical features; it is also the operettas and the songs and the suites and fantasies and novels and miscellaneous writings and all the Sousa works that are so little known today. One might say that Mr. Bierley has found some esoterica of his own right in the mainstream.

The author is quite aware that much of Sousa's work, apart from the marches, seems very dated at present, that the taste of the moment is not for period pieces of that vintage. This situation may very well change with time, and Paul Bierley freely admits that he sees his role partly as that of missionary, bringing the message of Sousa to the unaware as well as to the many devotees, bandmasters, players, and others who are aware. For myself, as a person, I am content to thrill to the marches and not worry about the long view. As a reference librarian, however, I am grateful for Paul Bierley's ardent enthusiasm for and dedication to the works of Sousa, all the works of Sousa. They have resulted in this book — a vast treasure of information patiently gathered and engagingly presented. Information is, of course, only as good as it is accurate. Over the years, when confronted with seemingly unanswerable Sousa questions, I have had frequent occasion to give thanks for the accuracy as well as for the breadth and variety of Paul Bierley's information — and most of all for his unfailing kindness in sharing with me his store of information, a unique store that now is happily available to all.

WILLIAM LICHTENWANGER

Music Division, Library of Congress
September, 1972

ACKNOWLEDGMENTS

This book had its beginnings in February, 1963, when I started research for a book about the marches of John Philip Sousa. Soon the need for a definitive catalog of all of Sousa's works, both musical and literary, became obvious. Such a catalog had never been possible, because many unknown or forgotten Sousa music manuscripts had lain unsorted in the basement archives of his home on Sands Point, Long Island. Thanks to the efforts of Dr. Frank Simon, I had the extreme good fortune of gaining the confidence of Sousa's younger daughter, Mrs. Helen Sousa Abert, and I am grateful to her for permission to study those manuscripts and other documents.

I soon realized that a book about Sousa's works could not be written without a detailed study of Sousa the man, because most of his compositions and literary works were related to events in his life. The resultant volume on Sousa's life and works grew too large, and a biography was written separately as *John Philip Sousa: American Phenomenon.*

There are many persons whose assistance in gathering information is gratefully acknowledged. Foremost is Dr. Kenneth Berger, author of *The March King and His Band;* his index of Sousa's works in that volume was of inestimable help in my early cataloguing efforts. And my undying thanks go to Dr. Leonard Smith, conductor of the Detroit Concert Band, for his generous programming of unfamiliar Sousa compositions and for his personal counseling. As a composer himself, he provided much insight into Sousa's composing processes.

Special thanks also go to Dr. Harold Spivacke and William Lichtenwanger of the Music Division and James Smart of the Recorded Sound Section of the Library of Congress — to Mr. Lichtenwanger in particular for guidance and personal sleuthing extending beyond his regular call of duty. Also thanks to Margaret Harman, James Boxley, and John Boyle of the Copyright Division. Others who helped in the collection of copyright data include my wife Pauline, my daughter Lois, and Nancy Aitel.

Of much importance was the study of various sections of the Sousa Band library and the widely scattered Sousa music manuscripts. In this capacity I am grateful to Professors Richard Feasel, Guy Duker, Mark Hindsley, Leonard Meretta, and Wesley Shepard, Major Dale Harpham, Major E. L. Kirby, Chief Warrant Officer Joan Ambrose, Joseph Frantik, Richard Leonard, and Marietta Ward.

Those who played under John Philip Sousa's direction provided a wealth of useful information regarding the performance of Sousa's music, as well as encouragement and inspiration. Among them were Dr. Frank Simon, Louis Morris, Edmund Wall, James Friberg, Eugene Slick, Harold Stephens, John Heney, Meredith Willson, William Bell, Donald Bassett, and Vane Kensinger.

Friendships are strengthened when a common interest is shared; my research would have been much less complete had it not been for the understanding and help of Dr. Mark Foutch, Dr. Harry Begian, Robert Hoe, Richard Harris, T. H. Corrie,

Oliver Graham, Glenn Bridges, Major Edward Connin, Captain Frank McGuire, Thomas Bardwell, Herbert Johnston, and David Stackhouse. And one person in particular whose encouragement went a long way toward making this a better book is Dr. Raymond Dvorak.

An undertaking such as this would be more tedious were it not for the cooperation of many dedicated librarians. I am particularly grateful to Elizabeth Hartman, Ruth Bleeker, Olga Buth, John Miller, Philip Miller, Richard Jackson, Shirley Solvick, William Donovan, Dougal Pendergast, Alice Paulin, Petta Khouw, and the following staff members of the Library of Congress Music Division: Edward Waters, Carroll Wade, William Parsons, Jon Newsom, Wayne Shirley, Rodney Mill, Anthony Doherty, and Elizabeth Auman.

Among many other persons who helped in various capacities, I express my thanks to Sir Vivian Dunn, Major James Howe, Drs. M. E. Wilson and Richard Franko Goldman, Sid Rosen, Uno Andersson, Darwin Maurer, Harold Hudson, Loyd Bulmer, Steve Gilman, Sergeant James Hedges, my son John, and a gentleman who prefers to be known only as Gidaon.

I am grateful to countless persons for assistance in collecting background information on Sousa's works, but especially to the following: John Smucker, Edward Kasten, Gerald Whitaker, William O'Brien, Stanley Adams, Professor Harold Shanet, Walter Ross, Katherine Spencer, Ann McCormick, Philip Lundeberg, Margaret Stace, Micki McDonald, Milton Hallman, Wyman Spano, Robert Lopez, Virginia Hawley, John Kilbourne, Allan Ottley, Martina Brown, Dorothy Ginn, Charles Andrews, K. C. Harrison, Howard Ferguson, Gordon Mapes, Robert McCarthy, Kay Hardesty, R. N. Hamilton, H. J. Comenech, Colonel John Stone, Colonel Lewis Hittemore, Major Leslie Pletcher, Lieutenant Glendon Wier, H. Durston II, Julius Frandsen, Alfred Lief, Mark Fisher, J. F. McGlinchy, Walter Buechele, Harry Schwartz, Patrick Foley, Calvin Hawkinson, W. B. Schroeder, and J. T. Willingham.

For critical examination of many parts of this manuscript I am especially grateful to Jane Koerner and Ainsley Smithyman, and also to Daniel Stevens, James Porter, Elmer Stasney, John Callender, Enoch Balcer, Samuel Jackson, Frank Koerner, Kenneth Mackay, Charles Pearce, Paul Matthews, Gilbert Lester, Samuel Ghianni, Charles Bailey, Frederick McQuilken, Harry Fuller, Pierce Robinson, Clyde Greer, Walter Crusoe, and Thomas Banks.

CONTENTS

INTRODUCTION

The purpose of this book is to make known to the world all the musical and literary works of the American composer John Philip Sousa. In discussing each musical work, background information is presented to be used conveniently for concert program material and for analytical studies. I have made every attempt to answer questions about each composition: When and where was it written? Who or what inspired it? What is the origin of the title? To whom or what was it dedicated? How popular did it become? Who published it? Are there interesting stories associated with it?

I have endeavored to be objective; this book should in no way be construed as a critique of Sousa's works. It was my sincere desire to present these works in such a manner that the way will be paved for future scholars who wish to analyze or pass judgment on them. No comprehensive catalog of Sousa's efforts has previously existed.

John Philip Sousa earned his rank in the world of music by doing two things better than anyone else. First, he was unsurpassed as a composer of marches; second, he was the most successful bandmaster who ever lived.

It is unfortunate that Sousa has become stereotyped as a march writer, because his creativity extended into many other areas. He actually composed a greater total volume of music than almost any other American. He composed for so many different media that it is indeed remarkable that he is remembered only as a march composer and bandmaster.

Sousa was one of the pioneers of American operetta. His early stage works, *The Smugglers* (1882), *Desiree* (1883), and *The Queen of Hearts* (1885), made scarcely a ripple in the music world, but they were landmarks among American theater productions of that era. In contrast, his later operettas, *El Capitan* (1895), *The Bride Elect* (1897), *The Free Lance* (1905), and *The American Maid* (1909), met with much greater success and rivaled the works of more prominent composers in the field.

Next to the operettas, the suites are the most important. They are programmatic in content and were all written originally for band. Like most of his songs, they faded into perhaps undeserved oblivion because they were period pieces. His humoresques and fantasies, although also unique and highly entertaining, likewise met their fate because they bore the stamp of a specific period. Most of these pieces are considered obsolete today, but one should not assume that they will be shelved forever, because they are rich in Americana and are not devoid of musical value.

Despite the abundance of his other compositions, Sousa will always be remembered for his marches. These compact pieces have stood the test of time, and few would question his right to the title "March King." Many writers have observed that Sousa was to the march what Strauss was to the waltz.

Over the years, the familiar Sousa favorites have served to standardize the march form as it is known today, and several of his marches may correctly be classified as miniature masterpieces. With these stirring

1

melodies he expressed love for a native land as few other composers ever have. In particular, "The Stars and Stripes Forever" is a priceless expression of patriotism and is generally regarded as the greatest march ever written. Sousa was a product of the era during which the United States became a world power, and his marches proudly heralded the glory of that era.

It is a strange phenomenon of musical history that if there had been a "hit parade" of popular tunes in the 1890's, several of Sousa's marches would have been at the top of the list. This is particularly true of "The Washington Post" (1889), which was adopted by dancemasters for use as a "two-step" and vaulted into international fame. Because of the widespread use of this and other marches, and because of his reputation as a touring bandmaster, he was probably the most popular musician the world had ever known.

Sousa had considerable impact on America's musical taste. Ever the pioneer in the cause of good music, he personally performed before more live audiences than almost any other individual in the history of entertainment. At the turn of the century, the Sousa Band was actually the artistic equal of most of the country's leading symphony orchestras, and in its many travels the band did much to convince the world that the United States was no longer a cultural void.

Sousa's impact on the music world was multifaceted. He had a profound influence on the status and development of bands throughout the world, and he made his mark in operetta. But his influence was also felt in other areas — such as jazz, for instance, for it was he who awakened Europe to ragtime, and he also contributed to the acceptance of jazz by programming it regularly before millions of listeners.

He also had a considerable influence on the recording industry, thanks to hundreds of recordings of the studio organizations called Sousa's Band and the early recordings made by the U.S. Marine Band while he was director. Recordings of his music by many other organizations added to his laurels. It now seems strange that for most

of his career he was opposed to recording and that he declined to conduct at recording sessions except on rare occasions. In 1906 he berated the recording empire in a series of derisive magazine articles and coined the phrase "canned music."

His influence also extended to radio, although not to any appreciable extent. He fought the broadcasting industry through the American Society of Composers, Authors, and Publishers (ASCAP), in which he was a charter member, but near the end of his career he consented to a series of broadcasts.

Sousa was so active as a traveling entertainer that it is astonishing that he found time to compose such a large quantity of music and to write books and articles as well. It must be remembered that he toured extensively over a thirty-nine-year period and that he also spent over nineteen years of his life in military service. Moreover, his arrangements and transcriptions of other composers' music are almost as numerous as his own compositions.

Entertainment has changed so drastically in the present century that it is difficult to imagine that John Philip Sousa was once the most widely known musician in the world. This he was because of the almost unbelievable popularity of his marches and because he had an obsession for giving audiences what they wanted to hear.

One must think of Sousa as an entertainer as well as a composer, because he appeared on stages throughout the world for over six decades. As such he was an active promoter of his own music. His popularity was insured by the sale of his sheet music, which at the turn of the century was being played on almost every imaginable instrument. This was an era without radio, television, movies, or a mobile population. With his fame thus preceding him, it was a big event when the "March King" came to town.

It is interesting to note that more people today can watch a television program of national interest than saw the Sousa Band perform in its entire thirty-nine-year history. However, the point to remember is that Sousa personally took his music to his audiences, traveling well over a million miles. He became an American institution — and a millionaire — in a period in which this would seem highly unlikely, and he carried with him a group of several dozen performers.

The Sousa Band was strictly a concert organization presenting formal programs; it was not a marching band. It was the acknowledged model of perfection in popular entertainment, primarily because Sousa paid salaries high enough to attract some of the finest musicians in the world. No small number of the performers were established artists.

Variety and timing were partly responsible for the Sousa Band's success in programming. The progressive Sousa even featured violinists and vocalists at his concerts, and virtually no musical form was slighted, traditional or contemporary. The most common melody was performed with precision and finesse. As for the classical selections which were sprinkled through his programs, it is well to remember that Sousa brought classics to dozens of cities and towns where the sound of a symphony orchestra had never been heard. Sousa also played a considerable amount of contemporary music. He was perhaps a bit forward in pointing out that his band had done more for the cause of good music than any symphony orchestra in existence at that time, but it was indeed true. Since he was one of the most polished conductors of his era, he captured the fancy of an audience with nearly anything he chose to play.

Showmanship also contributed to the success of the Sousa Band. Sousa was a showman par excellence, and he gathered about him a corps of show-wise musicians. Musicianship was paramount, but each candidate for the band also had to display outstanding stage presence. Since humor played a vital part in most concerts, showmanship was necessary for the success of humoresques and novelty numbers.

Another factor which contributed to Sousa's success was his contagious patriotism. His was not a superficial patriotism; he lived and breathed it, and it was obvi-

ous in both his music and his personal conduct. His love of country blossomed during the Spanish-American War and World War I, when he inspired huge audiences to patriotic demonstrations. And strangely, during those periods America was at war with the lands of his parents. Sousa clearly was born at an opportune moment in history. It is safe to assume that the world would not have accepted his brand of music so enthusiastically had he lived at any other time.

All facets of Sousa's personality found their way into his music at one time or another — his optimism, his determination, his high moral standards, his kindliness, his sense of justice, his self-discipline, his love of sports, his subtle humor. But something of extreme importance not reflected in much of his music was his humility and unassuming manner. He composed only when caught up by genuine inspirations, and his writings are full of references to the "Higher Power" which he credited with being the source of all his creativity. He composed because he felt obliged to compose, not because of mercenary motives. Seldom did he accept commissions for new works.

Had Sousa not been appointed leader of the U.S. Marine Band, he likely would have distinguished himself in the field of operetta. And had he not passed up an opportunity for a European musical education, his music would surely have been of a different nature. Although he had an uncanny knowledge of serious music, he was straightforward and independent, and he often remarked that he would rather be the composer of an inspired march than of a manufactured symphony.

Most of Sousa's music is in a lighter vein; this is partially explained by his love of the theater. He was outspoken in his view that music for entertainment was of more value to the world than music for education.

There is no substance to the story that Sousa was an alien by the name of Sam Ogden or Sigmund Ochs, etc., and that his American name was derived from the markings "S.O., U.S.A." on his luggage. He was born at 636 G Street, S.E., in Washington, D.C., on November 6, 1854.

His father, Antonio Sousa, was born in Spain of Portuguese parents. His mother, Elisabeth Trinkhaus, was born in Bavaria. Antonio and Elisabeth met and were married in Brooklyn; they later moved to Washington, where Antonio enlisted as a musician in the U.S. Marine Band. The Sousas had ten children, John Philip being the third. Four died in infancy.

John Philip received a grammar school education in Washington, and for several of his school years he was also enrolled in a private conservatory of music operated by John Esputa, Jr. He was an excellent student in both his academic studies and his musical training. He gained some proficiency on most orchestral instruments and on the piano, but his first love was the violin.

At the age of thirteen Sousa was about to run off with a circus band when his father intervened and enlisted him in the U.S. Marine Band as an apprentice musician. Except for a period of six months, he remained in the band until he was twenty. In addition to his musical training in the Marine Corps, he also studied theory and composition with George Felix Benkert, a noted Washington orchestra leader and teacher.

After his discharge from the Marine Corps Sousa remained in Washington, conducting and playing the violin in various theater orchestras. By this time he was composing minor pieces, most of which did get published. He toured with two traveling theater groups and settled in Philadelphia for four years beginning in 1876. Here again he conducted and played the violin in theater orchestras. His first position was in the first violin section of an orchestra conducted by the French composer Jacques Offenbach.

While in Philadelphia, Sousa became more active as a composer and did arranging and proofreading for publishing houses. He was fascinated by the operetta form, particularly the works of Gilbert and Sullivan. He conducted an *H.M.S. Pinafore* company which began as an amateur group

and eventually turned professional. He fell in love with a member of the cast, Jane van Middlesworth Bellis. After the company toured the east coast they returned to Philadelphia and were married on December 30, 1879.

Sousa resumed his theater work in Philadelphia and subsequently toured with a company producing the musical comedy *Our Flirtations*. While in St. Louis he received a telegram offering him the leadership of the U.S. Marine Band in Washington. He accepted and reported for duty on October 1, 1880, becoming the band's fourteenth leader.

Although by now Sousa had composed several pieces for band, he was totally inexperienced as a conductor of a military band. But he was young and ambitious, and within two years the Marine Band had risen to new heights. He now had the inspiration for composing quickstep marches, and they appeared in rapid succession. He also tried his hand at other musical forms, most notably operetta. By the mid-1880's three of his operettas had been produced, and he had started work on at least two others.

At the end of this decade the Marine Band was a very popular organization and was in demand for concert work. In 1891 and 1892 it made cross-country tours. The first left Sousa in a state of exhaustion, and he recuperated by vacationing in Europe. The manager of the tours was the impresario David Blakely, who encouraged Sousa to study the renowned bands of Europe while there. Blakely was grooming him for greater things. Before the second tour was completed he had persuaded Sousa to resign from the Marine Corps to form his own civilian concert band. Blakely offered two incentives: greater freedom of artistic expression, and a salary four times that which he earned as a Marine.

The Sousa Band began its rehearsals in New York. No expense was spared in engaging stellar performers, and contracts were signed with several artists of renown. The first public concert was presented in Plainfield, New Jersey, on September 26, 1892. Sousa was quite an attraction himself, for several of his marches ("The Gladiator," "Semper Fidelis," and "The Washington Post") were widely known, and already he was being referred to as the "March King."

The band's first tour was nearly a financial failure because of ineffective booking on the part of an assistant manager. But the next tour was highly successful, as were subsequent tours. The band soon became the talk of the country, and it was in constant demand. Talent attracted even more talent; Sousa could select his men from the finest musicians available, many of them giving up positions in leading symphony and theater orchestras.

Meanwhile, Sousa's operettas were catching the public fancy. After the smashing success of *El Capitan,* he was offered $100,000 for exclusive rights to *The Bride Elect.* At the outbreak of the Spanish-American War he attempted to enlist in the army as a bandmaster, but he was stricken with typhoid fever and pneumonia and could not serve.

By the turn of the century the Sousa Band could name its own price. Eager to prove to the world that America was coming into its own culturally, Sousa took the band to Europe in 1900. They caught the continent completely by surprise. Other European tours were made in 1901, 1903, and 1905, the 1903 tour extending into Russia. Then in 1910-11 the band completed a triumphal world tour, traveling from west to east and covering approximately forty thousand miles over a period of thirteen months.

The Sousa Band remained active most of each year, with time off usually only during the late winter and early spring. Most of the summer engagements were at resorts, expositions, and fairs. These summer engagements were difficult for the bandsmen because they normally presented four concerts each day, seven days per week, with very few repeats of selections and absolutely no rehearsals. Only a few musicians in the country could meet Sousa's demands, but their rewards were many.

The only long interruption in the Sousa Band schedule came during World War I, when Sousa enlisted in the navy to organize band units at the Great Lakes Naval Training Center. But here again he found himself touring, this time with a navy band of more than three hundred sailors. The "Jackie" band assisted in Liberty Loan and Red Cross drives. Sousa was sixty-two years old when he enlisted, as a lieutenant, and he declined several promotions. He set his own salary at one dollar per month. His navy work was highly effective, resulting in many splendidly prepared bands for the fleet. He was discharged shortly after the armistice and given the rank of lieutenant commander in the U.S. Naval Reserve.

The Sousa Band's operations were resumed after the war. Many had expected Sousa to retire, but his schedule was as full as ever. The tours did not diminish noticeably in length until the late 1920's. After a short tour in 1931, the Sousa Band fell victim of the Depression; it was losing money for the first time. Sousa was aging, although he appeared to be in good health. But after rehearsing for a guest appearance with the Ringgold Band of Reading, Pennsylvania, he died suddenly of a heart attack in his hotel room there. The date was March 6, 1932, and Sousa was seventy-seven years of age. Fittingly, the last composition he conducted was his own "The Stars and Stripes Forever."

His body was taken to Washington, D.C., for burial. Meanwhile, the nation paid tribute in many ways. The volume of eulogies appearing in the press was evidence of the admiration and sincere love of the public he had served so faithfully for more than sixty years. Both houses of Congress paused to pay tribute, and numerous radio memorial concerts and programs were broadcast. A simple, dignified military funeral was held in the band auditorium at the Marine Barracks. In one final parade the body was escorted to Congressional Cemetery.

Sousa's memory has been honored in many ways. Among structures named after him have been public schools in Washington, D.C., Chicago, New York, and Port Washington, Long Island; a bridge across the Anacostia River in Washington; a bandshell in Port Washington; a public fountain in Philadelphia; and numerous other shrines. By far the most impressive memorial is the Sousa Stage in the concert hall of the John F. Kennedy Center for the Performing Arts in Washington, dedicated in 1971. Several hundred memorial concerts were held by bands and orchestras throughout the world to raise money for this. Corporations and individuals also contributed, and the total amount contributed was matched by government funds.

His memory has also been perpetuated in other ways, such as by countless Sousa memorial concerts, salutes by bands on the football field, and by the ever-present musical instrument known as the sousaphone — originally built to his specifications. Another appropriate tribute to his memory is the coveted Sousa Award, presented to several thousand outstanding high school musicians each year.

But perhaps the most sincere tribute ever afforded an American composer is the living memorial known as the Sousa Band Fraternal Society. This is an organization of former members of Sousa's Band. Each year the members of this diminishing group make pilgrimages to New York to hold a memorial dinner on the anniversary of Sousa's birth. Seldom has a musician of any era commanded such a devoted following so many years after his death.

One of two focal points of the research for this book was a master file on each composition. The other was a day-by-day log of Sousa's life which was pieced together over a period of many years. The simple theory behind constructing such a log was that it was easier to understand how and why each Sousa composition came into being once the patterns of his career and personal life were laid out. The careful study of Sousa Band itineraries proved invaluable in this endeavor. These were collected from some fifty former members of Sousa's Band who were interviewed personally in all four corners of the continental United States.

It was essential to seek out, identify, and study each individual Sousa manuscript. The same was true for all known sections of his band's huge library. This led to considerable personal involvement (not to say

expense), but the rewards far outweighed the inconveniences.

I learned that the more I circulated, the more people became interested in the fact that the forgotten works of one of America's foremost composers were finally being brought to light. This brought about unexpected assistance. Direct personal contact was of great importance, but it would have been impractical to have conducted all research in this manner. Thus the typewriter and the telephone were used extensively; over three thousand letters of inquiry were written, and over four hundred long-distance calls were made.

Clues to the existence of several forgotten, unpublished works were found in the Sousa Band press books, which were studied in detail. Concert programs, many of which were found in the press books, provided other clues. Sousa's own writings, which were compiled only after considerable searching, hinted at still other works, although the search for these was usually fruitless.

The most time-consuming single area of research was the study of copyrights of Sousa's compositions. A complete search was made of all original-edition copyrights and renewals of the same. Most of this was done at the Library of Congress, and I learned why research librarians sometimes go "stare-crazy."

There is neither sufficient space to elaborate on each facet of research, nor room to list all the persons, organizations, and institutions providing the data upon which this book was founded. However, the Acknowledgments give the reader further insight into the depth of my investigations.

Notation Used in This Book

"(Reference)" beside a title indicates that it should not be numbered with the Sousa compositions, and the reason is stated in the discussion.

Manuscript, publishing, and copyright data on each Sousa work is given at the end of the discussion of the work. To avoid unnecessary repetition and to conserve space, the following abbreviations are used:

arr	arrangement; arranged
bd	band score; band
©	copyright(s); copyrighted
HSA	Sousa's younger daughter, Helen Sousa Abert
inc	incomplete — some pages missing from this manuscript
JPS	John Philip Sousa
JPrS	Sousa's older daughter, Jane Priscilla Sousa
JvMS	Sousa's widow, Jane van Middlesworth Sousa
MSS	manuscript(s)
N/A	not accounted for
nd	no date indicated on this manuscript
np	no place indicated on this manuscript
opa	operetta score; operetta
orch	orchestra score; orchestra
pi	piano score; piano
pp	page(s)
pub	publisher; published
ren	renewed by
rev	revision(s); revised
Sands Pt.	Sands Point, near Port Washington, Sousa's Long Island home. Some manuscripts are inscribed "Port Washington" or "Barker's Point."
unpub	unpublished
v	vocal score; voice, usually soprano
v/pi	vocal/piano score; for voice and piano
v/orch	vocal/orchestra score; for voice and orchestra
vi	violin
[ ]	present location of this manuscript
[LC]	Library of Congress, Washington, D.C.
[Morton]	J. Sterling Morton High School, Cicero, Illinois
[UI]	John Philip Sousa Library, Band Department, University of Illinois, Urbana
[USMC]	U.S. Marine Corps Museum Band Americana Collection, Navy Yard, Washington, D.C.

Below are examples of how the abbreviations are used.

Example 1

MSS: Bd 46pp; 12Oct1886 Washington, D.C. [LC]
Pub: Coleman
©: Bd: Coleman 13Dec1886; ren JPS 11Nov1914

The first line refers to a band manuscript forty-six pages long. It is dated October 12, 1886, and the place where the manuscript was completed, as indicated on the manuscript, is Washington, D.C. The manuscript is presently at the Library of Congress. The second line refers to the publisher of the original edition(s). The third line states that the band edition was copyrighted by Coleman on December 13, 1886, and renewed by John Philip Sousa on November 11, 1914.

Example 2

MSS: V/pi 3pp inc; nd np [UI]
Pub: Church
©: V/pi: Church 4Mar1920; ren JPrS & HSA 3Feb1948

The first line refers to three pages of a manuscript for voice and piano, with the remaining pages not accounted for. There is no date or place of writing indicated on the manuscript, which is presently at the University of Illinois. The second line refers to the publisher. The third line states that the piece was copyrighted for voice and piano by Church on March 4, 1920, and renewed by Sousa's two daughters on February 3, 1948.

Many additional Sousa music manuscripts have not been listed in the data sections. These are sketches or fragments of unidentified compositions which are now at the Library of Congress or the repositories of the Sousa Band library.

The publishers listed throughout the book refer only to the publishers of the original editions. Their complete names and locations are given in Appendix II. In many instances the original publishers subsequently merged with other companies or are no longer in business.

It should be noted that several early Sousa compositions may never come to light. Evidence of this is found in a study of his opus system of numbering: only sixteen opus numbers have been identified. The earliest is Opus 3 and the latest Opus 131, covering only the period from 1872 to 1881. Inasmuch as these numbers evidently were irregularly assigned, and since the whereabouts of so many of Sousa's early manuscripts are unknown, I have made no attempt to assign opus numbers to all the Sousa compositions.

OPERETTAS

If Sousa had not become leader of the U.S. Marine Band in 1880, he probably would have chosen a career in theater music. By the time Gilbert and Sullivan's operettas (or comic operas, depending on whose definition is preferred) gained their footing in the United States, Sousa was willing to provide an American counterpart. But there were no William Gilberts available to write his librettos, and it was the mid-1890's before first-class librettos were being written on this side of the Atlantic. Nevertheless, Sousa had a definite influence on the acceptance and growth of the American operetta. There was little in the way of precedent when his first two operettas were produced. After *The Smugglers* (1882) failed and *Desiree* (1883) and *The Queen of Hearts* (1885) met with only mild success, another Sousa operetta was not produced until *El Capitan* was performed in 1896. Then, within four years, he created *The Bride Elect* (1897), *The Charlatan* (1898), and *Chris and the Wonderful Lamp* (1899). After the latter he relaxed his operetta ambitions, partly because of the Sousa Band's European tours and partly because of competition from Victor Herbert and other contemporaries.

Sousa's operettas, all in English, clearly show the influence of Gilbert and Sullivan. This is particularly true of his early efforts. Sousa adopted their style as characterized by improbable characters and plots, short recitatives, chorus finales, and ensemble episodes where the individual singers voice their separate messages contrapuntally. In addition, Sousa's music has Sullivan's gaiety. But for the most part the similarity ends there. The best of Sousa's collaborators could not match the timeless, esoteric wit of Gilbert, but the fact remains that for a decade the Sousa operettas competed vigorously with anything from abroad.

With their abundance of martial rhythms, the Sousa operettas are distinctive. They have a constant undertone of optimism. Critics always expected at least one rousing march melody to add excitement to climactic scenes, and they were never disappointed. These marches always outlived the operettas, just as the hit songs of other operettas lived on after the productions had run their courses.

The songs from the Sousa operettas, while fresh and melodic, were sometimes handicapped by his unfortunate choice of awkward musical intervals and extremes of range. This was the price of his originality, and it often burdened the singers. A comparison between the songs of Victor Herbert and John Philip Sousa provides an insight into the demise of Sousa's. While there is no question that both were masters of melody, their melodies are different in character. Herbert's songs possess more warmth and charm and are more singable. One must conclude that Sousa's forte was the march, not the song. When audiences left a Herbert operetta, they were humming and whistling a beautiful song; when they left a Sousa operetta, they were humming and whistling a stirring march.

Sousa's operettas display a high standard of morality. They are a far cry from many other theatrical offerings of that day or this. Sousa once expressed his disgust at the trend:

"After a considerable period of decadence, the stage seems again to be assuming its rightful aspect. We have had too many risque farces, too many suggestive comedies, too many exhibitions of nudity and near nudity. The time has come for a revision to the clean, high thinking drama, and I believe that that is the kind the people will demand in the future. As for myself, I have no sympathy for anything that borders on the indecent, and I am especially antagonistic toward it when it is presented on the stage, where it may work to corrupt the morals of the younger generation. Why, for a long time, there, one might have supposed that some Grand Rapids furniture company was backing the plays, so many bedroom scenes were shown."[1]

Several celebrated stage personalities starred in the Sousa operettas. The most notable was De Wolf Hopper, who made his operetta debut as Pomaret in *Desiree,*[2] and who later starred in the title roles of *El Capitan* and *The Charlatan.* Two of Hopper's wives were also principals in Sousa operettas. Edna Wallace, his second, was Estrelda in *El Capitan* and Chris in *Chris and the Wonderful Lamp.* Nella Bergen, his third, was Isabel in *El Capitan,* La Pastorella in *The Bride Elect,* and Princess Yolande in *The Free Lance.* Sousa often joked that his operettas seemed to be matrimonial bureaus for Hopper. Among the other celebrated performers were Joseph Cawthorn, who played Sigmund Lump in *The Free Lance,* and many other popular names such as Alfred Klein, Jerome Sykes, Edmund Stanley, and Edna Blanche Showalter. Sousa did not compose his operettas with a given actor or actress in mind — with the exception of *The Charlatan,* which was created specifically for De Wolf Hopper.

The typical operetta composer complains of a shortage of superior librettos. Sousa, too, had his share of difficulties, and after

the success of *El Capitan* he was deluged with scenarios by both amateurs and professionals. Reviewers of the Sousa operettas usually remarked that the librettos were not equal to the music. Sousa seldom commented on this, because he had learned something of the librettist's difficulties while writing his own book for *The Wolf* (1888). A libretto can make or break any operetta, and Sousa was fortunate in securing the Anglo-American dramatist Charles Klein as librettist on his two most successful efforts, *El Capitan* and *The Charlatan.* The next most successful of the Sousa operettas was *The Free Lance,* with a libretto by Harry B. Smith, best remembered for his collaborations with Victor Herbert.

One art form Sousa longed to tackle was grand opera. For many years he considered writing an opera with an American theme, preferably set in the days of Dolly Madison. In 1913 newspapers hinted that he was about to commence such a work, but these ambitions were never realized. About this time his daughter Helen had translated a French play for his consideration. This was *The Demi-Monde* by Alexandre Dumas (the younger).[3]

With the post–World War II trend away from nonsensical plots and toward realism, the traditional operettas have, for the most part, fallen by the wayside. However, they paved the way for the musical comedy, which shares the scene with the modern operetta. Today's public does not have an appreciable appetite for period music, but music scholars have often surmised that a revival of Sousa's operettas might succeed if updated.

THE AMERICAN MAID (1909)
(THE GLASS BLOWERS)
In three acts
LIBRETTO BY LEONARD LIEBLING
First produced at the Schubert Theatre, Rochester, New York, January 27, 1913

Sousa's "All American" grand opera never materialized, but his collaboration with

---

[1] *Watertown* (N.Y.) *Daily Times,* August 1, 1921.

[2] Hopper was a principal with the McCaull Opera Comique Company for several years, but he did not play in *Desiree* when that Company premiered it in Washington.

[3] "Sousa's Daughter Finds 'Forgotten' Operetta Score" [*El Capitan*]. *Philadelphia Inquirer,* January 3, 1965.

Leonard Liebling on *The American Maid* was more serious in nature than his previous operettas. It was indeed "All American" and had a strong patriotic flavor. The recurring march themes, from which the march "From Maine to Oregon" was later developed, dominated several scenes. While giving generous amounts of praise, critics commented that the production was too long, mostly because of the inclusion of comical incidents which had little to do with the story. They generally agreed that the music was lively, if not outstanding, and that the libretto did not match the standard of the music.

Leonard Liebling, editor of the *Musical Courier,* was not widely recognized as a librettist. He was the brother of the famed operatic soprano Estelle Liebling, who had traveled extensively with the Sousa Band a few years earlier. In his libretto, Liebling was satirical in the treatment of a labor-capital dispute, but he cautiously avoided involved controversies. He wrote all the lyrics except the verses to "When You Change Your Name to Mine," which were written by R. M. Skinner.

The ingenious use of stage props was heralded by reviewers. To depict a battle scene of the Spanish-American War, actual movies of the battle of San Juan Hill were shown. This may have been the first such use of movies in a musical production of this proportion, and Sousa's musical setting was equal to the occasion. Another distinctive novelty was a scene inside a glass factory in which actual glassware was blown by several skilled artisans. For one song in this scene a glass harmonica was used for accompaniment, perhaps for the first time in an American operetta.

Sousa reached back nineteen years and resurrected one of his old songs called "Reveille" (set to a poem of R. J. Burdette) and used it to good advantage in Act III. He had once referred to the song as one of the better ballads of the day[4] (a view not shared by the public), and he took this opportunity to put it to further use.

----

[4] *York* [Pa.?] *Advertiser,* August 27, 1893[?] (clipping in the Sousa Band press book of of 1893).

The American Maid was the last Sousa operetta produced. Although completed in 1909, its premiere was postponed first because of the Sousa Band world tour and then because of difficulties in securing suitable principals. The name was changed from *The Glass Blowers* to *The American Maid* in February, 1913, while the company was on a tour of the midwest. Sousa felt that the former title was less attractive, thus accounting for poor box office receipts in some cities. The change was a wise one, because business then rose sharply.

CAST:

Jack Bartlett, a playboy
Annabelle Van de Veer, a society girl
Colonel Van de Veer, Annabelle's father
Mrs. Van de Veer, Annabelle's mother
Geraldine Pompton, a society girl
Silas Pompton, Geraldine's father and glassworks tycoon
Mrs. Pompton, Geraldine's mother
Duke of Branford
Stumpy, Jack Bartlett's valet
Rose Green ⎫
Nellie   ⎬ employees in Pompton's factory
Gawkins, head servant at the Van de Veer mansion
Count and Countess Hohenstaupellaufenwitz ⎫
John, James, and Jerry Smith, brothers ⎬ guests of the Van de Veers
Lefty McCarty
Hans Hippel
Pietro Nuttini ⎭
Gladys ⎫
Helen
Veronica
Alice   ⎬ society friends of Annabelle Van de Veer
Marion
Mabel
Edith ⎭
Domestic help of the Van de Veer mansion
Glassblowers at Pompton's factory
Red Cross nurses
Cuban girls

SYNOPSIS:

The Duke of Branford, an eligible British bachelor, is the target of New York's millionaire society ladies. The glassworks industrialist Silas Pompton is particularly anxious to arrange a marriage between the duke and his own daughter Geraldine. A romance is promoted at a reception held

in the home of Colonel Van de Veer, but
the colonel's pretty daughter Annabelle
catches the duke's eye. Annabelle, however, has another romance going with the
wealthy playboy Jack Bartlett.

Complications arise at the reception,
which is attended by all four of the young
principals. Through a misunderstanding,
the duke falls in love with Annabelle, and
their wedding is announced. This disgusts
Geraldine and Jack, and they laboriously
generate a romance of their own out of a
common spite.

Pompton plans retaliation for his daughter's disappointment and his own lost pride.
Just at the time Colonel Van de Veer in-
vests all his capital in a mining venture, the
financially powerful Pompton arranges for
his complete ruin. Penniless but confident
that her father's star will rise again, Annabelle goes to work in Pompton's factory.

Jack's romance with Geraldine was
largely superficial, and he had not given
up hope of gaining Annabelle's affection.
Annabelle had once vigorously disapproved
of his life of ease, so he reasons that if he
were to go to work as a common laborer,
he can win her back. He casts aside his
affluence and also goes to work in Pompton's factory.

The Spanish-American War breaks out
just at this time, and the next scene finds
the factory workers at the battlefront in
Cuba — the men as soldiers and the girls
as Red Cross nurses. There the problems
of the principals are straightened out: the
men return from the battlefield as heroes,
word arrives that Colonel Van de Veer's
mining stock has skyrocketed, and the ro-
mantic entanglements are resolved to everyone's satisfaction.

SONGS:

The American Girl (The American Maid)
The Bivouac
The Brotherhood of the Union
Cheer Up
Cleopatra's a Strawb'ry Blonde
The Crystal Lute
The Dinner Pail
I Can't Get 'Em Up (The Reveille)
In the Dimness of Twilight He Told His
   Love (Ten Thousand a Year)
It Would Be Very Hard to Get

Marconigrams
The Matrimonial Mart
My Love Is a Blower
Nevermore
The Sleeping Soldiers (The Belted Sleepers
   on the Ground)
The Red Cross Nurse
This Is My Busy Day
We Chant a Song of Labor
When You Change Your Name to Mine
You Do Not Need a Doctor

MSS: a) (Complete opa) 333pp in 3 bound
         volumes; Act I 2Jul1907 np; Act II
         nd np; Act III 2Aug1909 New
         York City [LC]
      b) ("Marconigrams") opa 8pp;
         13Jan1913 np [LC]
      c) ("The Belted Sleepers on the
         Ground") bd 4pp; 21May1913 New
         York City [LC]
      d) ("You Do Not Need a Doctor") bd
         23pp; 24Jun1913 New York City [LC]
      e) ("The Brotherhood of the Union")
         opa 3pp inc; nd np [LC]
      f) (Untitled song) v/pi 3pp; nd np [LC]
Pub: Church
©: (Complete) v/pi: Church 5Nov1909
         again 23Jan1913 again 20Mar1914;
         ren JvMS 28Dec1940 again
         12Dec1941
"The American Girl," "The Crystal Lute," "The
Dinner Pail," "In the Dimness of Twilight,"
"The Red Cross Nurse," and "When You
Change Your Name to Mine" also pub for v/pi
but not ©
(Also see Marches: "From Maine to Oregon")

THE BRIDE ELECT (1897)
In three acts
LIBRETTO BY JOHN PHILIP SOUSA
*First produced at the Hyperion Theatre,
New Haven, Connecticut,
December 28, 1897*

The Bride Elect had the misfortune of falling in the wake of the highly successful
El Capitan (1895). Charles Klein, the librettist of *El Capitan*, had been temporarily obliged to give up his literary work
because of ill health, and Sousa decided
to write his own book. Critics were quick
to point out that this was a mistake. The
operetta nevertheless met with mild success, and Sousa unwisely refused an offer
of $100,000 from the manager of the Hy-
perion Theatre for the exclusive rights.[5]

---
[5] John Philip Sousa, *Marching Along*, p. 163.

He also turned down an offer of $10,000 from the *New York Journal* for permission to publish the march alone.[6]

As usual, the march far outlived the operetta from which it was extracted. After the production had run its course, Sousa also took some of the individual songs and made wide use of these with the Sousa Band. For many years his sopranos were called upon to sing "The Card Song," "The Snow Baby," and "Love, Light of My Heart." The sextet which ends Act II, "An Awkward Complication This," was rewritten for six brass instruments and featured quite often. This apparently was Sousa's answer to the "Sextet" from *Lucia* (Donizetti), which was a very popular brass ensemble number at the time.

The Bride Elect had one important revival when it was produced in Philadelphia on January 30, 1923. For this production Sousa composed another song, "Hope On," and also included an adaptation of a song by Emerson Dresden called "You Cannot Tell How Old They Are by Looking at Their Skirts." An exceptionally fine ballet scene was also added, and for this Sousa transcribed one of his suites, "People Who Live in Glass Houses" (1909).

Much of *The Bride Elect* was drawn from two earlier Sousa operettas, *The Smugglers* (1882) and *The Wolf* (1888). The former was not successful and the latter was never produced. A sizable amount of music from *The Wolf* was appropriated, as can be seen by comparing the individual lists of songs, and there are similarities in the plots of all three operettas.

CAST:

Papagallo, King of Timberio
Guido, Duke of Ventroso (Kingdom of Timberio)
Frescobaldi, Prime Minister of Timberio
Bianca, Queen of Capri
Minutezza, Princess of Capri (the bride elect)
La Pastorella, widowed bandit leader
Gamba ⎱ bandits in La Pastorella's gang
Buscato ⎰
Pietro, an innkeeper
Sardinia, a jailer

------

[6] "Sousa's 'Bride Elect,'" *Music*, February, 1898.

Margherita
Rea
Zadena
Rosamonda

SYNOPSIS:

A war has been fought between the kingdoms of Timberio and Capri, because Capri's king had reportedly shot a goat belonging to Timberio's king. Timberio's forces win, and a peace commission decrees that, as spoils, Princess Minutezza must wed the king of Timberio when she reaches the age of eighteen. If not, the entire kingdom of Capri is to be forfeited. Minutezza is nearing that fateful age, and the operetta opens as Bianca and the chorus sing a brief history of the preceding events and announce that Papagallo will soon arrive.

Two members of a gang of robbers, Gamba and Buscato, are introduced in the disguises of a peddler and a bystander. Gamba poses as a detergent salesman who accidentally shrinks the coat of Buscato in a demonstration. Buscato goads the other by-standers into betting their gold on him in a duel with Gamba. A mock swordfight takes place, Buscato fakes a wound, Gamba collects the gold, and together they go merrily off. The by-standers realize that they have been duped and are about to seek revenge. But Minutezza appears, telling of her woes, and they realize that her plight is worse than theirs.

Just before Minutezza's eighteenth birthday, Papagallo arrives. He attempts to make friends by telling a funny story about how he was thrown from a donkey and then announces that the wedding will take place the following morning. A complication not realized by Papagallo is that his own nephew, Guido, is in love with Minutezza. Minutezza tries to convince Papagallo that she would snub him daily and not be faithful. She says that her mother, the Queen, would instead be more suitable as his bride, but Papagallo disagrees.

The gang of robbers are introduced next as they sing of their accomplishments and their admiration for their lady leader, La Pastorella. La Pastorella has recently been widowed, and Gamba, encouraged by Buscato, is wooing her.

A detail of the peace commission's decree is that Papagallo must marry Minutezza on or before her eighteenth birthday or else she is free of the obligation. Minutezza, together with La Pastorella and her gang, plot to kidnap Papagallo and hold him prisoner until after the wedding date. Later, the kidnapping takes place as Papagallo is singing a comical song about the shortcomings of a hotel he once frequented.

Act II begins as Guido tells Minutezza of his love for her, and they sing a duet. Meanwhile, La Pastorella is putting her own matrimonial future in the cards. According to the cards, she must wed a king, not Gamba. Papagallo has been delivered to her by the hands of fate, she reasons. Neither the gang nor Papagallo approve, but Gamba comes up with a solution. He discovers an old law of the gang stating that one cannot become their king until he has killed someone. But Frescobaldi, who was also abducted with Papagallo, points out that Papagallo technically had killed his three earlier wives by smothering them with kindness. In the meantime, the queen has missed the principal parties and concludes that Papagallo has kidnapped Minutezza, instead of vice versa. She locates the gang's hideout and marches on it, capturing them all.

In the short third act, news arrives that Papagallo's kingdom has had an insurrection and that Guido has been proclaimed king. This, of course, solves everyone's problems except Papagallo's. Since La Pastorella's cards had foretold that she would marry a king, she is no longer obligated to marry Papagallo, now an ex-king. Minutezza marries Guido, fulfilling the peace commission's original decree.

SONGS:

An Act to Purify Our Band
An Awkward Complication This (When Eve)
Before the Moor Was Master of the Hills of Old Iberia
Bright Star of Love
Come, Cavalier
Cuckoo
The Goat (The Goat and the Phonograph)
The God of Love Presides
Here's a Pack (The Card Song)

He's Here
Hope On
The Iceman Works (Why They Work)
If Ninety-nine Per Cent the Papers Print
In a Matter of Such Grave Import
Kind Friends This Deference
Let Poets Sing (The Highwayman)
Love, Light of My Heart
Oh, Stars That Form the Milky Way (The Jay Hotel)
Oh, Princess Minutezza
One Day King Papagallo Sent a Note
Our Customary Attitude
The Rose Tint Leaves the Sky
Should You Marry Ma
The Snow Baby
These Are Our Sentiments
Unchain the Dogs of War
We Cannot See the Reason Why
When This Old Goat Was in Style
You Cannot Tell How Old They Are by Looking at Their Skirts
You Remember T'was Six Months Ago

MSS: a) (Complete opa) 234pp in 2 bound volumes; 1897 np [LC]
b) ("You Cannot Tell How Old They Are by Looking at Their Skirts") v/pi 3pp; 8Jun1922 np [LC]
c) (Unidentified sections) opa 27pp inc; nd np [LC]
d) ("You Cannot Tell How Old They Are by Looking at Their Skirts") v/pi 2pp; nd np [LC]
e) ("You Cannot Tell How Old They Are by Looking at Their Skirts") v/pi 1pp; nd np [LC]
f) ("Love, Light of My Heart") several bd parts in Sousa's hand; nd np [UI]
g) ("Snow Baby") several bd parts in Sousa's hand; nd np [UI]

Pub: Church
©: (Complete) v/pi: Church 9Nov1897; ren JPS 17Oct1925
("The Snow Baby") v/pi: Church 13Jan1898; ren JPS 28Dec1925
(Selections) pi: Church 3Feb1898; ren JPS 30Jan1926
(Waltzes) pi: Church 3Feb1898; ren JPS 30Jan1926
(Lancers) pi: Church 10Feb1898; ren JPS 30Jan1926
("Unchain the Dogs of War") v/pi: Church 17Feb1898; ren JPS 30Jan1926
(Lancers; Waltzes) orch: Church 12Mar1898; ren JPS 19Feb1926
(Selections) bd: Church 19May1898; ren JPS 12Apr1926
(Selections) orch: Church 22Oct1898; ren JPS 4Sep1926
(Caprian Tarantella) pi: Church 17Feb1899; ren JPS 29Jan1927

("You Cannot Tell How Old They Are by Looking at Their Skirts") v/pi: Church 15Jan1923; ren JPrS & HSA 24Aug1950
(Also see Marches: "The Bride Elect")

EL CAPITAN (1895)
In three acts
LIBRETTO BY CHARLES KLEIN
LYRICS BY TOM FROST
AND JOHN PHILIP SOUSA

*First produced at the Tremont Theatre,
Boston, April 13, 1896*

El Capitan earned a place among the great operettas of its day and was by far the most successful of Sousa's stage works. It played almost continuously for four years in the United States and Canada and for another six months in England. It has been produced in several other countries and still enjoys an occasional revival.

The libretto of *El Capitan* was the first libretto written by the dramatist Charles Klein. It was read by comedian De Wolf Hopper, who immediately wanted it for himself, and then by Sousa, who was equally enthusiastic. Sousa's enthusiasm did not wear off; a quarter century later he was still referring to it as the finest libretto ever produced in America.[7] Inasmuch as Klein had never written lyrics, Sousa teamed up with Tom Frost to produce them, each furnishing approximately half the total. Sousa's most notable contribution to this effort was "Typical Tune of Zanzibar," which was set to the words of an old poem he reportedly had written for a periodical.[8]

As was the case in several of his other operettas, Sousa inserted some earlier works. "The Legend of the Frogs" had appeared earlier as "The Fable of the Frogs" in *The Queen of Hearts* (1885). This was cut early in the production and replaced with "Typical Tune of Zanzibar." And perhaps the operetta's most beautiful melody, "Sweetheart, I'm Waiting," was an adaptation of "Sighing, Ah Sighing," from the unsuccessful *The Smugglers* (1882). Since *El Capitan* experienced such a long life, there was little need for transplanting any of its tunes into later works, and Sousa made the most of its popularity by programming many excerpts with the Sousa Band. Outstanding among these was the "El Capitan" march, which still ranks as one of Sousa's most popular compositions.

CAST:

Don Errico Medigua, recently appointed Viceroy of Peru
Princess Marghanza, Don Medigua's wife
Isabel, Don Medigua's daughter
Luiz Cazarro, former Viceroy of Peru
Estrelda, Cazarro's daughter
Senor Pozzo, Chamberlain of Peru
Count Hernando Verrada, a Peruvian gentleman
Scaramba ⎫
Nevado ⎬ rebels
Montalba ⎭
General Herbano, commander of the Spanish army in Peru
Spanish and Peruvian ladies and gentlemen; soldiers, etc.

SYNOPSIS:

At the time of the Spanish possession of Peru, Don Medigua has been appointed viceroy. His predecessor, Luiz Cazarro, is attempting to regain power. Rebel forces are planning an attack on the palace, and Don Medigua, who is not at all inclined toward fighting, fears assassination. The rebels are soon to be joined by the dauntless leader El Capitan, whose exploits have often been broadcast even by Don Medigua. Medigua manages to have El Capitan secretly exterminated, however. He then disguises himself as El Capitan with the intent of leading the rebel forces to defeat, revealing his true identity, and then hanging the rebel leaders. He reasons that he could not lose, even in the unlikely event that the rebels should win.

Medigua's masquerade passes the test, and he takes his place at the head of the rebel forces. The rebels capture Pozzo, believing him to be the viceroy. Princess Marghanza and Isabel are aghast upon hearing the false report that the viceroy is in rebel hands. They organize a search party and

---

[7] *Boston Post,* October 1, 1922. This opinion is also expressed in Sousa, *Marching Along,* p. 150.

[8] Sousa, *Marching Along,* p. 150. Sousa states that the poem was written for a then (1928) defunct magazine. The author has been unable to trace this.

seek out El Capitan to plead for their
loved one's release. But there is a complication. Estrelda, daughter of the former viceroy, has been charmed by the many tales
of El Capitan's bravery and falls in love
with him. Since El Capitan (i.e., Don
Medigua) is already a married man, he is
quite uncomfortable. And one of the rebels, Scaramba, is quite jealous because he
is himself in love with Estrelda.

When confronted by his wife and daughter, Medigua is unable to conceal his real
identity for long. He privately tells them
the whole story, and they have no choice
but to accept the situation. Before these
internal matters can be straightened out,
a Spanish army is discovered nearby, and
Medigua is obligated to lead the rebels
against it. In the midst of all this, Isabel
is being courted by Count Hernando Verrada, who has accompanied the search
party.

Medigua purposely leads the rebels in
circles until they are too tired to fight, and
the Spanish army overtakes them. The
Spaniards are honoring Pozzo as the lib-
erated viceroy when Princess Marghanza
arrives to properly identify Pozzo and Don
Medigua and end the confusion. She is
then reunited with her husband, and he
offers the hand of Isabel to Verrada. Scaramba wins Estrelda, and all ends happily.

SONGS:

The Army
Bah! Bah!
Bowed with Tribulation
Ditty of the Drill
Don Medigua, All for Thy Coming Wait
Don Medigua, Here's Your Wife
The God of Wine
He Can Not, Must Not, Shall Not
I Remarked to You Before
If You Examine Human Kind
I've a Most Decided Notion
The Legend of the Frogs
Lo, the Awful Man Approaches
Nobles of Castilian Birth
Oh, Beautiful Land of Spain
Oh, Spare a Daughter
Oh, Warrior Grim (The Bell Song)
Sweetheart, I'm Waiting
Typical Tune of Zanzibar
We Beg Your Kind Consideration
When Laughing Eyes

When Some Serious Affliction
When We Hear the Call for Battle
You See in Me (El Capitan's Song)

MSS: a) (Complete opa) 320pp in 3 bound
volumes; 29Aug1895 Manhattan
Beach, N.Y. [LC]
b) ("The Army," "When Laughing
Eyes," and untitled sections) 50pp inc;
29Jul1895 Manhattan Beach, N.Y.
[LC]
c) (Valses) bd 11pp; 6Jun1896
Montreal [LC]
d) (Selections) bd 23pp; 15Jul1896
New York City [LC]
e) ("A Typical Tune of Zanzibar")
v/pi 7pp; nd np [LC]
f) ("When Laughing Eyes") v/pi 3pp;
nd np [LC]
g) (Valses) orch 2pp inc; nd np [LC]

Pub: Church
©: (Complete) v/pi: Church 4Feb1896;
not ren
("Oh, Warrior Grim") bd: Church
4Feb1896; not ren
("Sweetheart, I'm Waiting") v duet &
chorus with pi: Church 4May1896;
ren JPS 30Apr1924
("Typical Tune of Zanzibar") pi;
guitar; mandolin: Church 4May1896;
ren JPS 30Apr1924
(Waltzes) pi: Church 14May1896; ren
JPS 30Apr1924
(Selections) pi: Church 6Jun1896;
ren JPS 3May1924
("El Capitan's Song") pi: Church
26Jun1896; ren JPS 3May1924
(Lancers) pi: Church 2Jul1896; ren
JPS 3May1924
(Waltzes) bd: Church 20Jul1896; ren
JPS 31May1924
(Lancers) orch: Church 21Aug1896;
not ren
(Waltzes) orch: Church 21Aug1896;
ren JPS 7Jun1924
(Selections) bd: Church 21Sep1896;
ren JPS 1Aug1924
(Selections) orch: Church 15Oct1896;
ren JPS 20Sep1924
("Oh, Warrior Grim") cornet solo with
bd: Chappell 26Jan1920; ren
Chappell 28Jan1947
(Also see Marches: "El Capitan")

THE CHARLATAN (1898)
(THE MYSTICAL MISS)
In three acts

LIBRETTO BY CHARLES KLEIN
LYRICS BY JOHN PHILIP SOUSA

*First produced at the Academy of Music,
Montreal, August 29, 1898*

After Sousa's own efforts at writing a libretto for *The Bride Elect* (1897) had fallen short of his expectations, he once again turned to Charles Klein, with whom he had collaborated on the highly successful *El Capitan* (1895). *The Charlatan* became the second most successful Sousa operetta, attesting to the wisdom of his choice. It was written specifically for De Wolf Hopper and the De Wolf Hopper Opera Company, and the original company played in the principal eastern cities of the United States and in London for a total of over sixteen months. In London *The Charlatan* was known as *The Mystical Miss*.

For years Sousa had been labeled as a composer of strongly rhythmical works. He tried to change this by deemphasizing march melodies when he wrote *The Charlatan,* leading some reviewers to observe that it lacked the gaiety of other Sousa operettas. Still, the inevitable Sousa march came through. From Klein's libretto, Sousa developed the lyrics of all the individual songs except "The Ammonia Song," which was eventually replaced with "The Golden Cars." "The Ammonia Song" had been transplanted from *The Queen of Hearts* (1885), and "The Golden Cars" was taken from *The Wolf* (1888). "The Legend of the Frogs," another transplant from *The Queen of Hearts* (there as "Fable of the Frogs"), had also been used in *El Capitan* but had been cut early in its production. For effect, Sousa inserted an adaptation of the Russian national anthem into the finale of Act II. Additional songs, "Have You Got That Tired Feeling?" and "Right up on the Firing Line," were added as the production was refined.

The operetta was composed during the Spanish-American War, mostly while Sousa was recuperating from a near nervous collapse after a strenuous tour. At his physician's advice he leased a farm near Suffern, New York, where he could rest and work without interruption.

The original production was richly costumed, and handsome settings were provided. Critics were widely varied on their opinions, but the operetta's relatively long life was the final judgment.

CAST:

Prince Boris
Gogul, uncle of Prince Boris
Demidoff, a traveling magician (the charlatan)
Anna, Demidoff's daughter
Sophia, daughter of Gogul
Princess Ruchkowski
Grand Duke
Grand Duchess
Katrinka
Captain Peshofki
Jelikoff
Koreff

SYNOPSIS:

Prince Boris of the kingdom of Bokhara, a province of southern Russia, had been pledged in marriage to a peasant girl by an arrangement of his father's. This angered the czar, who had not been told of the arrangement, because he did not wish the prince to marry beneath his station. A decree was then issued to the effect that if the prince married anyone of less rank than a princess, he would forfeit his title and estate.

Gogul is the only living relative of Prince Boris and realizes that he would inherit the prince's title and estate if misfortune should befall him. He conceives of a plan whereby the prince would marry a peasant girl disguised as a princess. Just at this time, Demidoff and his caravan come upon the scene. He is an unscrupulous charlatan and is approached by Gogul with the prospect of marrying his daughter to a prince. This appeals to Demidoff, but he is not told of the czar's decree. Demidoff presents his daughter, Anna, to the prince as "Princess Ruchkowski." Both Demidoff and Gogul believe that "Princess Ruchkowski" is an extinct title. Through Demidoff's trickery, the prince is married to Anna.

Gloating over his success in tricking both Prince Boris and Demidoff, Gogul informs Demidoff of the czar's decree and reveals that Anna is thus married to a beggar, not a prince. At the same time, however, a complication arises — the real Princess Ruchkowski appears, accompanied by the grand duke and grand duchess. Demidoff pretends to apply magic in making Anna disappear into space, and the grand duke charges him with witchcraft and has him arrested. Actually, Anna has fled in guilt because of the disgrace she brought upon Prince Boris.

Anna's timely return at Demidoff's trial sets off a chain of events that brings about a happy ending. Demidoff exposes Gogul for his trickery, the grand duke promises to restore Prince Boris to his original fortunes, and all ends well.

SONGS:

After Due Consideration
As the Agent
Before the Twilight Shadows Change
The College Man
Day of Joy
The Golden Cars
Have You Got That Tired Feeling?
I Am the Seventh Son of a Seventh Son
It Is a Well Established Fact (The Ammonia Song)
The Legend of the Frogs
The Lilies of Your Love May Die (Will You Love When the Lilies Are Dead?)
Love's the Pleasure
The Matrimonial Guards
Mountbanks, Come Waken from Your Dreaming
Oh, Sunlit Sea beyond the West
The Philosophic Tale Is Told (The Faithless Knight and the Philosophic Maid) (The Philosophic Maid)
Pluto's Partner I
Right up on the Firing Line
She Was a Maid of Sweet Simplicitee
Social Laws
Venus, Goddess of Love
When the Wintry Moon Is Bright

MSS: a) (Complete opa) 210pp in 1 bound volume; 27Jul1898 Suffern, N.Y. [LC]
b) ("The Golden Cars") bd 6pp; 26Mar1903 Waenerhampton, England [UI]
c) ("The Faithless Knight and the Philosophic Maid") bd 5pp; 1Jun1922 Sands Pt. [UI]
d) (Untitled section) opa 7pp inc; nd np [LC]
e) ("The Faithless Knight and the Philosophic Maid") several bd parts in Sousa's hand; nd np [UI]
f) ("Social Laws") bd 3pp inc; nd np [LC]
g) ("Social Laws") bd 2pp inc; nd np [LC]

Pub: Church
©: (Complete) v/pi: Church 1Sep1898; ren JPS 6May1926
(Lancers) orch: Church 10Nov1898; ren JPS 23Sep1926
(Waltzes) orch: Church 30Dec1898; ren JPS 30Oct1926
(Waltzes) pi; Church 20Jan1899; ren JPS 1Nov1926
(Russian Peasant's Dance) pi: Church 17Feb1899; ren JPS 29Jan1927
("Will You Love When the Lilies Are Dead?") v/pi: Church 17Feb1899 ren JPS 29Jan1927
(Selections) orch: Church 20Mar1899; ren JPS 29Jan1927
(Lancers) pi: Church 3Apr1899; ren JPS 30Oct1926
(Selections) pi: Church 3Apr1899; ren JPS 1Feb1927
(Waltzes) bd: Church 4May1899; ren JPS 23Mar1927
("The Golden Cars") v/pi: Church 11May1899; ren JPS 23Mar1927
("Have You Got That Tired Feeling?") v/pi: Church 11May1899; ren JPS 23Mar1927
("Right up on the Firing Line") v/pi: Church 11May1899; ren JPS 23Mar1927
("The Philosophic Maid") v/pi: Church 6Sep1898 again 10Sep1898 again 12Sep1902; ren JPS 6May1926 again 1Mar1930
("The Matrimonial Guards") v duet & pi: Church 28Sep1899; ren JPS 8Sep1927
(Also see Marches: "The Charlatan")

CHRIS AND THE WONDERFUL LAMP
(1899)
In three acts
LIBRETTO BY GLEN MacDONOUGH
First produced at the Hyperion Theatre, New Haven, Connecticut, October 23, 1899

Before its premiere, Sousa told newsmen that *Chris* was his best work to date. He was obviously pleased with several of the songs and predicted a successful run — something he seldom dared do. It had a run of only five months, however, falling far behind *El Capitan* and *The Charlatan,* which were both going strong when *Chris* closed. It was a more extravagant production than any of Sousa's earlier operettas and was characterized by lavish scenery and costuming, and for its distinctive choreography. In particular, the Electric Ballet of Act II caused much favorable comment from the press.

Sousa was disappointed with public acceptance of the operetta as a whole and was determined not to let all the individual melodies pass into disuse. He extracted one march, "The Man Behind the Gun," and there were still enough melodies for half of another march. Around these he built "Jack Tar" (1905), which became much more popular than "The Man Behind the Gun." He also used parts of Act II in his instrumental suites, *Looking Upward* (1902) and *Dwellers of the Western World* (1911). In addition to the songs which the publisher issued as separate compositions, the Sousa Band often programmed the Overture, "Mama, Papa," "Where Is Love?" and the Electric Ballet.

The young librettist Glen MacDonough was just beginning to distinguish himself at the time of *Chris,* and he went on to collaborate with Victor Herbert and others on several successful productions. He was one of the founders of ASCAP, and he and Sousa were charter members.

CAST:

Chris Wagstaff
Fanny Wiggins
The genie of Aladdin's lamp
Miss Prisms, principal of the Prisms Academy
Scotty Jones, boy-of-all-work at the Prisms Academy
Aladdin, the mythological character
Queen of Dreams
Amine ⎫
Sofie ⎪
Zobeide ⎬ talking dolls
Diana ⎪
Haydee ⎪
Hebe ⎭
Auctioneer
Mr. Lovemony, a money-lender and bidder at the auction
Mr. Pettingill, bidder at the auction
Katie Clancy, maid-of-all-work at the Prisms Academy
Stella ⎫
Della ⎪
Bella ⎬ pupils at the Prisms Academy
Ella ⎪
Nella ⎭
Captain of the Guard
Al Khizar, chief of secret police of Etheria

SYNOPSIS:

The belongings of a deceased New England schoolteacher are being sold at an auction in 1899. Bidding on one small casket climbs, but the buyer is disgusted to learn that the casket contains only a dusty old lamp. Chris, a former student of the deceased, obtains the lamp from the distraught buyer. He soon learns that it is the same magical lamp which was once owned by the Aladdin of storybook fame.

Chris's first request of the lamp's genie is that he be enabled to see his sweetheart, Fanny. Fanny is inaccessible because her parents have enrolled her in an exclusive boarding school for girls run by the stern Miss Prisms. The resourceful genie gains entrance for them both in the guise of college professors.

The two phony professors are eventually unmasked, and Miss Prisms threatens arrest. But the genie transports all present to Aladdin's court in the ancient kingdom of Etheria, which is awakened by their arrival. Aladdin promptly falls in love with Fanny, but she is not responsive. Meanwhile, the genie amazes the court by the introduction of cigarettes, champagne, and other modern marvels which they had not known in their sleep of two thousand years.

Aladdin is eager to gain possession of his lamp. He seizes it by trickery and orders the execution of Chris and his friends. But Fanny recaptures the lamp and saves them. Chris and his party then return to modern times.

Once back in New England, the genie springs a surprise by sacrificing his supernatural powers to marry Miss Prisms. And, of course, Chris wins Fanny.

SONGS:

Above the Slim Minaret
Awake, Aladdin
Awake, Sleepers
The Bobolink
The Brooding Is the Only Street
The College of Hoop-De-Doo
Fanny
The Fourth of July Has Its Meed of Joy
He Couldn't Do a Blessed Thing without Me
I Am a High-Toned Genie
In Posterland

The Lamp (The Yankee Boy)
Mama, Papa
The Patient Egg
The Patter of the Shingle
Prepare to Receive with a Crook of Your
    Knees
She Was Dainty as a Fairy
Sweetest of All the Words of Love
We Seniors Are
We'll Proceed
Where Is Love? (Ah! Sighing)
Young Torah Tep Was the Boy for Me

MSS: a) (Complete opa) 138pp in 2 bound
            volumes; 2Sep1899 Manhattan Beach,
            N.Y. [LC]
       b) (Misc. opa) 56pp, bearing dates and
            places as follows: Overture 9Jan1899
            New York City; untitled section
            9Jan1899 New York City; Act I
            27July1899 Manhattan Beach, N.Y.;
            untitled sections 7Oct1899 New York
            City; Act II 3Nov1899 Phila.; untitled
            section 6Nov1899 New York City;
            Act II 26Jan1900 New York City
            [LC]
       c) ("The Brooding Is the Only Street")
            v/pi 2pp; 17Oct1899 Boston [LC]
       d) (Fanny) opa 6pp; 3Nov1899 Phila.
            [LC]
       e) ("Mama, Papa") bd 4pp; 27Jul1914
            Sands Pt. [LC]
       f) ("She Was Dainty as a Fairy") opa
            2pp; nd np [LC]
Pub: Church
©:   (Complete) v/pi: Church 20Oct1899;
            ren JPS 15Sep1927
       (Fanny) v/pi: Church 11Dec1899; ren
            JPS 15Oct1927
       "The Patient Egg" was pub for v/pi but
            not ©
(Also see Marches: "The Man Behind the
Gun")

DESIREE (1883)
In two acts

LIBRETTO BY EDWARD M. TABER

*First produced at the National Theatre,
Washington, D.C., May 1, 1884*

Written in 1882 and 1883 and produced in
1884, *Desiree* played in Washington and
Philadelphia for a total of approximately
forty days. The first three performances, in
Washington, were under the supervision of
Sousa and Taber. The operetta was fash-
ioned after an old English comedy, *Our
Wife*, by John Maddison Morton.

CAST:

Pomaret, proprietor of a dry goods store
Desiree, Pomaret's daughter and a clerk in
    his store
Marquis de LaVaree, colonel of a contin-
    gent of French musketeers
Count de Courville, lieutenant of the mus-
    keteers
Marie, Pomaret's niece and also a clerk in
    his store
Laurie, a schoolteacher at Desiree's school
    and also the beau of Pomaret
Gertrude }
Rose   } school companions of Desiree
Dumont, sergeant of the musketeers and
    Marquis's orderly
Corporal of musketeers

SYNOPSIS:

The action takes place in Amiens, France,
during the time of Cardinal de Richelieu.
A group of French musketeers are gathered
in Pomaret's shop admiring Desiree. Desiree's cousin, Marie, who is not quite as
attractive, is all but ignored. The musketeers are dismissed by the Count de Courville, who then woos Desiree and asks her
hand in marriage. But the count's father
disapproves of his marriage to a commoner
and threatens to imprison Pomaret if he
permits the marriage to take place.

The Marquis de Lavaree, the count's
superior officer, appears after the count's
departure and conceives of a solution. He
offers to marry Desiree, revealing that she
will soon be a widow and thus free to
marry the count. He explains that he has
recently been convicted of killing a rival in
a duel and has been sentenced to death.
Cardinal Richelieu has condescended to
permit him to die in battle against the
Spaniards instead of on the gallows. Pomaret and Desiree agree to his plan. The
count is infuriated upon learning of the
marriage plan and challenges the marquis
to a duel. The marquis has him arrested
for his own good and does not tell him of
the fateful future.

The marquis seems disinterested at the
wedding banquet, and Desiree is very much
slighted. She sends a note the to cardinal
requesting annulment of her marriage.
Meanwhile, the count has escaped and

confronts the marquis. The marquis then reveals to him that Desiree will soon be a wealthy widow and will be free to marry him. A messenger arrives with surprising news from the cardinal. The rival whom the marquis had killed had turned out to be a traitor, and the marquis was thereupon pardoned. He had already been obliged to lead a battle, however, and he departs — but not before finally telling Desiree of his love for her.

The marquis is not killed in battle, as was expected. He returns victorious and is reunited with Desiree, but Desiree's request for the annulment has been approved. The count solves this problem neatly by tearing up the annulment paper and announcing that he is marrying Marie — now eligible to be his wife because she is the cousin of a marquis.

SONGS:

As Perhaps You're Not Acquainted
The Average Man
The Bastille, the Bastille, Oh Horrible Fate
The Battle Is Won
For All of Which My Son-in-Law Will Pay
The Foreman Awaits
Girls Should Have Lovers Plenty
Hold, or Your Blood Shall All Be Shed
I Pity You, but Still What Can I Do?
I Will, in a Word, Tell What Has Occurred
I Wonder
If to Gossiping You Ever Find Your Mind
    Inclined
In This Most Stately Sort of Measure
It's Sad to Love a Man You Cannot Find
Let Me Not in Vain, Entreat You Explain
Long Life to the Marquis and His Bride
Love May Wander
The Men Are at Their Wine
My Son's Request I've Read with Care
My Soul Is Filled with Love for You
Never Seemed the World More Fair
Now, Traitor, Face to Face We Stand
Now We Will Hear the Joyful News
A Star Shone Softly from the Sky Afar
The Student of Love
The Sword, the Musket and the Lance
Tell Me
This Is, Indeed, an Awkward Situation
Three Quarters of an Hour, You Say
'Tis Bliss to Him Who Sips
True Friendship Is Something as You Are
    Aware
'Twas So Always

We're Ardent in Geography
Will I Regret
Untitled song

MSS: a) Opa 18pp inc; one section dated
        7Feb1882 Washington, D.C.; final
        page dated 7Dec1883 np [LC]
      b) (Selections) bd 11pp inc; 26May1894
        New York City [UI]
      c) (Waltz) orch 7pp inc; nd np [LC]
Pub: Pepper
©:   (Complete) v/pi: Pepper 30Dec1882;
        not ren

THE DEVIL'S DEPUTY (1893)
Unfinished

Comedian Francis Wilson engaged Sousa to compose the music for this three-act operetta, the libretto having been written by J. Cheever Goodwin. After Act I and part of Act II had been completed, Wilson and Sousa could not agree on terms. Wilson wanted to purchase the music outright rather than divide the royalties. Sousa asked $1,500, and Wilson offered $1,000. Neither would yield, so negotiations were broken off. The music was subsequently written by another composer, but that production was not a notable success.[9] Sousa later used part of his score in "The Liberty Bell" march.

Only fragments of the score are known to exist. From these, the only characters noted are Melissen, Elnerine, Larenzo, and Karamatoff. The only song titles indicated are "Matrimony" and "Romance."

MSS: v/pi 11pp inc; nd np [LC]
Not pub or ©

FLORINE (1881)
Unfinished

Mary Andrews Denison, one of Sousa's violin students, had collaborated with him on two songs and was the librettist of this operetta. Her husband died while *Florine* was still in the first act, and she lost interest. Later in life, Mrs. Denison authored several books.[10]

MSS: N/A
Not pub or ©

---

[9] *Denver Times,* February 19, 1899.
[10] John Philip Sousa, "Keeping Time (Part 2)," *Saturday Evening Post,* November 7, 1925.

THE FREE LANCE (1905)
In two acts
LIBRETTO BY HARRY BACHE SMITH
*First produced at the Court Square
Theatre, Springfield, Massachusetts,
March 26, 1906*

Sousa's happy collaboration with Harry B. Smith was reflected in the exuberance of *The Free Lance*. Both audiences and critics received it so enthusiastically that its relatively short run of only seven months is difficult to explain. On October 12, 1906, when Sousa personally conducted a performance in Philadelphia, the performers — including the orchestra members — were so moved by their reception that they paraded through the audience.[11]

Sousa's orchestration is clever. Some themes and instrumentation are in character with the motives assigned to the singers, perhaps showing the influence of Wagner. Before the premiere, Sousa and Smith had planned to call the operetta *King for a Day* but decided that *The Free Lance* was more in keeping with the capers of the mercenary principal of the operetta, Sigmund Lump. The publisher made the most of the operetta's immediate popularity by printing many of the songs and other selections as separate compositions. Even as late as 1939, "The Goose Girl's Song" was rearranged for piano in the style of Mozart and published as "Petit Minuet."

CAST:

Emperor of Braggadocia
Princess Yolanda, daughter of the Emperor
Duke of Graftiana
Prince Florian, son of the Duke
Griselda, a goose girl
Sigmund Lump, a goatherd, Griselda's husband and a former bandit chief (the "free lance")
Pertinax, court censor of Braggadocia
Dragonet, Minister of the Interior of Graftiana
Mopsa, a sorceress
Leandre ⎱ pages
Silvandre ⎰
Jacqueline ⎱ maids of honor
Diane ⎰

----

11 *Philadelphia Press*, April 13, 1906.

Lords and ladies of the courts
Other pages and maids of honor
Amazons of Braggadocia
Warriors of Graftiana
Bandits

SYNOPSIS:

The neighboring kingdoms of Braggadocia and Graftiana are bankrupt, but ambassadors of each country report to their respective rulers that the other kingdom is exceedingly wealthy. The emperor of Braggadocia plans to marry off his daughter, Princess Yolanda, to Prince Florian of Graftiana in the hope of borrowing money to save his kingdom. The duke of Graftiana is agreeable, naturally, thinking he can salvage his own kingdom. Yolanda and Florian have not yet met. They both object to being made into merchandise in this manner and flee.

The emperor and the duke separately resolve not to be disappointed, and each resorts to trickery. The emperor secretly prevails upon Griselda to disguise herself as the princess. Likewise, the duke forcefully persuades Sigmund Lump to impersonate the prince. The imposters are actually man and wife, but they carry on the deception in expectation of financial rewards.

After the wedding, each ruler learns of the fraudulence of the other, and a war is declared. Griselda is made leader of Braggadocia's army of Amazons, and Sigmund is made leader of Graftiana's army. But Sigmund's disguise is discovered, and his execution is ordered.

Sigmund is no ordinary goatherd, however. It happens that he was once a bandit chief who, like Sampson, had great strength in his hair. He had lost his power when a sorceress had shorn him, and his gang had deserted him. The sorceress reappears at this time, restoring his former power.

The clever Sigmund then hires himself out as a mercenary leader to both sides. He is thus a "free lance." He carefully maneuvers his forces so that neither side can win. A truce is called, and he demands ransom from both kingdoms. Neither side can pay, so he declares himself ruler of both countries as Sigmund I.

Yolanda and Florian, in the meantime, have met as commoners. They fall in love, marry, and all ends happily.

SONGS:

All Lovely Art, We Worship at Thy Shrine
The Carrier Pigeon
Come, My Dear
Conundrums
Drums Are Beating
The Emperor's War Song
Friendship's Sacred Touch
The Goose Girl's Song
I Am a Salaried Warrior (The Free Lance Song)
I Was Never Right in My Life
I'm the Potentate
It Depends upon the Hair (Hair)
Keep the Mums If You Please
The Legend of the Sons of Sampson
Let Us Greet with Joy Pretended
Little Bas Bleu
The Mystery of History (Girls Who Have Loved)
On to Victory
Release That Man
Three Love Stories
We Do It All by Proxy
Youth Must Have Its Fling

MSS: a) (Complete opa) 388pp in 2 bound volumes; 27Dec1905 np [LC]
b) ("Keep the Mums If You Please") v/pi 2pp; 15May1906 np [LC]
c) (Untitled section) opa 18pp inc; 6Jul1906 Shelter Island [LC]
d) (Untitled section) v/pi 3pp inc; nd np [LC]

Pub: Church; Presser (for "Petit Minuet" only)

©: ("The Carrier Pigeon"; "Girls Who Have Loved"; "The Goose Girl's Song"; "Hair") v/pi: Church 26Mar1906; ren JvMS 23Jan1934
("The Free Lance Song") v/pi: Church 26Mar1906; ren JvMS 19Feb1934
(Selections) pi: Church 26Mar1906; ren JvMS 23Jan1934
(Complete) v/pi: Church 30Apr1906; ren JvMS 23Jan1934
("I Was Never Right in My Life") v/pi: Church 8Oct1906; not ren
(Selections) bd: Church 12Nov1906; ren JvMS 23Jan1934
(Selections) orch: Church 19Nov1906; ren JvMS 23Jan1934
("Petit Minuet") pi: Presser 9Aug1939; not ren
Selections also pub for v/pi but not ©
(Also see Marches: "The Free Lance")

THE GLASS BLOWERS
(See THE AMERICAN MAID)

THE IRISH DRAGOON (1915)
In three acts
LIBRETTO BY JOSEPH W. HERBERT
(Not produced)

Two nearly complete versions of this operetta were discovered in the basement of Sousa's Sands Point estate in 1965. One version is written in the hand of another composer, not identified on the manuscripts. The other is in Sousa's hand. His daughter Helen revealed that he had purchased the libretto from Joseph Herbert and that the first composer's work was part of the package received. Sousa evidently set this aside and composed his own music. Among the songs given titles are "The Blarney Stone," "The Showman's Song," "Their Life and Joy," and "Whish! Hiroo!" The only other selections with titles are the overture and a piece called "Circus Galop."

The libretto was based on Charles Lever's novel, *Charles O'Malley*. The leading role was created for Andrew Mack, and the operetta was to have been produced in October, 1915.[12]

MSS: Opa 384pp inc; overture dated 17Jul1915 np [LC]
Not pub or ©

KATHERINE (1879)
In three acts
LIBRETTO BY WILSON J. VANCE
(Not produced)

Although this obscure work was perhaps never completed, it was at least copyrighted — at a time when copies were not required for registration. Sousa made occasional unflattering references to it when queried about his early operettas, and very little was known about it until recently. The only selection ever known to have been performed was the overture, which appeared in a few Sousa Band concert programs of the late 1920's.

[12] *Birmingham* (Ala.) *Age-Herald,* May 16, 1915.

In all probability Sousa appropriated some of the better melodies for use in later works, because only fragments of the manuscript have survived. Constructing a synopsis from these fragments would be impractical, but the names of the principal characters and some of the songs are known.

CAST:

Katherine (Kate)
Wyvern
Clotilde
Lucius
Brown
Smith
Lottie
Begoor
Doodles

SONGS:

Ah, Sad Is the Heart
Call Me Your Darling, Your Love
Love Is Young
Now the Author's Got Us into His Libretto
She Sat Amid the Red Red Roses There
This Sad Misguided Old Man Behold!
Waiting for a Lover
We Thought
When Love the Young Archer
Why Nothing Could Be Plainer

MSS: Opa 148pp inc & 12pp sketches; sketches dated 14Nov1878 np, 15Nov1878 np, 20Nov1878 np, 5Dec1878 np, & 11Dec1878 np [LC]
Not pub
©: "Opera in three acts": JPS & Wilson J. Vance 18Sep1879; not ren

THE MYSTICAL MISS
(See THE CHARLATAN)

THE QUEEN OF HEARTS (1885)
(ROYALTY AND ROGUERY)
In one act, three scenes
LIBRETTO BY EDWARD M. TABER

First produced at Albaugh's Opera House, Washington, D.C., April 12, 1886

This "juvenile jingle," as it was called, had the shortest run of any of the Sousa operettas which were produced. This was probably due to the unusually large cast required — all costumed as various members of a deck of cards. The only three performances, by amateurs in Washington, were conducted by Sousa, then the popular leader of the U.S. Marine Band.

The work was enthusiastically received, but, as one newspaper remarked, ". . . Some allowance must necessarily be made for the evident friendliness of the audience. . . ."[13] Taber was at his best in his clever, pun-filled libretto, based on the Mother Goose rhyme:

> The Queen of Hearts
>   She made some tarts
> Upon a summer day;
>   The Knave of Hearts,
> He found the tarts,
>   And with them ran away.

Because of its brevity, *The Queen of Hearts* shared the bill with Gilbert and Sullivan's *Trial by Jury*.

Sousa often thought of revising his score for a smaller cast, but there is no evidence that he ever made definite plans. Had he made such a decision, it would have been necessary to compose some new music, because several pieces were conscripted for later use. Most of the operetta's manuscript is unaccounted for, so we may never know how much of this was done. "Ammonia" turned up in *The Charlatan* (1898). "Fable of the Frogs" reappeared in *El Capitan* (1895) and also in *The Charlatan*. And "March of the Cards" was the basis for "The Loyal Legion" march (1890).

CAST: (Total eighty-six)
King of Hearts
Queen of Hearts
Knave of Hearts
Ten of Hearts
Nine of Hearts
Eight of Hearts
Seven of Hearts
Six of Hearts
Five of Hearts
Four of Hearts
Trey of Hearts
Deuce of Hearts
Ace of Hearts
King of Spades, Queen of Spades, etc.

---

[13] *Washington Post*, April 13, 1886.

King of Diamonds, Queen of Diamonds, etc.
King of Clubs, Queen of Clubs, etc.
Little Joker
Cooks (sixteen)
Kitchen Maids (sixteen)
Headsman

SYNOPSIS:

The Queen of Hearts has a fondness for huckleberry tarts, which are expertly prepared from the finest ingredients of foreign lands by her staff of royal cooks. A banquet and reception is held for the courts of Spades, Diamonds, and Clubs so that they too may enjoy the delicious pastry.

The Knave of Hearts shares the Queen's love for the tarts, and he steals them. The Knaves of Spades, Diamonds, and Clubs are shocked by this, but they do not hesitate to help him dispose of them.

At the banquet the Queen faints when it is discovered that the tarts are missing. The Little Joker revives her with ammonia, and it is noticed that the Knave of Hearts is acting suspiciously. The King of Hearts tricks him into confessing and orders him beheaded. But the Queen intercedes, and the Knave's sentence is commuted to the punishment of having his head doused with water beneath a pump. The other Knaves, although accessories to the crime, go undetected and unpunished, and the Queen decrees that at the next banquet the tarts will be protected by the royal army.

SONGS:

Ammonia
Chorus of Cooks and Kitchen Maids
Chorus of the Courts
Fable of the Frogs
It's Really Too Hard to Tell
March of the Cards
Moral Abberation
Now List While I Confess
O Spare This Wretched Knave
Sweet Is Life When One's a Queen
We All Are Waiting

MSS: a) Opa 7pp inc; 18Jan1885 Washington, D.C. [LC]
b) Opa rev 4pp inc; nd np [UI]
c) V/pi 77pp inc; nd np [LC]
Pub: (Libretto only) R. O. Polkinhorn, Washington, D.C.

©: "A juvenile jingle in one act": JPS & Edward M. Taber 16May1885; not ren
(Also see Marches: "The Loyal Legion")

THE SMUGGLERS (1882)
In two acts

LIBRETTO BY WILSON J. VANCE

First produced at Lincoln Hall, Washington, D.C., March 25, 1882

Together with *Desiree* (1883), *The Smugglers* was one of the forerunners of the American operetta. It was the first of Sousa's operettas to be produced, and the music actually was written twice.

While Sousa was conducting the Philadelphia Church Choir Company on a tour of the New England states with Gilbert and Sullivan's *H.M.S. Pinafore* late in 1879, the company tired of that production. They hurriedly prepared Burnand and Sullivan's *The Contrabandista* as a replacement. It was short-lived. Sousa made the orchestration, including several of his own compositions. This orchestration was not published but was copyrighted as "The Musical Numbers of Smugglers." There is no record of copies being sent to the Copyright Office of the Library of Congress, but a few orchestral parts have survived and are now at the Sousa Museum at the University of Illinois. There are twenty-one numbered (although unnamed) selections on these parts, four of which are accredited to Sousa by markings in another's handwriting.

Nearly two years later, after unsuccessfully attempting to launch *Katherine* (1879) and *Florine* (1881), Sousa was ready to try operetta again. With Wilson J. Vance, a Washington journalist and his collaborator on *Katherine,* he wrote the second version of *The Smugglers*. Vance's libretto was based on the plot of *The Contrabandista,* but Sousa's music was entirely his own.[14] It bears an exceptional resem-

---

[14] Sousa apparently felt that the plot of *The Contrabandista* was ineffective but still too good to go to waste. Rather than to rework his earlier

blance to Sullivan's style, however — much more so than in any other Sousa work. Sousa probably felt obliged to do this, out of respect for Sullivan. Imitating another's style deliberately was very much out of character for him, but he evidently made an exception in this case. He was thoroughly familiar with the Sullivan operetta style, having previously made several arrangements and transcriptions of his works. Presumably included in the new production were the four songs of Sousa's from the 1879 version.

With a mostly amateur cast, *The Smugglers* was produced once in Washington, five times in Philadelphia, and once in Lancaster, Pennsylvania. Although it received favorable reviews, it was a financial failure, and the company was transported back to Washington on borrowed money.[15] Sousa was much upset over the failure, but he felt that some of the melodies had sufficient merit to be transferred to later works. Part of the stately song "We Hail Our New-Found King" was used in the suite *At the King's Court* (1904). And the song "Sighing, Ah, Sighing," after revision, was entitled "Sweetheart, I'm Waiting" and included in *El Capitan* (1895). Also, the soldier's chorus, "Let Us March Along," was the basis for "The Lambs' March" (1914).

CAST:

Stubbs, an English photographer
Queen of the smugglers
Violante, a maiden held hostage by the smugglers' gang
Enrique, Violante's fiance
Tito, member of the smugglers' gang in love with the Queen
Mateo, member of the smugglers' gang
Other members of the smugglers' gang
Captain of the Spanish soldiers

---

orchestration, which would have been a mixture of his and Sullivan's music, he composed his own. Had he not, he would probably have encountered copyright ownership problems. Apparently others also felt that the libretto of *The Contrabandista* was weak, because it was rewritten and produced in London as *The Chieftain* in 1894. The plot of *The Chieftain* deviates widely from the plot of *The Contrabandista*, while that of *The Smugglers* does not.

[15] Sousa, *Marching Along*, p. 82.

SYNOPSIS:

Stubbs is photographing the Spanish countryside and becomes lost in a mountainous area. He wanders into the smugglers' hideout and is captured. For the queen of the smugglers this is a timely arrival, because her husband disappeared some time before and has been presumed dead. She has spurned the affections of Tito because the cards foretold that a stranger would appear and become the next king of the gang. Stubbs explains that he is already married, but he is told to comply with their demands or be shot. He is eventually married to the queen, and his own camera records his bigamy.

Another captive of the smugglers, Violante, has been kidnapped and is being held for ransom. Her lover, Enrique, had disguised himself as a smuggler and has been recruited by the gang. He is recognized only by Violante and is dismayed to learn that Mateo is also courting her.

In a coronation ceremony Stubbs is conditionally crowned king of the smugglers. An ancient law of the gang states that each king must prove his allegiance by committing an act of bloodshed. All the smugglers become intoxicated in the celebration, and Violante escapes. She returns with Spanish soldiers, and both sides prepare for battle. But it turns out that the captain of the soldiers is none other than the queen's missing husband. He has brought with him a pardon for the smugglers, all of whom then enlist in the army. Violante and Enrique are reunited, as are the captain and the queen, and Stubbs is free to return home.[16]

SONGS: (published version)
Ah, Love, Kind Love
As They March Along
Canst Thou Turn Away?
Come to These Arms That Long to Hold Thee

---

[16] If inaccuracies are ever detected in this synopsis, it should be considered that no libretto or written description of the operetta was available for study. The synopsis was reconstructed from a study of the scores of *The Smugglers* and *The Contrabandista*, from newspaper reviews of the production in Philadelphia, and from a synopsis of *The Chieftain*.

Cut and Thrust
Do You with Your Flocks and Herds
Free Hearts of Spain
He Is a Spy
How Slowly Fades the Sun
I'm a Robber Free and Bold
It Matters Not
I've Leaped and I've Climbed Like a Blasted Goat
Let Us March Along
The Maiden Sat with Folded Hands
Rouse Thee, and Put Thine Armor On
Sighing, Ah, Sighing
Silence, and to Your Stations Hie
Smugglers We
We Hail Our New-Found King
When the Storms of Life
A Widow's Life
Wine — Wine

MSS: a) Opa 29pp inc; 1pp of rev dated 7Feb1882 Washington, D.C. [LC]
b) V/pi 4pp inc; nd np [LC]
Pub: Shaw
©: "The musical numbers of Smugglers": JPS 11Dec1879; not ren
(Complete) v/pi: JPS & Wilson J. Vance 2Feb1881; not ren
(Also see Marches: "The Lambs' March")

THE VICTORY (1915)
Unfinished

Evidently while still working on *The Irish Dragoon*, Sousa commenced work on *The Victory*. *The Victory* was a play by Ella Wheeler Wilcox and Ruth Helen Davis, and Mrs. Wilcox undertook adapting it as an operetta. The fairy-tale plot, reportedly inspired by World War I, takes place in the land of "One-upon-a-Time" and concerns the victory of love over many vices.

The two-act work was scheduled to be produced in August, 1915,[17] but for reasons never explained publicly it was not completed. None of Sousa's music has ever been found, but a typed libretto was among volumes of his personal library which his family bequeathed to the U.S. Marine Corps Museum in 1969.

MSS: N/A
Not pub or ©

---

[17] *New York Morning Telegraph,* April 21, 1915.

THE WOLF (1888)
In three acts
LIBRETTO BY JOHN PHILIP SOUSA
(Not produced)

The Wolf should be regarded as a "transition" operetta. Sousa borrowed much of the plot and music from his unsuccessful *The Smugglers* (1882). Then, since *The Wolf* was not produced in the nine years of its existence, much of the plot and music were used later for *The Bride Elect* (1897). Some of the songs were also used in *El Capitan* (1895) and *The Charlatan* (1898). This accounts for the fact that only fragments of the manuscript are known to exist under the original title.

Little is known of the reasons for the operetta's demise except for some information given in a faded clipping from a newspaper called the *Advertiser,* found on p. 76 of the Sousa Band press book for 1893. It reads as follows:

> ... The fifth [*sic*] and most ambitious effort of Sousa in the operatic line is entitled "The Wolf." This he sold to Francis Wilson, who forfeited his contract. Then he sold it to Locke and Davis for De Wolf Hopper, who did likewise. The failure of these two comedians to produce the opera was, in the estimation of Mr. Sousa, because the leading role is for a primadonna and it consequently does not afford an opportunity for the male comedian to occupy the center of the stage from the rise of the curtain until its fall. ...

CAST:

Maraquita
Lombriz, elderly, miserly banker betrothed to Maraquita
Gabriel, Maraquita's true lover
Binks, an English photographer
The Wolf (La Loba), widowed bandit leader
Gandul
Sapo } bandits in the Wolf's gang
Balthazar, an innkeeper
Argelles, a notary
Sarasate, a jailer
Captain of the household troops
Villette, Maraquita's maid
Teresa
Ester } friends of Maraquita
Jacinta

SYNOPSIS:

In the village of Pontacasa, Spain, the pretty maid Maraquita is about to become the victim of her late father's vindictiveness. Nearly eighteen years ago, he had wished for a boy instead of a girl. As though she were to blame for his disappointment, he willed her his fortune only on the condition that she wed the aging Lombriz before her eighteenth birthday. Another peculiar condition of the will is that she must forfeit her inheritance if she marries someone other than Lombriz — before her eighteenth birthday. In spite of these conditions she is in love with the youthful Gabriel.

Argelles, the local notary, is in sympathy with Maraquita and secretly suggests that Lombriz be kidnapped and held hostage until after she turns eighteen. Then she will be free to marry Gabriel. The marriage to Lombriz is to be consummated two days hence.

Binks, a traveling photographer in search of scenery to photograph, appears in the village and checks into Balthazar's hotel. The Wolf and her bandits also make an appearance at the hotel, inquiring if any wealthy guests are registered. Balthazar has been most cooperative with the lovely bandit leader in the past, and he names Binks as a likely victim. The bandits then proceed to cheat him out of much of his money by confidence routines.

Maraquita takes Argelles's plot to heart, and she and her friends masquerade as bandits. To test the effectiveness of their disguises they attempt a robbery. But their first intended victims turn out to be none other than the Wolf and her two lieutenants, Gandul and Sapo. They are amused at their amateurishness and cause the ladies to panic merely by pretending to spot a mouse. Exposed and having lost her composure, Maraquita tells the Wolf of her woes, and the Wolf is hired to kidnap Lombriz in a more professional manner.

Meanwhile, Gabriel realizes that time is running out and formulates a plan of his own to prevent the marriage. He disguises as Lombriz and has engaged Argelles to marry him to Maraquita immediately.

The Wolf's gang, augmented by Maraquita and her friends, spreads out and searches for Lombriz. One group mistakenly kidnaps the disguised Gabriel, another group kidnaps the real Lombriz, and a third group mistakenly kidnaps the hapless Binks. After they meet and become aware of their multiple blunders, Lombriz is taken to their mountain hideout and Binks and Gabriel are released.

The next day, Binks sets out to photograph the countryside and accidentally wanders near the Wolf's hideout. The Wolf has just been seeing her fortune in the cards, and according to the cards her fate is that she must marry the next stranger she meets. Binks arrives at this moment, is captured, and the Wolf believes that he was directed to her by fate. A marriage is arranged, much to the consternation of Binks, because he has a wife and family back in England.

Gandul and Sapo have both been courting the Wolf and are jealous of Binks. They point out an ancient law of their band which states that a bandit king must have proved himself worthy by having been victorious in battle. The Wolf then arranges for a duel between Binks and the elderly Lombriz, knowing that Lombriz would come out the loser and she could then have Binks.

Both Binks and Lombriz are exceedingly reluctant to fight. Just as they are forced together, a corps of Spanish carbineers surrounds the camp and captures them all. It had been rumored that Lombriz had been in league with the bandits, that Maraquita had learned of it, and that he had kidnapped her and fled. When the carbineers ask who her abductor was, she cleverly points to Lombriz. All the men are then taken to prison.

The Wolf, Maraquita, and the girls later masquerade as a special contingent of carbineers and march to the prison with faked orders in an attempt to have Gabriel, Lombriz, and the bandits released in their custody. Lombriz is told that Maraquita had interceded in his behalf and had obtained his pardon — on the condition that she be freed of her obligation to marry him. He agrees, under duress. He is then led to a wine cellar which will serve as a "pardon ward," where he consumes several bottles of wine in an effort to forget the whole matter.

In his state of drunkenness, Lombriz has no appreciation of the fact that he has meanwhile been found innocent of the charge of abduction. So Maraquita is free to marry Gabriel. And Binks is declared unfit to be bandit king by virtue of his unwillingness to prove himself in battle, so the Wolf gives her hand to Gandul.

SONGS: [18]

Ay-ay de Mi!
Behold a Robber

---

[18] Not all the songs were titled. Titles have therefore been assigned, for the sake of documentation, in two ways. First, if an untitled song occurred both in *The Wolf* and in another operetta, the name used in the other operetta has been used here. Second, if an untitled song was not used in another operetta, the author assigned a logical title based on a repetitive phrase. The second group includes "Ay-ay de Mi!," "Contemplate Our Stride," "I Don't See It That Way," "A Man Outside Our Noble Band," "Oh Lover Tried and True," "She'll Find a Way to Cheat Him Yet," "Sympathetic Feelings We Repress," "Take Him up Tenderly," and "Yo t'amo Bien."

A Bird Reduced to Feather's Weight
Contemplate Our Stride
The God of Gold
The Golden Cars
Hail the Stranger
I Don't See It That Way
In a Matter
Knights of the King's Highway Are We
Love, Light of My Heart
A Man Outside Our Noble Band
May and December Are to Mate
Oh Lover Tried and True
Oh, Nature (The Photographer's Rhapsody)
Oh Save Us from the Monster's Rage
Oh Stars That Form the Milky Way
The Rose-Tint Leaves the Sky
She'll Find a Way to Cheat Him Yet
Sweetheart I'm Waiting
Sympathetic Feelings We Repress
Take Him up Tenderly
To Marry or Not to Marry
When This Old Coat Was in the Style
While You're Hardly Prepossessing
Yo t'amo Bien

MSS: a) Opa 26pp inc; nd np [LC]
     b) V/pi 86pp inc; nd np [LC]
     c) Typescript of libretto with rev in Sousa's hand 92pp; nd np [LC]
Not published
©:   "Comic opera in three acts": JPS 6Jul1888; not ren

MARCHES

When a person thinks of marches, the name of John Philip Sousa immediately comes to mind. It has always been generally agreed that Sousa is rightfully entitled to the cognomen "March King." He had worthy competition, however. Serious contestants from abroad included Carl Teike, Franz von Blon, and Herman Blankenburg of Germany, Louis Ganne of France, Julius Fucik of Czeckoslovakia, and Kenneth J. Alford (Major Fred J. Ricketts) of England. In the United States, the most significant writers were Henry Fillmore, Karl L. King, Edwin Franko Goldman, Robert B. Hall, and David W. Reeves. Next to Sousa, England's Alford (composer of "Colonel Bogey") emerges as the most important march writer, even though his output was small.

Sousa wrote 136 marches. The number is greater if we add other march melodies found in his suites and operettas and also a number of songs which he transformed into marches without the addition of new material. To avoid double listings, however, only the marches initially written as marches are listed in this section.

All of Sousa's marches have not had the same public appeal. Some of his early marches are almost never performed; while they are not substandard in workmanship, they do not have the mark of genius borne by his more significant works. Generally speaking, his marches of the 1880's and 1890's are military in character. Those written after the turn of the century are more sophisticated. This is especially true

of those written during his last decade; these are polished works when compared with his earliest efforts and are very definitely worthy of one called "March King."

Sousa gave his marches colorful, imaginative titles, and an investigation into the origins of these titles leads to some fascinating stories about his life and career. In spite of the fact that his public image is that of a military man, only thirty-two of his marches have military titles. Another twelve were composed for expositions and fairs, eleven for schools, and ten for stage productions. The remainder were written for organizations, events, etc. Thirty of these carried no specific dedications. He seldom accepted commissions, but twenty-two were dedicated exclusively to individuals.

If Sousa had a formula for composing successful marches, it was inspired simplicity. He was a master of counterpoint, but he used it prudently and in such a straightforward way that his countermelodies and obbligatos do not appear as mere embellishments or detract from melodic and rhythmic elements.

Sousa's marches are energetic, and in this respect they are said to be characteristically American. The typical Sousa march moves forward at all times. A brief introduction, often beginning with a unison of all instruments, is followed by two distinctly different sections. The first section is vigorous, and the second is still vigorous but broader in nature. Then comes a trio, or main melody, of a more subdued character. After the trio Sousa either inserts lively episodic material and repeats the trio or goes on to a fourth section to end the march. There is an unmistakable impression of finality in the last section, whether it is a repeat of the trio or a fourth, terminal section.

Sousa was a prolific melodist, and his march melodies are bouncy. It is often noted that they are easy to play on the violin — Sousa's instrument — and are difficult for brass instruments. The layman might observe that they are hard to whistle. Seldom were minor keys used, and even then they were quickly resolved to major keys. Minor keys appear only in the first sections, except for momentary excursions in some of the episodic passages. Even in Sousa's three dirges ("In Memoriam," "The Honored Dead," and "The Golden Star"), both major and minor keys are used.

A number of harmonic and rhythmic patterns appear often in Sousa's marches. These provide distinctive stylistic features for one attempting to analyze them from a musical standpoint; such an analysis is beyond the scope of this book, however. A study of the instrumentation he called for is excluded for the same reason.

Looking at the musical characteristics of the typical Sousa march, and excluding those marches of the dirge, medley, or "grand" variety, we find that the average length is two minutes and thirty-five seconds when played at 120 beats per minute. The shortest is "Guide Right" (1:28), and the longest is "The Free Lance" (4:07). Almost all are written in flat keys, rather than sharp keys, for the convenience of band musicians. (Exceptions to this are simplified versions published for piano.) Although the most frequently used keys are B-flat and E-flat major (two and three flats respectively), a bandsman may expect to find a Sousa march written in keys of from no flats to six flats. Sousa apparently had no favorite keys.

Regarding time signatures, nearly twice as many of Sousa's marches are written in alla breve ("cut time") or 2/4 time as in 6/8 time. However, five of his twelve most popular marches are exclusively 6/8 marches, primarily because this was the rhythm of the popular two-step dance with which several of his marches were identified. He used a combination of 6/8 and 2/4 in only six of his marches (excluding the medley types), and five of these were pieced together wholly or partly from various sections of his operettas.

Most of Sousa's marches (again excluding the medley, dirge, and "grand" types) may be broken down into these two basic forms:

	Introduction	First section (repeated)	Second section (repeated)	Trio	Episode	Trio	Episode	Trio
(a)	Introduction	First section (repeated)	Second section (repeated)	Trio	Episode	Trio	Episode	Trio
(b)	Introduction	First section (repeated)	Second section (repeated)	Trio (repeated)	Fourth section (repeated)			

Sousa did not take credit for originating these forms, but he did standardize them. They were then widely used by others, with or without variations, particularly by American march writers.

Three-fourths of his marches, including all but a few of his most successful ones, are of the form (a) above. This form was established with "Our Flirtation" (1880), was developed gradually, and then was used almost exclusively after World War I. A majority of his introductions were four measures long, and most of the remaining sections (episodes excepted) were either sixteen or thirty-two measures long. The key signature was nearly always changed at the trio by adding a flat and thereby raising the key by the interval of a perfect fourth. Sousa departed from march tradition by omitting a return to the first sections (da capo, or D.C.) on all but a few of his early marches. Likewise, he used a coda on only one of his marches, "Riders for the Flag" (1927).

Sousa's episodes, usually called break strains or interludes, are very interesting and are found in over eighty of his marches. They are used mostly in the form (a) above, but they are occasionally inserted between the trio and the fourth section in marches of the form (b). There is no set length, and the episodes are sometimes as long as or longer than the sections they separate. After changes of key, modulations, and usually unpredictable musical gyrations, the episodes lead up to the final section with a definite sense of direction.

In America, the common march is not played as often today as it was in Sousa's day. There was a time when practically every professional bandmaster was obliged to write marches, but this time has passed. Veteran bandsmen often observe that the performance of marches, particularly Sousa's, is becoming a lost art.

Many writers have said that no band could play a Sousa march like the Sousa Band, but it would probably be more accurate to state that no conductor ever swayed audiences with marches more dramatically than Sousa did. It was a thrilling experience to see Sousa conduct his own band in his own marches, and therein lies one of the secrets of the Sousa Band's phenomenal success. With Sousa on the podium, his marches had what is best described as a driving pulsation. This pulsation, or "lift," electrified audiences, and it has seldom been duplicated since Sousa's death.

Sousa did not insist that others duplicate his interpretations. In fact, he deliberately attempted to keep these to himself, perhaps to avoid undue competition from other bands. He would deviate from the printed score, mostly by adding accents, dynamics, and a few special effects to suit his own personal desires. He condoned no changes of tempo and consistently played the marches at tempos slightly faster than normal military marching tempos.

The pulsation effect he extracted from his players was largely due to a style of playing which he referred to as a marcato style. "Marcato," in musical language, means that the rhythm is emphasized,

marked, and accented, but by Sousa's definition it also meant playing in a separated or detached style, for the sake of clarity. Except for sustained passages, the Sousa Band played their notes slightly shorter or crisper so as to create an impression of cleanly separated rhythmic patterns. They also attacked each note with confidence.

When playing a march, the Band's effectiveness was increased by special artistry on the part of the bass drummer, who played in such a manner as to highlight the pulsation effect. Veteran bandsmen have often commented that his beat was felt rather than heard. For many years Sousa was fortunate in having August Helmecke, a true virtuoso of the bass drum, to provide this essential ingredient. The finale of each march was exciting and climactic, and often the cornets, trumpets, and trombones would come to the front of the stage. These various devices, coupled with great precision and Sousa's brighter tempos, gave the Sousa Band its unique musical personality.

Marches are, in many ways, highly difficult compositions to play well, and Sousa's are certainly no exception. But when a conductor adheres to Sousa's principles, and when he make a sincere effort to re-create marches in the spirit in which they were conceived, the results are most gratifying.

Sousa gave his marches the same care that a great symphony orchestra conductor would give to the works of the master composers. He believed that the march was the special heritage of the band, and he made a major contribution to that heritage.

ACROSS THE DANUBE (1877)

The Danube traditionally divided the Mediterranean world from the "barbarian hinterland." It was one of the borders of the Ottoman Empire, which was regularly at war with czarist Russia. In their fourth extended war, the Russians gained one decisive victory by crossing the Danube in June and July, 1877. Sousa credits the inspiration for "Across the Danube" to one such victory of Christendom over the

Turks, and it was probably the news of this particular battle which caught his fancy.

MSS: N/A
Pub: Stoddart (piano); Hitchcock (piano); Coleman (band)
©: Pi: Stoddart 17Nov1877; not ren

AMERICA FIRST (1916)

The subtitle of this piece, "A March of the States," caused confusion because Sousa's incidental music for the "Hip Hip Hooray" show at the New York Hippodrome was also called "March of the States" and was written at approximately the same time. The inspiration came from the text of a 1915 speech by President Woodrow Wilson in which he declared, "Our whole duty for the present is summed up in the motto 'America First.' "

A dual premiere took place as Washington's birthday was celebrated on February 22, 1916. Sousa's Band played the march at the Hippodrome while the U.S. Marine Band played it in Washington at the national convention of the Daughters of the American Revolution. The march was dedicated to Mrs. William Cumming Story, president of the D.A.R., and included brief passages of "Maryland, My Maryland" and "Dixie."

MSS: N/A
Pub: Harms
©: Pi: Harms 18Mar1916; ren JvMS 19Mar1943
Bd: Harms 6Dec1940; ren Warner Brothers-Seven Arts 8Aug1968

THE AMERICAN LEGION
(See COMRADES OF THE LEGION)

THE AMERICAN WEDDING MARCH
(See WEDDING MARCH)

ANCHOR AND STAR (1918)

While leading the U.S. Navy Battalion Band at the Great Lakes Naval Training Center during World War I, Sousa composed this march and dedicated it "To the U.S. Navy." It is often compared with "Semper Fidelis" because it bears a resemblance in construction, rhythm, key, and

contrapuntal devices. Just as "Globe and Eagle" was named after the U.S. Marine Corps emblem, this march was named after the U.S. Navy emblem.

MSS: N/A
Pub: Fischer
©: Bd; orch; pi: JPS 22Aug1918; ren JPrS & HSA 10Sep1945

ANCIENT AND HONORABLE ARTILLERY COMPANY
(1924)

"I have always found a great deal of inspiration in these old songs. . . . We cannot improve simple straightforward melodies, but we can give them a more adequate, full-throated expression. . . ." Sousa made this statement to a newspaper reporter in discussing the new march he had just built around "Auld Lang Syne."[1]

"Auld Lang Syne" happened to be the marching song of the Ancient and Honorable Artillery Company of Boston, the oldest military organization in the United States. When the Sousa Band visited Boston in 1923, a delegation from the "Ancients" requested that Sousa compose a march incorporating the song so dear to them. He gave them his word. Formal solicitation by Governor Cox of Massachusetts and the commander of the company, Capt. Clarence J. McKenzie, followed shortly.[2]

The Sousa Band's strenuous thirty-second annual tour lay ahead of Sousa, but he wasted no time in penning the new march when the tour ended, and it was promptly published. "Ancient and Honorable Artillery Company" was the featured march of the next tour, and a formal presentation was made to the "Ancients" at Symphony Hall in Boston on September 21, 1924.[3]

MSS: a) Pi 1pp inc; 18Mar1924 np [LC]
b) Bd 15pp; 19Mar1924 Sands Pt. [UI]
Pub: Fox
©: Pi: Fox 23Jul1924; ren JPrS & HSA 1Aug1951
Also pub for bd but not ©

---

[1] *Philadelphia Inquirer,* June 29, 1924.
[2] *Boston Evening Transcript,* August 15, 1923.
[3] *Boston Leader,* September 13, 1924. The combined bands of Sousa and the "Ancients" played the march for the first time in Boston's Symphony Hall on September 21, 1924.

THE ATLANTIC CITY PAGEANT (1927)

In the late 1920's it became increasingly difficult for professional concert bands to find employment at amusement parks or expositions, even for a few days. As the engagements at Philadelphia's Willow Grove Park were coming to an end, the Sousa Band was happy to extend its regular tour by playing at the Steel Pier in Atlantic City, New Jersey. They began regular seasons there in 1926, and Sousa penned this almost-forgotten march to celebrate their second annual engagement. The march was reportedly written at the suggestion of Atlantic City's mayor, Anthony M. Ruffu. Sousa probably had the Miss America Pageant in mind; at that time it was known as the Atlantic City Beauty Pageant.

MSS: N/A
Pub: Fox
©:   Bd: Fox 26Sep1927; ren JPrS & HSA
      13Jun1955
Also pub for pi but not ©

THE AVIATORS (1931)

Friends and associates of Sousa were constantly telling of his subtle wit. The object of one of his rare pranks was Captain William A. Moffett, the man responsible for his enlistment and commission in the U.S. Navy during World War I. Moffett needed a musician with considerable administrative ability to organize navy band units at the Great Lakes Naval Training Center. Sousa's brother-in-law happened to be on Moffett's staff.[4] He arranged a meeting between Moffett and Sousa to discuss the possibility of obtaining Sousa's services.

Sousa arrived at a decision quickly but decided to have fun at Moffett's expense. He indicated that he would like to accept the position but raised the question as to whether or not the navy could meet his salary demand. Moffett realized that Sousa was a wealthy man but had not expected such a blunt approach. He apologized for the navy's relatively low pay scale and offered Sousa $2,500 per year. Sousa replied: "I refuse to take such a sum! Tell Secretary Daniels that if he wishes for my

help in this war he will have to part with not less than one dollar a month for the duration of the conflict."[5]

Moffett and Sousa became warm friends. Moffett had a distinguished military career, rising to the rank of rear admiral as chief of the navy's Bureau of Aeronautics. He was later nicknamed "Father of the flat-top." In one of his last musical efforts, Sousa dedicated "The Aviators" to him.

MSS: a) Bd 11pp; 2Jun1931 Sands Pt. [LC]
     b) Pi 1pp inc; 9Jul1931 np [LC]
     c) Pi 2pp; nd np [LC]
     d) Pi 2pp inc; nd np [LC]
Pub: Presser
©:   Bd: Presser 4Sep1931; ren JPrS & HSA
      15Sep1958
      Pi: Presser 18Feb1932; ren HSA
      31Aug1959
      Orch: Presser 18Apr1932; ren Presser
      13Apr1960
      Pi duet: Presser 10May1932; not ren

THE BEAU IDEAL (1893)

"Sousa is the joy of the masses, the beautiful musician."[6] The expression "beau ideal" was used in the early 1890's to describe anything that had caught the public fancy. An inscription on the original sheet music indicates that the "beau ideal" in the title was a newly formed organization called The National League of Musicians of the United States.

MSS: Pi 2pp; nd np [LC]
Pub: Coleman
©:   Pi: Coleman 7Apr1893 again 4May1894;
      ren JPS 7Mar1921 again 6Feb1922
      Bd: Coleman 17Apr1893; ren JPS
      7Mar1921
      Pi duet: Coleman 7Jun1893 again
      4May1894; ren JPS 6Feb1922
      Orch: Coleman 7Jun1893; not ren
      Pi 6 hands: Coleman 4May1894; ren
      JPS 6Feb1922
      Cornet & pi: Coleman 4May1894; ren
      JPS 6Feb1922

THE BELLE OF CHICAGO (1892)

Sousa was soundly criticized for this march,

---

[4] Lieutenant James M. Bower, second husband of Sousa's youngest sister, Elise.

[5] *Albany* (N.Y.) *Journal,* circa July, 1922; in Sousa Band press book of 1922. Also other clippings in same book.
[6] *Chicago Journal,* sometime prior to 1897. Quoted in a book of testimonials distributed for promotional purposes by David Blakely, Sousa Band manager.

which he composed as a salute to the ladies of Chicago. Among the protests made by Chicago newsmen were these:

> "Mr. Sousa evidently regards the Chicago belle as a powerful creature, with the swinging stride of a giant, a voice like a fog-horn, and feet like sugar-cured hams."

> "The maiden who inspired it would seem to be . . . a giantess . . . whose motto . . . might have been 'I will make a noise.' "

> "Mr. Sousa has made his Chicago belle a strappling kitchen wench. . . ."[7]

The march outlived its criticism and is probably more popular overseas than it is in the United States.

MSS: Bd 5pp; 23Jul1892 Washington, D.C. [LC]
Pub: Coleman
©: Bd: Coleman 2Sep1892; not ren
Pi: Coleman 21Sep1892 again 4May1894; ren JPS 6Feb1922
Orch: Coleman 6Oct1892; not ren
Cornet & pi; 3 zithers: Coleman 4May1894; ren JPS 6Feb1922

THE BELLE OF PITTSBURGH
(See THE PRIDE OF PITTSBURGH)

BEN BOLT (1888)

Public acceptance of the Sousa marches which were entirely of his own creation was almost always greater than those in which he incorporated melodies of others. "Ben Bolt," which was constructed around a popular song of the same name, is practically unknown today. It included several songs of the day: "The Daisy," "Go Down Moses," "Sally in Our Alley," "O Fond Dove, O Fond Dove," and "Ben Bolt" ("Sweet Alice Ben Bolt").

MSS: Bd 1pp inc; nd np [LC]
Pub: Coleman
©: Bd: Coleman 27Dec1888; ren JPS 26Dec1916

THE BLACK HORSE TROOP (1924)

Sousa's love for horses is reflected in this march dedicated to the mounted troops of a Cleveland National Guard unit. Their exclusive use of black horses was the inspiration for the title. Troop A, once known as the First City Troop of Cleveland, was originally an independent militia group and has had a long, distinguished history since its formation in 1877. Sousa's most noteworthy association with the troop came in 1898. The Sousa Band, having arrived in Cleveland just as the troop was preparing to leave for the Spanish-American War, marched in a parade escorting them from the Armory to the train depot. His first association was much earlier, however. As leader of the U.S. Marine Band in 1881, he marched with the organization in the funeral cortege of President James A. Garfield.

At a dinner held in Sousa's honor in November, 1924, the march was requested by Captain Walker Nye of Troop A.[8] The request was fulfilled promptly, and the march was presented in Cleveland on October 17, 1925, at a Sousa Band concert which also marked the forty-eighth anniversary of Troop A. For the occasion, the mounted troopers were dressed in the blue uniforms of 1877, complete with black fur busbies. They rode right up onto the stage with the band. Sousa presented a manuscript of the march to Captain Nye. After the concert a reception was held at the Armory, and Sousa was presented with a bronze plaque.

Many of the former Sousa Band members expressed their fondness for this composition and commented on the descriptive character it assumed when performed by Sousa himself. Part of the effect was due to the 6/8 rhythm, which suggests the canter of horses. Also contributing to the effect was Sousa's use of simulated hoofbeats.

MSS: Bd 16pp; 30Dec1924 np [UI]
Pub: Fox
©: Pi: Fox 6Jul1925; ren JPrS & HSA 6Aug1952
Also pub for bd but not ©

THE BLUDSO MARCH
(See THE PHOENIX MARCH)

BLUE RIDGE
(See THE NAVAL RESERVE)

---

[7] Undated clippings from Chicago newspapers in Sousa Band press books of 1892-93.

[8] "Troop A March," *Cleveland Topics,* July 11, 1925.

BONNIE ANNIE LAURIE (1883)

Sousa often remarked that the old Scottish ballad "Annie Laurie" was the most beautiful of all folk songs. He wrote this march around it in 1883, but in spite of several printings it was soon forgotten.

MSS: N/A
Pub: Pepper
©:   Bd: Pepper 8Jun1883 again 17Dec1883; not ren
      Pi: Pepper 22Jan1897; not ren
      Orch: Pepper 28Jul1897; not ren

BOY SCOUTS OF AMERICA (1916)

Sousa received three silver loving cups for his sixty-second birthday in 1916 when the Sousa Band was performing in the *Hip Hip Hooray* show in Philadelphia. One of the cups was presented by the members of his band, another by the 1,200 employees of the show, and the third by the Boy Scouts of America, for whom he had just written this march.

Dr. Charles D. Hunt, president of the national Scout organization, had earlier made the request of Sousa. Sousa responded with a march that ". . . absolutely breathes the boy; it visualizes the supple step of the boy marching, and not the heavy tread of the man."[9] He also wrote lyrics, as did author Booth Tarkington, and it was announced that the march was to be officially adopted by the Boy Scouts of America.[10] For the premiere, the Scouts were represented by delegations from several cities.

MSS: Bd 11pp; 30Sep1916 Sands Pt. [LC]
Pub: Harms
©:   Pi: Harms 16Dec1916; ren JvMS 18Dec1943
      Bd: Harms 26Dec1940; not ren

THE BOYS ARE HOME AGAIN
(See Songs — Words by Others: WHEN THE BOYS COME SAILING HOME!)

THE BOYS IN NAVY BLUE
(See THE NAVAL RESERVE)

THE BRIDE ELECT (1897)

After the widespread success of his operetta *El Capitan,* Sousa regrettably declined an offer of $100,000 for *The Bride Elect,* from which this march was extracted. The operetta soon passed from the musical scene, but the march was a favorite of bandsmen for many years to come.

The march was pieced together from various sections of the operetta. The principal theme was developed from the song, "Unchain the Dogs of War," which ended Act II. The march was sometimes programmed by the Sousa Band under that title.

According to Frank Simon, cornetist of the Sousa Band from 1914 to 1920, "The Bride Elect" was among Sousa's own favorites.[11] He once referred to it as the best march he had ever written.[12]

MSS: N/A
Pub: Church
©:   Pi: Church 20Dec1897; ren JPS 11Nov1925
      Bd: Church 27Dec1898; ren JPS 11Dec1925
      Orch: Church 27Dec1898; ren JPS 11Nov1925
      Pi duet; pi six hands; banjo; banjo duet; banjo & pi; guitar; guitar duet; mandolin; mandolin & pi; mandolin & guitar; mandolin & pi & guitar; two mandolins & pi; two mandolins & guitar: Church 6Jan1898; no renewals of any

BRITISH TARS
(See JACK TAR)

BULLETS AND BAYONETS (1918)

More than many of Sousa's other marches, this World War I composition has a distinctly military character. In studying the music, Sousa's apparent inspiration by visions of battlefield glory is not difficult to imagine. But perhaps its war-like title accounted for the relative lack of popularity.

There is no record of solicitation by a specific regiment, but the march was dedi-

---

[9] Quoted from an unidentified Boston newspaper in Sousa Band press book of 1916.
[10] *Musical Courier,* October 12, 1916.

[11] Interview with author, June 29, 1963.
[12] *Trenton* (N.J.) *Evening Times,* April 4, 1899.

cated "To the officers and men of the U.S. Infantry."

MSS: Pi 2pp; nd np [LC]
Pub: Schirmer
©: Pi: Schirmer 8Feb1919 again 12Sep1919 again 20Feb1922; not ren
Also pub for bd and for orch but not ©

EL CAPITAN (1896)

One of the perennial Sousa favorites, this march has enjoyed exceptional popularity with bands since it first appeared. It was extracted from the most successful of the Sousa operettas, *El Capitan*. El Capitan of the operetta was the comical and cowardly Don Medigua, the early seventeenth-century viceroy of Peru. Some of the themes appear in more than one act, and the closing theme of the march is the same rousing theme which ends the operetta.

This was the march played by the Sousa Band, augmented to over a hundred men and all at Sousa's personal expense, as they led Admiral Dewey's victory parade in New York on September 30, 1899. It was a matter of sentiment with Sousa, because the same march had been played by the band on Dewey's warship *Olympia* as it sailed out of Mirs Bay on the way to attack Manila during the Spanish-American War.

MSS: Bd 6pp; 30Apr1896 Exeter, N.Y. [LC]
Pub: Church
©: Pi: Church 18May1896; ren JPS 30Apr1924
Bd: Church 21May1896; ren JPS 30Apr1924
Orch: Church 20Jun1896; ren JPS 3May1924
Pi duet; pi six hands: Church 30Jul1896; ren JPS 31May1924
Banjo; banjo duet; banjo & pi: Church 20Aug1896; not ren
Guitar; guitar duet; mandolin; mandolin & pi; mandolin & pi & guitar; mandolin & guitar; two mandolins & pi; two mandolins & guitar; zither; zither duet: Church 10Sep1896; no renewals of any

CARMEN MARCH

(See Arrangements and Transcriptions — Instrumental Solos or Ensembles: EVENING PASTIME)

A CENTURY OF PROGRESS (1931)

In the span of a century, the city of Chicago grew from a small fort and a handful of crude cabins to a thriving metropolis. The World's Fair was held there in 1933 to celebrate this extraordinary expansion. The Sousa Band was to be engaged as the official band, and Sousa was asked to compose a march specifically for the fair. He responded with "A Century of Progress," using the motto of the fair for the title.

Although he once expressed a wish that he could some day celebrate his own century of progress, thereby being enabled to write more marches, Sousa passed away at the age of seventy-seven, prior to the fair's opening. His cousin Lennox Lohr, general manager of the fair, saw to it that the Sousa composition was named the official march of the fair. Strangely, however, no band was hired in the absence of the Sousa Band.

MSS: a) Pi 1pp inc; 30Mar1931 np [LC]
b) Bd 10pp; 1May1931 Sands Pt. [LC]
c) Bd 10pp; nd np [LC]
d) Pi 2pp; nd np [UI]
Pub: Presser
©: Bd: Presser 4Sep1931 again 3Nov1931; ren JPrS & HSA 15Sep1958 again by HSA 31Aug1959
Orch: Presser 3Nov1931; ren HSA 31Aug1959
Pi: Presser 19Nov1931; ren HSA 31Aug1959
Pi duet: Presser 16Jul1932; not ren

THE CHANTYMAN'S MARCH (1918)

After enlisting in the U.S. Navy in 1917, Sousa made a study of sea chanteys and then wrote an article for *The Great Lakes Recruit* entitled "Songs of the Sea." He made further use of the study while on a brief leave from the navy the following spring by composing one of his medley-type marches and calling it "The Chantyman's March." The march incorporates eight chanteys, in this order: "Knock a Man Down," "Away for Rio," "Haul the Bowline," "The Ballad of Billy Taylor," "It's Time for Us to Leave Her," "Put up Clearing Gear," "Hoodah Day," and "A-Roving."

MSS: Pi 2pp; 21Mar1918 Sands Pt. [LC]

Pub: Fischer
©:   Bd; pi: JPS 13Jul1918; ren JPrS &
       HSA 29Jul1945
       Orch: JPS 23Aug1918; ren JPrS &
       HSA 10Sep1945

THE CHARLATAN (1898)

It would seem that a march taken from
one of Sousa's most musically interesting
operettas would rank among his better
efforts, but such was not the case with this
march. It was extracted from Acts II and
III of *The Charlatan,* and despite a wealth
of published editions it was soon all but
forgotten.

MSS: a) Pi 1pp inc; 14Aug1898 Suffern, N.Y.
       [LC]
       b) Pi 1pp inc; nd np [UI]
Pub: Church
©:   Bd; orch; pi: Church 6Sep1898; ren
       JPS 6May1926
       Pi duet; two mandolins & pi; two
       mandolins & guitar: Church
       24Sep1898; ren JPS 9Aug1926
       Guitar: Church 15Oct1898; ren JPS
       4Sep1926
       Banjo: Church 17Oct1898; ren JPS
       4Sep1926
       Banjo duet: Church 17Oct1898; ren
       JPS 23Sep1926
       Guitar duet; zither duet: Church
       12Nov1898; ren JPS 23Sep1926

C.I.A. MARCH
(See DAUGHTERS OF TEXAS)

THE CIRCUMNAVIGATORS CLUB
(1931)

To be admitted to the exclusive Circumnavigators Club of New York City, one
must have "traveled around the world and
have a sincere interest in foreign countries." Sousa met these requirements easily.
His fascination with countries abroad was
obvious in his writings, speeches, and in
the titles of his compositions. As for his
circumnavigating the globe, he did it in
a big way — with a band of fifty-three
musicians on his payroll.

According to the dates of his manu-
scripts, this was Sousa's last composition.
He typed a note to the Circumnavigators
Club, and this is filed at the Library of

Congress with one of the two known manuscripts. The manuscript shows little un-
steadiness of hand, but Sousa added a
humorous apology at the end of the typed
note, which reads in full:

"I am a member of Circumnavigators
Club for the following reasons: I went
from New York to London, from London
on a tour in England, Ireland, Scotland, and
Wales; sailed from Plymouth to Teneriffe,
sailed again from Teneriffe to Capetown,
toured South Africa, sailed from Capetown
to Australia, toured that country, sailed from
Melbourne to Tasmania, toured that country and sailed from there to New Zealand,
toured that country and went from New
Zealand to Suva, from Suva to Honolulu,
from Honolulu to Vancouver, British Columbia, from British Columbia to New
York. John Philip Sousa. Port Washington,
Oct. 29th, 1931. God forgive my mistakes.
I hope the copyist will."

With Sousa as one of the honored guests,
the new march was played for the Circumnavigators Club at their annual meeting on December 10, 1931, and was wildly
applauded.

MSS: a) Bd 6pp; 29Oct1931 Sands Pt. [LC]
       b) Pi 4pp; nd np [LC]
Pub: Presser
©:   Bd; pi: Presser 27Nov1931; ren HSA
       31Aug1959

(Reference) CIRCUS MARCH (no date)

This short, lively march obviously was
written for a stage production, but which
one may never be known. The undated
manuscript was among others presented to
the Library of Congress by Sousa's heirs
in 1970. Page numbers and other notations
indicate that it belongs in an operetta, but
this type of composition does not seem to
fit any of the scenes of Sousa's operettas.
Neither does it seem to belong in any of
the stage productions for which he composed the music. One marking reads "On
Stage," and the instrumentation called for
is two cornets, two alto horns, one baritone horn, one tuba, and percussion.

MSS: Bd 2 pp; nd np [LC]
Not pub or ©

COLUMBIA'S PRIDE (1914)

This march grew from Sousa's 1890 song, "Nail the Flag to the Mast," the lyrics being a poem by William Russell Frisbe. Sousa deleted the words, modified the melody and rhythm, added a change of key, and shortened it. The result was a march for piano called "Columbia's Pride," which he apparently never arranged for band or orchestra.

MSS: N/A
Pub: Presser
©:   Pi; pi duet: Presser 21Dec1914; ren JvMS 13Feb1942

COMRADES OF THE LEGION (1920)

Immediately after World War I, Sousa was besieged by such a flood of requests for new marches that he could scarcely have fulfilled them all. One, however, took top priority — a solicitation from the executive staff of the newly formed American Legion. The request was filled promptly. Sousa was enthusiastic about the American Legion because it promoted 100 percent Americanism and because it was a veteran's group. Little could have appealed to him more. On the first piano manuscript was this notation:

> To the American Legion
> Comrades of the Legion

The title was changed on a later manuscript:

> To my comrades of the American Legion
> The American Legion March

When the published version appeared, the original title was used. By the time it was printed and distributed, Sousa was an honorary member of five different Legion posts.

A recording of the new march was made by the Sousa Band, and half a million copies were sold in advance of the actual pressing. The sale was no doubt helped along because the composition was one of the featured numbers of the 1920 Sousa Band tour.

MSS: a) Bd 10pp; 8Mar1920 Sands Pt. [UI]
    b) Pi 4pp; Mar1920 np [LC]
    c) Pi 2pp; 11Feb[?]1920 np [LC]
Pub: Fox
©:   Bd; pi: Fox 1Jun1920; not ren

CONGRESS HALL (1882)

Congress Hall is the name of a historic inn at Cape May, New Jersey. Cape May was and is today a popular east coast resort area, and in 1882 the U.S. Marine Band made its first appearance there under Sousa's direction. The band had created little interest outside Washington until Sousa assumed leadership in 1880. News of its surprising excellence spread, and it was invited to play this engagement at Cape May from August 20 to 26, 1882. Sousa returned the compliment by composing this march and dedicating it to the proprietors of the inn, H. J. and G. R. Crump.

MSS: N/A
Pub: Coleman (bd; pi); Ellis (pi)
©:   Bd: Coleman 31Dec1895; ren JPS 13Dec1913
    Pi: JPS 10Apr1901; not ren

CORCORAN CADETS (1890)

The Corcoran Cadets drill team was the pet of Washington, D.C., being the most notable of the drill teams which flourished there after the Civil War. Their average age was sixteen, and they presented a snappy picture with their colorful uniforms, wooden rifles, and youthful enthusiasm. They competed vigorously with units from Washington and other towns and were the first company of cadets to be mustered into the National Guard. Their esprit de corps was high, and the Corcoran Cadets Veterans' Association held annual reunions for many years.

The "Corcorans" had their own band. Although it is not recorded, they probably made a formal request for this march. Sousa's affirmative response, "to the officers and men of the Corcoran Cadets," was no doubt tendered by an earlier association with William W. Corcoran, for whom the Cadets were named. It was he who nearly changed American musical history by considering Sousa for a musical education in Europe. Sousa had declined this opportunity, and the march was probably a belated expression of appreciation.

MSS: a) Bd 6pp; 8May1890 Washington, D.C. [LC]

b) Pi 1pp; nd np [LC]
Pub: Coleman
©:   Pi: Coleman 31Dec1890 again
          4May1894; ren JPS 31Aug1918 again
          6Feb1922
       Orch: Coleman 29Dec1891; not ren
Also pub for bd; 1st & 2nd banjo; 1st mandolin
  but not ©

THE CORNHUSKERS
(See UNIVERSITY OF NEBRASKA)

CORONATION MARCH
(See Suites: TALES OF A TRAVELER)

THE CRUSADER (1888)

Only those who receive certain degrees in
Masonry may fully appreciate the meaning
of this composition, which was written
shortly after Sousa was "knighted" in
Columbia Commandery No. 2, Knights
Templar, Washington, D.C. The Knights
Templar is theoretically derived from the
Crusades, and a number of their secret
rituals and ceremonies relate to the period
when the Crusaders were battling the
Turks. Thus the Knights Templar organization itself is probably the "Crusader,"
unless Sousa had some individual in mind
whose identity has escaped historians.

The march was one of several sold outright to the Philadelphia publisher Harry
Coleman for $35.00. It is interesting har-
monically, yet straightforward and simple.
If Sousa secretly used fragments of any
Masonic music in the march, he concealed
it so well that Masonic historians have
been unable to bring it to the public's
attention.

MSS: a) Bd 5pp inc; 5Jan1888 Washington,
           D.C. [LC]
       b) Pi 1pp; 4Sep1888 nd np [LC]
       c) Pi 1pp; 5Sep1888 np [LC]
Pub: Coleman
©:   Orch: Coleman 1Mar1889; ren JPS
          17Feb1917
       Pi: Coleman 1Mar1889 again
          4May1894; ren JPS 17Feb1917 again
          6Feb1922
Also pub for bd but not ©

DAUGHTERS OF TEXAS (1929)

A curious fact about "Daughters of Texas,"

which was dedicated to a Texas college, is
that two completely different marches were
written. The college never knew of the first
version, which was conscripted for another
use. This fact has not heretofore been
made public.[13]

After an evening concert in Denton,
Texas, on October 19, 1928, Sousa was
approached by Marion Benson and Margaret Marable and other representatives
of an all-girls school; they presented him
with a petition signed by seventeen hundred students asking him to compose a
march for them. The school was the
College of Industrial Arts, now known as
the Texas Woman's University. Flattered,
Sousa beamed one of his seldom-seen
smiles and replied: "It is impossible to
resist the request of seventeen hundred
charming Texas girls, and if you will send
me some of your college songs I will incorporate them into a march."[14]

Either the college songs were not sent
or else Sousa decided against using them,
because he proceeded to compose the first
version of the march without them. At
the head of the first band score was the
inscription "Daughters of Denton." "Denton" was scratched out and replaced by
"Texas" in another person's handwriting.
A piano manuscript of the same march,
apparently made later, was titled "Daughters of Texas."

This version of the march was never
published, becoming Sousa's "mystery"
march. Just at this time, a Sousa Band tour
for the 1929 season was hurriedly scheduled. There were no plans for a tour that
year, but an attractive offer to appear in
Minneapolis was made by utilities magnate
Wilbur B. Foshay of that city, and a tour

---

[13] The mix-up in titles was discovered by
accident. I examined the band score at the
Sands Point home in 1965. The Library of Congress also listed a band score. Thinking it unlikely that there would be two such scores, I
examined the one at the Library of Congress
and found that it was actually the "Foshay
Tower Washington Memorial" march.

[14] This story was told to the author by
former Sousa Bandsman Edward J. Heney in an
interview on February 8, 1964, and verified by a
story in the *Fort Worth Record-Telegram* of
November 20, 1928.

was built around that engagement. A sky-scraper fashioned after the Washington Monument was being completed, the building now known as the Foshay Tower. A fabulous four-day celebration was to be held, one of the main attractions being Sousa and his band. Realizing the importance of this engagement, Sousa decided to dedicate a march to Foshay and his impressive building. Apparently thinking there was insufficient time to compose a new one, he took the school march and used it in Minneapolis as the "Foshay Tower Washington Memorial" march.

As it turned out, there was sufficient time to compose a second march, because the second version was completed before the tour began, and both marches were featured on tour programs. The second march was published as "Daughters of Texas," but the "Foshay Tower Washington Memorial" march was never published, for reasons given in the discussion of that march.

MSS: Bd 12pp; 19Aug1929 Sands Pt. [LC]
Pub: Church (pi); Presser (bd; pi)
©: Pi: Church 2Apr1930; ren JPrS & HSA 10May1957 again 19Jul1957

THE DAUNTLESS BATTALION (1922)

President Warren G. Harding and band-master John Philip Sousa — two Americans who served their country in totally different capacities — were awarded honorary doctorates by the Pennsylvania Military College in Chester on February 7, 1920. Sousa saluted the cadets in his own inimitable way, by composing a march in their honor. The band score was dedicated "To Col. Hyatt, the Faculty and Cadets of the Pennsylvania Military College" and was entitled "The Pennsylvania Military College March." An orchestra score, presumably made later, was entitled "The Pennsylvania Military March." But by the time the march was published, Sousa had provided the more colorful title.

MSS: a) Orch 10pp inc; 28Dec1922 Sands Pt. [LC]
b) Bd 8pp; 1Jan1923 Sands Pt. [LC]
Pub: Church
©: Pi: Church 15Mar1923; ren JPrS & HSA 24Apr1950

Bd; orch: Church 10Apr1923; ren JPrS & HSA 24Apr1950

(Reference) DESIREE

The march from the operetta *Desiree* is not classified as a separate composition because there is no evidence that it was ever extracted and used as a quickstep march by that or any other name.

THE DEVIL'S DEPUTY
(See THE LIBERTY BELL)

THE DIPLOMAT (1904)

"What is the inspiration for many of the suites and arrangements, for which Lieutenant Commander John Philip Sousa, the famous bandmaster, who comes to Bangor, Wednesday, September 19th, would have won a place in the American musical history, had he never written a single march?

" 'A good tenderloin steak, German fried potatoes and plenty of bread and butter,' answers the March King.

"... 'I remember that one of my best marches, from the standpoint of lasting popularity, was written with the best tenderloin I ever had tasted for an inspiration. The march was "The Diplomat" and the city was Mitchell, South Dakota, and mentally at least, I dedicated the march to the unseen cook who prepared that tenderloin.' "[15]

While mentally dedicated to Mitchell's unnamed chef, the march was in actuality dedicated to Secretary of State John Milton Hay, whose diplomatic skill had impressed the composer.

When performing this march in the prime of his career, Sousa gave a subtle but highly pleasing display of conducting excellence for the benefit of both his audiences and his musicians. The first section of the march has a catchy melody which he had the band phrase and accent in a style different from the printed music. As the late Dr. Frank Simon, former Sousa Band solo cornetist, remarked: "When the 'Governor' conducted this march, we could literally visualize the graceful swagger of

---

[15] *Bangor* (Maine) *Commercial,* September 7, 1923.

a handsome diplomat, top hat, tux, striped trousers and all, strutting down the street, nodding cheerfully here and there."[16]

MSS: a) Pi 2pp; 30Sept1904 Mitchell, S.D. [LC]
       b) Bd 11pp; 26Oct1904 San Buenaventura, Calif. [LC]
Pub: Church
©: Pi: Church 21Nov1904; ren JPS 1Mar1932
     Bd; orch: Church 5Dec1904; ren JPS 1Mar1932
     Banjo; guitar; mandolin: Church 29Jan1905; not ren
Also pub for pi duet but not ©

THE DIRECTORATE (1894)

Not dedicated to band directors, as the title might imply, this march was written in appreciation of an honor bestowed upon Sousa by the Board of Directors of the 1893 St. Louis Exposition. The Sousa Band had been in existence for less than a year at that time but had created such a sensation at the exposition that the directorate held a special ceremony in his honor during the final week. In the brief ceremony, the governor of Missouri presented the "March King" with an elaborate medal of gold, rubies, and diamonds. To add the finishing touch, the Sousa Band struck up "For He's a Jolly Good Fellow."

MSS: a) Pi 2pp; 15Sep1894 np [UI]
      b) Orch 9pp; 21Sep1894 St. Louis [LC]
      c) Bd 8pp; 30Sep1894 St. Louis [LC]
      d) Pi 1pp; nd np [LC]
      e) 2nd pi part of pi duet 1pp; nd np [LC]
Pub: Church
©: Pi: Church 29Sep1894; ren JPS 16Mar1922
     Bd: Church 1Dec1894; ren JPS 30Oct1922
     Orch: Church 15Dec1894; ren JPS 30Oct1922
Also pub for pi duet; pi six hands; banjo; banjo duet; banjo & pi; guitar; guitar duet; mandolin; mandolin & pi; mandolin & guitar; mandolin & pi & guitar; two mandolins & guitar; zither; zither duet but not ©

(Reference) THE DRAGOONS

Presumably this march would have been

---

[16] Discussed in an interview with the author in 1963.

taken from the operetta *The Irish Dragoon*. Although the title appears on the inaccurate list of compositions appended to Sousa's autobiography, there is no evidence of the existence of such a march. The unpublished, unproduced operetta contains no significant march melodies, but several pages are missing. It must be assumed that, if a march was extracted, it reappeared under another title.

ESPRIT DE CORPS (1878)
(ESPRIT DU CORPS)

The U.S. Marine Band was not known for having outstanding esprit de corps before Sousa's twelve-year period of leadership, but since that time its honor, enthusiasm, and devotion to duty have been marks of distinction. Inspiration for this composition might seem obvious had it been written while Sousa was in service, but it was not. Curiously, it was not published for band until the year after he resigned from the Marine Corps.

MSS: N/A
Pub: Shaw (pi); Pond (pi); Pepper (bd); Coleman (bd)
©: Pi: Shaw 23Aug1878; not ren
     Bd: Pepper 24May1893; not ren

THE FAIREST OF THE FAIR (1908)

"The Fairest of the Fair" is generally regarded as one of Sousa's finest and most melodic marches, and its inspirations came from the sight of a pretty girl with whom he was not even acquainted. It was an immediate success and has remained one of his most popular compositions. It stands out as one of the finest examples of the application of pleasing melodies to the restrictive framework of a military march.

The Boston Food Fair was an annual exposition and music jubilee held by the Boston Retail Grocers' Association. The Sousa Band was the main musical attraction for several seasons, so the creation of a new march honoring the sponsors of the 1908 Boston Food Fair was the natural outgrowth of a pleasant business relationship.

In fairs before 1908, Sousa had been impressed by the beauty and charm of one particular young lady who was the center of attention of the displays in which she was employed. He made a mental note that he would some day transfer his impressions of her into music. When the invitation came for the Sousa Band to play a twenty-day engagement in 1908, he wrote this march. Remembering the comely girl, he entitled the new march "The Fairest of the Fair."[17]

Because of an oversight, the march almost missed its premiere. Nearly three months before the fair, Sousa had completed a sketch of the march for the publisher. He also wrote out a full conductor's score from which the individual band parts were to have been extracted. The band had just finished an engagement the night before the fair's opening and had boarded a sleeper train for Boston. Louis Morris, the band's copyist, was helping the librarian sort music for the first concert, and he discovered that the most important piece on the program — "The Fairest of the Fair" — had not been prepared.

According to Morris's own story, the librarian, whose job it had been to prepare the parts, went into a panic. There was good reason; considerable advance publicity had been given to the new march, and the fair patrons would be expecting to hear it. In addition, the piano sheet music had already been published, and copies were to be distributed free to the first five hundred ladies entering the gates of the fair.

Morris rose to the occasion. He asked the porter of the train to bring a portable desk, which he placed on a pillow across his lap. He worked the entire night, and the parts were nearly finished when dawn broke. Both were greatly surprised by the appearance of Sousa, who had arisen to take his usual early morning walk. When asked about the frenzied activity, they had no choice but to tell exactly what had happened.

There were many times in the life of John Philip Sousa when he demonstrated

his benevolence and magnanimity, and this was surely one of them. After recognizing Morris's extraordinary effort and remarking that it was saving the band from considerable embarrassment, he instructed him to complete his work and to take a well-deserved rest, even if it meant sleeping through the first concert.

With no one the wiser, Louis Morris — hero of the day — was asleep in his hotel as Sousa's Band played "The Fairest of the Fair" for the first time on September 28, 1908. Sousa did not mention the subject again, but Morris found an extra fifty dollars in his next pay envelope — the equivalent of two weeks salary.[18]

MSS: a) Pi 2pp; 6Jul1908 Saranac Lake, N.Y. & 7Jul1908 np [LC]
 b) Bd 16pp; 8Jul1908 Saranac Lake, N.Y. [LC]
Pub: Church
©: Pi: Church 18Aug1908; ren JvMS 2Jan1936
 Bd: Church 28Aug1908; ren JvMS 2Jan1936
 Pi duet: Church 14Sep1908; ren JvMS 2Jan1936

THE FEDERAL (1910)

Just before embarking on his world tour of 1910-11, Sousa composed this march in honor of the people of Australia and New Zealand, including both in his dedication, "to the Australasians." The title was to have been "The Land of the Golden Fleece," but "The Federal" was suggested to Sousa by Sir George Reid, the High Commissioner for Australia, who heard it in London at the beginning of the tour. The original title was not wasted; Sousa used "In the Land of the Golden Fleece" later for the second movement of his suite, *Tales of a Traveler*.

MSS: a) Bd 7pp; 16Dec1910 New York City [LC]

---

[17] Sousa told this story when interviewed by a reporter from a Boston newspaper. The undated clipping is in the Sousa Band press book of 1908.

[18] The account of the near-catastrophic premiere of the march was given to the author by Louis Morris in interviews on September 16, 1963, and September 26, 1964. "The Fairest of the Fair" was listed as a selection in Willow Grove programs at a date earlier than the Boston Food Fair engagement, but these programs were printed in advance and were probably in error.

b) Orch 9pp; 9Apr1912 Montgomery,
Ala. [LC]
Pub: Church
©:   Pi: Church 13Jan1911; ren JvMS
      30Dec1938 again 12Jan1939
      Bd: Church 31Jan1911; ren JvMS
      30Dec1938 again 12Jan1939

FLAGS OF FREEDOM (1918)

Sousa composed this march at the request
of Joseph W. Gannon, Division of Associated Flags chairman of the Fourth Liberty Loan drive of World War I.[19] Gannon
asked Sousa to incorporate national airs
of the twenty-one nations at war with Germany, but Sousa thought this impractical
and decided upon five. The countries represented were Belgium, Italy, France,
Great Britain, and America, in that order.
In a letter to Gannon dated August 25,
1918, Sousa suggested that the march be
royalty free. This would have made little
difference, because it was written just at
the war's end and consequently sold very
few copies.

MSS: N/A
Pub: Fischer
©:   Bd: Fischer 19Oct1918; ren JPrS &
      HSA 31Oct1945
      Pi: Fischer 20Oct1918 again 29Jul1926;
      ren Fischer 1Mar1946

LA FLOR DE SEVILLA (1929)

"Quien no ha visto Sevilla no ha visto
maravilla" ("He who has not seen Seville
has not seen beauty") — thus read a quotation on printed copies of this march,
which was composed at the request of the
directors of the Ibero-American Exposition held in Seville in 1929. No doubt the
publisher added the inscription without
Sousa's knowledge, because Sousa had
never visited Seville, the city of his father's
birth. According to the dedication on the
band manuscript it was "written for and
dedicated to the people of Spain."

MSS: Bd 8pp; 9Apr1929 New York City [LC]
Pub: Church
©:   Bd; pi: Church 3May1929; ren JPrS &
      HSA 10Oct1956

FOSHAY TOWER WASHINGTON MEMORIAL (1929)

This obscure march has perhaps the most
interesting history of any of Sousa's compositions. It might well be called his "mystery march," and it has never been published.[20]

Sousa and the managers of the band
were undecided about making a tour in
the fall of 1929, but Wilbur B. Foshay of
Minneapolis resolved their dilemma by
making a lucrative offer for the band's
services over the Labor Day weekend.
Foshay was a public utilities magnate and
had constructed a unique thirty-two-story
building in downtown Minneapolis which
came to be known as the Foshay Tower.
Because of his fascination with the Washington Monument, Foshay had the building fashioned after it. A gala celebration
was planned for the dedication. Governors
of all the states and many other dignitaries
were invited to Minneapolis at Foshay's
expense.

Sousa wanted a new march for such an
event but felt there was insufficient time
to compose one. So he borrowed one he
had just written for the College of Industrial Arts in Denton, Texas, and later
wrote another one for that institution.[21]
The new march was entitled "Foshay
Tower Washington Memorial" and was
played at each of several concerts held
every day at the celebration.

The stock market crash came two
months later, and Foshay's financial empire collapsed. In an ensuing investigation
it came out that the W. B. Foshay Company had misrepresented its stock and had
been guilty of illegal manipulation. In an
eventful trial, one of Foshay's former sec-
retaries managed to seat herself as a juror
and caused a hung jury.[22] Later, however,
Foshay was convicted of mail fraud and
imprisoned.

---

[19] Correspondence between Sousa and Gannon dating August, 1918, in custody of the
Sousa family.

[20] A more detailed story of this composition
may be found in my "Sousa's Mystery March,"
Instrumentalist, February, 1966.

[21] "Daughters of Texas."

[22] The secretary was convicted of perjury.
She and her husband apparently consummated
a suicide pact, and they were found dead with
their children.

Sousa did not want his name associated with the Foshay scandal and quietly withdrew his march from the public. He died before Foshay was imprisoned, and his family has since withheld the march from publication. Meanwhile, Foshay was serving a fifteen-year term in a federal prison. After three years, President Roosevelt commuted his sentence, and he was released on parole. Ten years later, President Truman granted him a complete pardon.

Once out of prison, Foshay copyrighted Sousa's march and made several attempts to have it published. Sousa had presented him with a copy in 1929, and Foshay had incorrectly reasoned that it was Sousa's last march. But apparently the Sousa family had informed several publishers of the circumstances, and Foshay was unable to find a publisher willing to go against their wishes.

More than three decades after the "Foshay Tower Washington Memorial" march had disappeared, Sousa's daughter Helen discovered the band parts in the archives of the Sands Point estate. Almost coincidentally, there was a movement in Minneapolis to convert the top floor of the Foshay Tower into a museum. The Apache Oil Corporation, new owners of the building, conducted a survey to determine public sentiment concerning Foshay's past history. The consensus was that Foshay had merely had the misfortune of being caught doing what many other corporation executives had done without detection. Because of this and Foshay's subsequent record of public service, the public had forgiven him. So the museum was begun.

Representatives of the Apache company explained the situation to Sousa's daughter Helen, who agreed to permit her father's march to be played at the opening of the museum. After preparations had begun, however, she changed her mind. The march was not played, other scheduled events were canceled, and the museum was quietly opened in the spring of 1967.

Today the Foshay Tower stands as a landmark in Minneapolis, tribute to Wilbur B. Foshay — and George Washington. In the museum may be found memorabilia attesting to Foshay's association with the "March King."

MSS: a) Bd (entitled "Daughters of Texas") 12pp; 4Jul1929 Sands Pt. [LC]
b) Orch 15pp; 19Sep1929 Urbana, Ill. [In possession of HSA, New York City]
c) Pi (entitled "Daughters of Texas") 2pp; nd np [LC]
Not pub
©: Pi: Wilbur B. Foshay 26Feb1951

THE FOURTH OF JULY MARCH
(See HAIL TO THE SPIRIT OF LIBERTY)

THE FREE LANCE (1906)

"The Free Lance" march, taken from Sousa's operetta of the same name, has a lengthy and unorthodox construction when compared with most other Sousa marches. There were so many spirited march tunes in the operetta that perhaps Sousa felt obligated to include most of them when piecing together the march. Actually, there were enough for two separate marches.

The "free lance" of the operetta was Sigmund Lump, a clever goatherd who hired himself out as a mercenary leader to two opposing armies, maneuvered his forces so that neither side could win, and then declared himself emperor of both nations.

The trio of the march corresponds to the song "On to Victory" in the operetta, and some editions of the march were published under that title.

MSS: Bd 14pp; 31Mar1906 Toronto [LC]
Pub: Church
©: Pi: Church 26Mar1906; ren JvMS 23Jan1934
Bd: Church 30Apr1906 again 12Nov1906; ren JvMS 23Jan1934
Orch: Church 19Nov1906; ren JvMS 23Jan1934

THE FREE LUNCH CADETS
(See Songs — Words by Sousa)

FROM MAINE TO OREGON (1913)

Sousa's "All American" operetta, *The American Maid* (*The Glass Blowers*), contains one recurring march theme, the title of which does not appear in the list of songs. Perhaps the publishers made this arrangement so that "reprise" would not appear so many times. The theme is the nucleus around which Sousa built the march "From Maine to Oregon." The march, like the operetta, met with only limited success.

MSS: Bd 11pp; 19Apr1913 Montgomery, Ala. [LC]
Pub: Church
©: Orch: Church 11Feb1913; ren JvMS 22Jan1941
    Bd: Church 29May1913; ren JvMS 21Mar1941

THE GALLANT SEVENTH (1922)

It is amazing that this march, regarded as one of Sousa's finest and certainly one of his most vigorous, was composed while he was recuperating from a broken neck. The march takes its title from the 7th Regiment, 107th Infantry, of the New York National Guard, whose history may be traced back to the Civil War. The conductor of the famous 7th Regiment Band was Major Francis Sutherland, a former Sousa Band cornetist.

Upon America's entry into World War I, Sutherland left his position with Sousa to enlist in the army; he was made a bandmaster in the U.S. Field Artillery. Several other Sousa men then secured their release to enlist, some for service with Sutherland's band.

Sutherland did not return to the Sousa Band at the war's end; he accepted the position of bandmaster of the 7th Regiment. The regiment's commanding officer, Colonel Wade H. Hayes, made a formal request of Sousa for a march. Sousa obliged, paying tribute to the organizational ability and professional standing of one of his band's alumni. For the official send-off of the new march at the New York Hippodrome on November 5, 1922, Sutherland's 7th Regiment Band augmented the Sousa Band on stage.

Although no less than seven other composers had also written marches for this regiment, Sousa's was the only one to gain wide acceptance, and Sousa was named honorary bandmaster of the regiment. Many years later, Sutherland repaid his debt to Sousa in an appropriate way. He was one of eight founders of the living Sousa memorial known as the Sousa Band Fraternal Society.

MSS: N/A
Pub: Fox
©: Bd: Fox 11Jul1922; ren JPrS & HSA 27Sep1949
    Pi: Fox 9Aug1922; ren JPrS & HSA 27Sep1949

GARFIELD'S FUNERAL MARCH
(See IN MEMORIAM)

GEORGE WASHINGTON
BICENTENNIAL (1930)

To commemorate the two hundredth anniversary of the birth of George Washington, a Bicentennial Commission in Washington, D.C., was formed. A gala celebration was held, the climax being an impressive ceremony at the Capitol Plaza on February 22, 1932. The commission had asked Sousa to take part in the final ceremony, and he composed this march for the occasion. In this affair, one of two final appearances before his death, Sousa conducted the combined bands of the U.S. Army, Navy, and Marine Corps in the new march.

MSS: a) Orch 14pp; 14May1930 Sands Pt. [LC]
    b) Bd 14pp; 2Jun1930 Sands Pt. [LC]
    c) Pi 4pp; nd np [LC]
    d) Pi 2pp inc; nd np [LC]
Pub: Fox
©: Violin (unpub): Fox 7Jun1930; ren JPrS & HSA 25Jun1957 again 19Jul1957
    Pi & accordian: Fox 2Jul1932; ren Fox 24Sep1959
    Pi: Fox 15Nov1930; ren JPrS & HSA 21Nov1957
Also pub for bd but not ©

THE GLADIATOR (1886)

Nothing among Sousa's memoirs reveals the identity of the "gladiator," but the first printing of the sheet music carried a dedication to Charles F. Towle of Boston. Towle was a journalist who was editor of the *Boston Traveller* at the time this march was written, but the nature of his association with Sousa is not known.[23]

---

[23] Research done by Ruth Bleecker, Curator of Music, Boston Public Library.

Sousa's daughter Helen conjectured that her father might have been inspired by a literary account of some particular gladiator.[24] It is unlikely that he would have dedicated a march to gladiators in general because of their ferocity and deeds of inhumanity, but perhaps one noble gladiator who had been a victim of circumstances might have been his inspiration. There has also been speculation that the march had some Masonic significance, inasmuch as it was written at the time he was "knighted" in Columbia Commandery No. 2, Knights Templar, but this lacks substantiation.

For Sousa, "The Gladiator" brought back both happy and unhappy memories. In 1885 he had written the dirge "The Honored Dead" for Stopper and Fisk, a music publisher in Williamsport, Pennsylvania. They were so pleased that they asked him to write a quickstep march. He responded with "The Gladiator," but they rejected it. Their shortsightedness cost them dearly; Sousa then sold it to Harry Coleman of Philadelphia, and it eventually sold over a million copies.

"The Gladiator" was the first Sousa composition to reach such wide circulation. He himself was unaware of its popularity until its strains startled him one day while in Philadelphia on business. Many years later he gave this dramatic account:

"I was taking a stroll along Broad Street. At a corner a hand-organ man was grinding out a melody which, somehow, seemed strangely familiar. As I listened more intently, I was surprised to recognize it as my own 'Gladiator' march. I believe that was one of the proudest moments of my life, as I stood there on the corner listening to the strains of that street organ!

"As the Italian, who was presiding over the crank, paused, I rushed up to him and seized him warmly by the hand. The man started back in amazement and stared at me as though he thought I had taken leave of my senses.

" 'My friend! My friend!' I cried. 'Let me thank you! Please take this as a little token of my appreciation!'

"I tore myself away, walking on air down the remainder of the street and leaving the organ grinder dazed by the coins I had thrust into his hand. I don't believe he can account for the gift to this day.

"But I was exultant. My music had made enough of a hit to be played on a street organ. At last I felt that it had struck a popular chord."[25]

MSS: N/A
Pub: Coleman
©   Bd; orch: Coleman 30Dec1886; ren JPS
          13Feb1914
      Pi: Coleman 30Dec1886 again
          4May1894; ren JPS 13Feb1914 again
          6Feb1922
      One or two banjos: Coleman 14Nov1888;
          ren JPS 19Jan1916
      Pi duet: Coleman 7Aug1891; not ren
      Cornet & pi: Coleman 4May1894; ren
          JPS 6Feb1922

GLOBE AND EAGLE (1879)

This march takes its title from the emblem of the U.S. Marine Corps. It was one of several military titles curiously chosen by Sousa while he was an orchestra conductor in Philadelphia. He might possibly have been bidding for the position of leader of the Marine Band, knowing that the leader at that time was about to be replaced.

MSS: Bd 1pp inc; 20Jul1879 Washington, D.C.
         [LC]
Pub: Shaw (bd); Coleman (bd); Pepper (bd)
©:   Bd: Shaw 26Nov1879 again Coleman
         12Dec1885; not ren

THE GLORY OF THE YANKEE NAVY (1909)

The musical comedy *The Yankee Girl* was in need of a spirited march, so Sousa was prevailed upon to provide one. The march, one of Sousa's most interesting musically, was dedicated to the star of the show, Blanche Ring. Lyrics were provided by Kenneth S. Clark. The title underwent a process of evolution. The earliest known manuscript was labeled "Uncle Sam's Navy." Prior to the opening, newspapers referred to the march as "The Honor of the Yankee Navy."

MSS: a) Pi 3pp; 7Apr1909 New York City
          [LC]
      b) Bd 11pp; 11Sep1909 Montreal [UI]

---

[24] Interview with the author, September, 1963.

[25] Interview in *The American Boy,* April, 1907.

Pub: Church
©:   V/pi: Church 23Sep1910; ren JvMS
       4Jan1937
       Bd: Church 4Oct1909; ren JvMS
       4Jan1937
       Orch: Church 4Oct1909; not ren

GOLDEN JUBILEE (1928)

To commemorate his fiftieth year as a conductor Sousa wrote this, one of his most brilliant marches. He was hesitant to compose anything for his own gratification but reasoned that his public might expect something special. The march was given its premiere by the Sousa Band at the beginning of its engagement at the Steel Pier in Atlantic City on July 29, 1928, and then featured on the 1928 "golden jubilee" tour.

Subtracting fifty from 1928 gives 1878 as Sousa's first year as a conductor. In actuality, he began his conducting career in 1875 as leader of the orchestra in a traveling company which featured Milton Nobles in the play *Bohemians and Detectives,* otherwise known as *The Phoenix.* But apparently Sousa did not consider this conducting per se, because he led the orchestra while playing first violin. As a conductor whose capacity was strictly conducting, his first position was with the Philadelphia Church Choir Company in their production of *H.M.S. Pinafore.* Their first rehearsals were held late in 1878, Sousa's apparent point of reference.

The inspiration came with considerable difficulty, even for Sousa. He searched for suitable melodies for five months, but nothing was forthcoming. Then suddenly the inspiration came, and within a day's time he had the march sketched in its entirety. His thoughts were recorded in the 1928 tour programs:

"I've always been inspired by an occasion and as I thought of the golden jubilee and of all it meant to me — fifty years of band [*sic*] leading — I seemed to see the world passing in review. There they were, peoples of every land — on parade, at great music festivals, going to war, at expositions, attending the opera, in the home — listening to a march. So the music took form and then 'The Golden Jubilee March' was ready for placing on paper."

MSS: a) Pi 1pp inc; 8Mar1928 np [LC]
      b) Pi 1pp inc; 9Mar1928 np [LC]
Pub: Fox
©:   Bd: Fox 26Jul1928; ren JPrS & HSA
      16Dec1955
      Pi: Fox 8Aug1928; ren JPrS & HSA
      16Dec1955

THE GOLDEN STAR (1919)

On the front cover of this World War I dirge is the following inscription:

"Dedicated to Mrs. Theodore Roosevelt
In memory of the brave
who gave their lives
That liberty shall not perish."

Specifically, the march was composed in memory of Theodore Roosevelt and his son Quentin Roosevelt, who was killed in France. Sousa summed up his sentiments in an interview. "It will not be a monetary success. One cannot write from his heart and write for rewards. I was thinking of those fine young boys who will never return."[26]

The composition was heartily but seriously received immediately after the war but was dropped from the Sousa Band repertoire gradually as the nation returned to normal. Taps was included in one section of the march, and this brought about several sorrowful reactions from audiences. At one concert in Reno, Nevada, for instance, women burst into tears and the band could scarcely hear itself play.[27]

MSS: N/A
Pub: Chappell
©:   Organ: Chappell 19Mar1919; ren JPrS
      & HSA 21Mar1946
      Pi: Chappell 19Mar1919; not ren
      Bd: Chappell 9May1919 again
      26Jan1920; ren JPrS & HSA
      10May1946 again Chappell 28Jan1947
      Orch: Chappell 9May1919; ren JPrS &
      HSA 10May1946

GRAND FESTIVAL MARCH
(See Suites: TALES OF A TRAVELER)

GRAND PROMENADE AT THE WHITE HOUSE
(See Suites: TALES OF A TRAVELER)

---

[26] *Winston-Salem* (N.C.) *Journal,* January 7, 1920.
[27] *New York Morning Telegraph,* December 2, 1919.

GREAT LAKES
(See THE NAVAL RESERVE)

THE GRIDIRON CLUB (1926)
(See also THE WILDCATS, UNTITLED
MARCH, and UNIVERSAL PEACE)

The piano score of a march called "Universal Peace" was discovered among old papers at Sousa's Sands Point estate in 1965. The title "National Defense" had been crossed out. Sections are almost identical to sections of the march now known as "The Gridiron Club," the march Sousa apparently composed shortly thereafter and dedicated to the Gridiron Club, the celebrated organization of journalists in Washington, D.C.

He did almost the same thing with still another march, one bearing no title. In this instance he used some sections for "The Gridiron Club" and later used most of the remainder for a march called "The Wildcats" (1930 or 1931). The end result of this musical juggling was that three separate marches grew from this nucleus: "The Gridiron Club," "Universal Peace," and "The Wildcats." Apparently he felt that "The Gridiron Club" was the best of the three, because the other two were never published.

Sousa had a long association with the "Griddies," attending their annual meetings faithfully for over forty years.[28] He had composed a humorous song for them, "Do We? We Do," thirty-five years earlier. When Sousa died in 1932, a sizable delegation of the organization attended his funeral, and the Gridiron Club Quartet provided the only music.

MSS: a) Pi (with sections of "Universal Peace") 2pp; nd np [LC]
     b) Orch 12pp; nd np [LC]
     c) Pi (with sections of "The Wildcats" and an unidentified march) 1pp; nd np [LC]
Pub: Fox
©: Vi: Fox 7Apr1926; ren JPrS & HSA 25Aug1953

---

[28] Sousa was made musical director and elected to limited membership on January 12, 1889, and transferred to associate membership on September 12, 1893. The musical director of the "Griddies" has, since Sousa's time, been the current leader of the U.S. Marine Band.

Bd: Fox 18Jun1926; ren JPrS & HSA 25Aug1953
Pi: Fox 26Jul1926; ren JPrS & HSA 25Aug1953

GUIDE RIGHT (1881)

Sousa marches had a banner year in 1881. Sousa had just reached his stride as leader of the U.S. Marine Band and wrote six that year. Two of these, "Guide Right" and "Right Forward," were written for parade use, and their names were derived from marching commands. Both were dedicated to a Captain R. S. Collum of the Marine Corps.

MSS: Bd 3 pp; 14Mar1881 Washington, D.C. [LC]
Pub: Pond (pi); Coleman (bd); Pepper (bd)
©: Pi: Pond 28Feb1881; not ren
    Bd: Coleman 31Dec1885; ren JPS 13Dec1913

HAIL TO THE SPIRIT OF LIBERTY (1900)

It was with great pride that Sousa and his band represented the United States at the Paris Exposition of 1900. This was the first overseas tour of the band, and it was received throughout Europe with enthusiasm. The band displayed the finest American musicianship Europe had seen and helped dispel the notion that the United States was an artistic void.

A statue of George Washington was unveiled on July 2, but the highlight of the Paris engagement was the unveiling of the Lafayette Monument on July 4. It was presented on behalf of the children of the United States by Ferdinand W. Peck, commissioner general of the Paris Exposition, as President Loubet of France looked on. The monument portrayed Lafayette on horseback offering his sword to the American cause in the Revolutionary War and was draped with a huge American flag. At the unveiling the Sousa Band gave the first performance of the march composed specifically for that moment: "Hail to the Spirit of Liberty." Immediately after the ceremony, the band made one of its rare appearances in a parade as it marched through the main streets of Paris.

Certain sections of the march evidently were taken from an unidentified earlier operetta and revised, because in 1965 fragments which were probably meant to be discarded were found in a stack of manuscripts at the Sands Point estate. The march was so successful that it is difficult to reconcile a story often told by Sousa's daughter Priscilla; she said that her father had entered the march in a contest shortly before it was published, and that the contest had been won by an "unknown" composer whose march was promptly forgotten.

MSS: 10pp of opa with themes of march inc; nd np [LC]
Pub: Church
©: Pi: Church 3Jul1900; ren JPS 25May1928
Pi duet: Church 15Aug1900; ren JPS 25May1928
Banjo; guitar; guitar & pi; mandolin & pi & guitar: Church 27Sep1900; ren JPS 27Aug1928
Bd: Church 22Oct1900; ren JPS 11Sep1928
Also pub for pi six hands; banjo duet; banjo & pi; guitar duet; mandolin; mandolin & pi; mandolin & guitar; two mandolins & pi; two mandolins & guitar; zither but not ©

HANDS ACROSS THE SEA (1899)

When played for the first time by Sousa's Band in Philadelphia's Academy of Music on April 21, 1899, "many feet were beating a tattoo."[29] The band was obliged to repeat it three times. "Hands Across the Sea" was off to a good start, and it has since remained a standard in band literature.

The march was addressed to no particular nation, but to all of America's friends abroad.[30] It has been suggested that Sousa was inspired by an incident in the Spanish-American War, in which Captain Chichester of the British Navy came to the support of Admiral Dewey at Manila Bay.[31] A second (and more likely) source is a line by Frere, which was printed on the front cover of the sheet music: "A sudden

thought strikes me — let us swear an eternal friendship."[32]

The line by Frere apparently appeared in a play which Sousa read. In answering questions sent to him while serving in the navy, he gave this account in the *Great Lakes Recruit* of March, 1918:

"After the Spanish war there was some feeling in Europe anent our republic regarding this war. Some of the nations . . . thought we were not justified while others gave us credit for the honesty of our purpose. One night I was reading an old play and I came across this line, 'A sudden thought strikes me, — let us swear an eternal friendship.' That almost immediately suggested the title 'Hands Across the Sea' for that composition and within a few weeks that now famous march became a living fact."

MSS: Bd 9 pp; 14Mar1899 Los Angeles [UI]
Pub: Church
©: Bd; orch: Church 28Apr1899; ren JPS 23Mar1927
Pi: Church 28Apr1899; not ren
Pi duet; pi six hands: Church 11May1899; ren JPS 23Mar1927
Guitar & pi; mandolin & pi & guitar; two mandolins & pi: Church 13May1899; ren JPS 23Mar1927
Banjo duet: Church 25May1899; ren JPS 23Mar1927
Guitar duet: Church 27May1899; ren JPS 23Mar1927
Zither duet: Church 18May1918; not ren
Also pub for banjo; banjo & pi; guitar; mandolin & pi; mandolin & guitar; two mandolins & guitar but not ©

HARMONICA WIZARD (1930)

Leading a harmonica band was a novel experience for Sousa when he was invited to conduct Albert N. Hoxie's fifty-two-member Philadelphia Harmonica Band in September, 1925. He was so impressed with their playing and the possibilities of the harmonica that he carried an endorsement for Hohner harmonicas in his 1928 programs and subsequently wrote this march for Hoxie's boys.

When the Sousa Band came to Phila-

---

[29] *Philadelphia Inquirer,* April 22, 1899.
[30] *Philadelphia Public Ledger,* April 18, 1899.
[31] G. Hollis Stewart, "The Royal Welch Fusiliers March," U.S. Marine Corps Historical Section publicity, December 16, 1930.

---

[32] *Rochester Herald,* April 17, 1899. The paper credits this line to Hoodman Frere, but this is probably John Hookham Frere, English diplomat.

Forty-member U.S. Marine Band, with leader Sousa (center), in 1889. Defense Department photo.

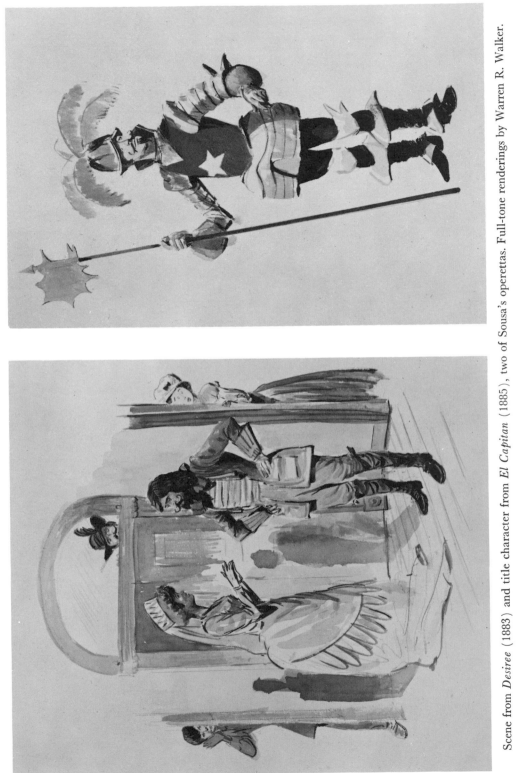

Scene from *Desiree* (1883) and title character from *El Capitan* (1885), two of Sousa's operettas. Full-tone renderings by Warren R. Walker.

Sousa Band and 7th Regiment New York National Guard performing "The Gallant Seventh" at the New York Hippodrome in 1922. Photo courtesy of Donald C. Gardner.

Manuscript of "The Stars and Stripes Forever." Note Sousa's initials and the date,

"Xmas '96," in the lower right corner. Photo courtesy of the Library of Congress.

Sousa conducting the 2nd Battalion of the Royal Welch Fusiliers, 1930.
Photo courtesy of Joan Ambrose.

Publicity photo for Sousa's march, "The Atlantic City Pageant" (1927). The event
named in the march's title later became known as the Miss America Pageant.

Sousa became a Shriner in 1922. The following year he wrote his march, "Nobles of the Mystic Shrine," in honor of the organization. United Press International photo.

University of Illinois Band in a salute to the "March King" at a halftime football program. Photo courtesy of the University of Illinois Archives.

delphia on November 21, 1930, the mayor proclaimed the day Sousa Day. Among other events was Sousa's leading the University of Pennsylvania Band, but the climax of the day was when Hoxie's boys came to the stage during the Sousa Band concert and performed the new march Sousa had written for them. A special commemorative medal, with the emblem of the Philadelphia Harmonica Band on one side and a tribute to Sousa on the other, was presented to the "March King" at the close of the concert.

MSS: a) Bd 9pp; 19May1930 Sands Pt. [LC]
    b) Orch 8pp; 22May1930 Sands Pt. [LC]
Pub: Presser
©: Pi (unpub): Presser 27Jun1930; ren JPrS & HSA 12Jul1957 again 19Jul1959
    Bd; pi: Presser 8Oct1930; ren JPrS & HSA 19Nov1957
    Orch: Presser 19Dec1930; ren JPrS & HSA 20Feb1958
    Pi duet: Presser 4Jun1931; ren JPrS & HSA 16Jul1958

THE HIGH SCHOOL CADETS (1890)

The mutual admiration which existed between John Philip Sousa and the school bands of America has caused many musicians and writers to conclude that this march was composed as a salute to the school band movement. However, it was written twenty years before that movement had begun. It was composed at the solicitation of the marching cadet corps of the one and only Washington, D.C., high school in 1890 (later called Central High School) and was dedicated to the teachers and pupils.

The High School Cadets was another of the drill teams which were an exciting part of the capital city scene for many years after the Civil War. The members requested the march of Sousa, asking that he make an effort to make it superior to his "National Fencibles" march, which he had written for a rival cadet corps. In Sousa's estimation, it was indeed a better march.[33]

[33] 1910 letter from Sousa to Ralph G. Waring, then editor of the *Central High School Review*. Quoted in a Washington newspaper of April 1, 1934. (Loose clipping at the Columbia Historical Society in Washington.)

The music world has concurred, because "The High School Cadets" has always been one of Sousa's most popular marches.

The Cadets were invited to a Marine Band rehearsal to hear the march played. They liked what they heard and produced $24 to cover the cost of having the march published and copyrighted.[34]

MSS: Bd 6pp inc; 12Feb1890 Washington, D.C. [LC]
Pub: Coleman
©: Pi: Coleman 20Feb1890 again 4May1894; ren JPS 26Nov1917 again 6Feb1922
    Pi duet: Coleman 7Aug1891; not ren
    Guitar: Coleman 7Jun1893; not ren
    Mandolin & Guitar: Coleman 17Jun1893; ren JPS 7Mar1921
    Pi six hands: Coleman 12Aug1893; ren JPS 7Mar1921
    Banjo; banjo duet: Coleman 28Dec1893; ren JPS 7Mar1921
    Cornet & pi: Coleman 4May1894; ren JPS 6Feb1922
Also pub for bd and for orch but not ©

THE HIPPODROME
(See THE NEW YORK HIPPODROME)

HOMAGE TO PITTSBURGH
(HOMAGE TO STEPHEN FOSTER and ETHELBERT NEVIN)
(See THE PRIDE OF PITTSBURGH)

HOMEWARD BOUND
(probably 1891 or 1892)

The only clue to the existence of this unpublished march was a mention in the list of compositions given in Sousa's autobiography, *Marching Along*, until manuscripts turned up in a trunk in the basement archives of the Sands Point home in 1965. Several copyist's manuscripts for band

[34] This story was told in the *El Paso* (Tex.) *Herald* of January 12, 1922, by H. D. Slater of that city, who was a member of the Cadet committee which had made the request for the march and which also heard the march rehearsed by the Marine Band. There are two minor inconsistencies in the story. One is that Slater gives 1888 as the date of the request and 1889 as the date of the initial hearing, whereas the date on the band score is 1890. The other is that the amount of money, which he reported as $24, is given by Sousa as $25 on p. 144 of *Marching Along*.

bearing the names of U.S. Marine Band musicians were found. Marine Corps enlistment records of these men are incomplete, so establishing an exact date for the composition is improbable unless other manuscripts are some day discovered. Inasmuch as it was written while Sousa was leader of the Marine Band, it would seem that it would have been written during the homeward leg of one of the Marine Band tours (1891 and 1892) or perhaps on the return from the engagement in Fayetteville, North Carolina (1889).

MSS: Bd 1pp inc; nd np [LC]
Not pub or ©

THE HONOR OF THE YANKEE NAVY
(See THE GLORY OF THE
YANKEE NAVY)

THE HONORED DEAD (1876)

The date of this march, as inscribed on the manuscript of a piano arrangement by C. H. Hattersley, is 1876. This manuscript is now at the U.S. Marine Corps Museum. The occasion for the march's composition is not known. When President U. S. Grant died in 1885, Sousa arranged the piece for band, apparently at the publisher's request. It has rarely been performed but was fittingly used by the U.S. Marine Band in Sousa's funeral procession.

MSS: Bd 4pp; 1886 Washington, D.C. [LC]
Pub: Fisk (Band; pi); Church (pi);
       Vandersloot (bd)
©:   Bd: Fisk 26May1886 again 12Nov1896;
       ren JPS 10Apr1914
      Pi: Fisk 8Sep1896 again Church
       10Dec1896; not ren

IMPERIAL EDWARD (1902)

On December 1, 1901, while on a tour of England, the Sousa Band played a command performance at Sandringham. In a conversation with the royal family after the concert Sousa requested and received permission to dedicate a march to His Majesty the King. The first draft was completed the following April while Sousa was vacationing at Hot Springs, Virginia, and the new march was premiered by the Sousa Band in

Montreal on May 21, 1902. A beautiful illuminated manuscript was made by the John Church Company, publishers of the march, and this was carried to England by George Frederick Hinton, manager of the Sousa Band. This manuscript is now at the British Museum in London.

Hidden in the trio of the march is a trombone solo consisting of a fragment of "God Save the King." When the piece was performed by the Sousa Band, it was customary for the trombone section to rise at this point, play the brief solo fortissimo, and then be seated.

For some reason, Sousa revealed his displeasure with the march almost twenty-two years after it was written. In the 1923 Sousa Band programs at Willow Grove was the following quotation:

> "I have never written a piece of music that I did not feel the inspiration. I have never turned out but one piece that I consider in any manner mechanical. That was 'Imperial Edward,' the march I dedicated to King Edward on my second [sic][35] command to play before him — and that had to be finished in a hurry. For a part of it I felt an inspiration. For the rest, instead of digging down to the vein of gold, I struck a vein of ashes and used it."

MSS: Bd 9pp; 13May1902 Syracuse, N.Y. [UI]
Pub: Church
©:   Pi: Church 21May1902; ren JPS
       21Feb1930
      Bd: Church 26May1902; ren JPS
       21Feb1930
      Orch: Church 5Jun1902; ren JPS
       21Feb1930
      Two mandolins & pi & guitar: Church
       15Jul1902; ren JPS 21Feb1930
      Pi duet: Church 16Jul1902; ren JPS
       21Feb1930
      Banjo duet; banjo & pi; guitar duet:
       Church 25Aug1902; ren JPS
       21Feb1930
Also pub for mandolin; mandolin duet; mandolin & pi; mandolin & pi & guitar; two mandolins & guitar; zither but not ©

IN MEMORIAM (1881)
(IN MEMORIAM: GARFIELD'S
FUNERAL MARCH)

Washington's best-known Mason in 1881

---

[35] This was the first command performance. The second was at Windsor Castle on January 31, 1903.

was President James A. Garfield, who was a member of Columbia Commandery No. 2, Knights Templar. Sousa was also to belong to this same organization five years later, but during Garfield's presidency he was being worked in the lower degrees of Masonry.

Sousa was not well acquainted with the President, but he was greatly shaken at the news of his assassination. In the autobiography he tells of hearing paperboys shouting the news of Garfield's death. It was unexpected, because the President had been recovering satisfactorily from the gunshot wound of two months earlier. Shocked, Sousa rose from his bed and went outside for a walk. With the event weighing heavily on his mind he walked all through the night and into the next morning. When he returned home he immediately committed the dirge "In Memoriam" to paper.

The dirge was played by the U.S. Marine Band as the President's body was received in Washington and then again at its final resting place in Cleveland. It was afterward played infrequently by the Marine Band until half a century later, when it was played while John Philip Sousa's body was being escorted to the grave in Congressional Cemetery.

MSS: N/A
Pub: Stoddart; Hitchcock
©: Pi: Stoddart 22Sep1881; not ren

THE INVINCIBLE EAGLE (1901)

Blanche Duffield, soprano of the Sousa Band in 1901, witnessed the creation of this march, and she provided this rare description of Sousa composing:

"It was [on] a train between Buffalo and New York.[36] Outside the coach the lights of towns along the route flashed by like ghosts fluttering at the window panes. The night was dark and the few stars above twinkled fitfully. Mr. Sousa sat in his chair in the dimly lit pullman. At the further end of the car a porter diligently brushed cushions. At intervals the engine whistled as if in pain.

"Suddenly and without previous warning Mr. Sousa began to describe circles in the air with a pencil, jerking back and forth in his seat meanwhile. Gradually the circumference of his pencil's arcs diminished and Mr. Sousa drew a notebook from his pocket, still humming to himself.

"Notebook and pencil met. Breves and semi-breves appeared on the page's virgin surface. Quarter notes and sixteenth notes followed in orderly array. Meanwhile Mr. Sousa furrowed his brow and from his pursed lips came a stirring air — rather a martial blare, as if hidden trombones, tubas, and saxophones were striving to gain utterance.

"Now Mr. Sousa's pencil traveled faster and faster, and page after page of the notebook were turned back, each filled with martial bars. [I] looked on from over the top of a magazine and listened with enthusiasm as Mr. Sousa's famous march, 'The Invincible Eagle,' took form.

"I tried to attract Mr. Sousa's attention while he was supplying the accompaniment of flutes, oboes, bassoons and piccolos, but it was not until he had picked out the march on a violin on his fingers, put his notebook in his pocket, his [imaginary] violin in his case and his cigar back in his mouth that he finally turned toward me and casually remarked that it was a very dark night outside."[37]

The march was dedicated to the Pan-American Exposition, held in Buffalo in the summer of 1901. It outlived a march entitled "The Electric Century" by Sousa's rival, Francesco Fanciulli, whose band also played at the Exposition.[38] At first Sousa thought "The Invincible Eagle" would surpass "The Stars and Stripes Forever" as a

[36] An apparent error. On March 26 and 27, 1901, according to route sheets, the Sousa Band was en route from Buffalo to Cleveland. After other engagements, it then returned to Buffalo for the Exposition. By this time, however, the march had already been arranged for band, and it was premiered at Willow Grove Park in Philadelphia on Memorial Day.

[37] *New York Tribune,* September 20, 1914.
[38] Fanciulli was former leader of the U.S. Marine Band, succeeding Sousa. He was subsequently court-martialed for not playing Sousa marches. After his discharge he led his own band for several seasons, and the rivalry between Sousa and Fanciulli existed for quite some time. The fact that they each wrote marches for the benefit of the Pan-American Exposition patrons is evidence of this rivalry.

patriotic march, although he nearly entitled it "Spirit of Niagara."

MSS: a) Bd 11pp; 8May1901 Marion, Ohio [UI]
     b) Orch 1pp inc; nd np [LC]
Pub: Church
©:   Pi; pi duet: Church 29May1901; ren JPS 27Mar1929
      Bd; orch; banjo duet; guitar duet; mandolin & pi & guitar; two mandolins & pi: Church 3Jun1901; ren JPS 27Mar1929
Also pub for pi six hands; banjo; guitar; banjo & pi; mandolin; mandolin & pi; mandolin & guitar; two mandolins & guitar; zither; zither duet but not ©

JACK TAR (1903)

When composing this march, which was originally to be called "British Tars," Sousa had hoped that it would be to naval men what "The Stars and Stripes Forever" was to army men. This ambition was not realized, however. The format of the march is slightly different from the usual Sousa march and contains traces of "Sailor's Hornpipe." The introduction and first two strains were taken from his operetta "Chris and the Wonderful Lamp" (1899).

Royalties from the sale of sheet music in Britain were turned over to the Union Jack Club, a newly formed service club organized for the benefit of Royal Navy men in London. With everyone waving miniature Union Jacks, the march was given a rousing premiere in London's Albert Hall on June 25, 1903. The King, Queen, and the Prince and Princess of Wales were present as the new march was played by the combined bands of the Coldstream Guards, Scots Guards, Irish Guards, Himenoa Band of New Zealand, Sousa's Band, and the Queen's Hall orchestra.

MSS: a) Bd 10pp; 1Jun1903 Hamburg, Germany [UI]
     b) Orch 8pp; 2Jun1903 Hamburg, Germany [UI]
     c) Pi 1pp inc; nd np [LC]
Pub: Church
©:   Pi: Church 29May1903; ren JPS 29May1931
      Bd: Church 13Aug1903; ren JPS 29May1931
      Orch: Church 22Aug1903; ren JPS 29May1931

Pi duet; banjo duet; guitar duet; mandolin & guitar & pi; two mandolins & guitar: Church 10Oct1903; ren JPS 22Jul1931

KANSAS WILDCATS (1931)
(Also see THE WILDCATS and UNTITLED MARCH)

On October 10, 1928, at a Sousa Band concert in Manhattan, Kansas, Sousa was presented a handsomely bound petition requesting that he compose a march for the Kansas State College of Agriculture and Applied Science. A march was subsequently dedicated to the college, but it was not the one written in response to the petition.

Fragments of two manuscripts of the march originally intended for the college bear the titles "The Wildcats" and "The Wildcats of Kansas March." A copyist's manuscript of a later march, the one which was eventually dedicated to the college, sheds light on what might have happened. The title of this march, "The Sword of San Jacinto," was crossed out, and above it was written "Kansas Wildcats." The retitled march was then published under its new name. A publisher's note penciled on the front page reads: "Mr. Sousa agrees in letter. Contract under way."[39]

The following conclusions have been reached from a study of the manuscripts. Sousa wrote a march for the Kansas State College of Agriculture and Applied Science and called it, at various times, "The Wildcats" or "The Wildcats of Kansas March." At the same time he was also writing two other marches. One of these was called "The Sword of San Jacinto," and the title of the other is unknown. When the copyist's score of "The Sword of San Jacinto" was sent to the publisher, two things might have happened. First, Sousa could have

---

[39] "The Sword of San Jacinto" was probably intended for the U.S. Army's Second Division, stationed at Fort Sam Houston, Texas. A clipping from the *Houston Dispatch* of December 31, 1925, tells of Sousa's promise to compose a march for this division. The title of the march apparently refers to the battle of San Jacinto in the struggle with Mexico for Texas's independence in 1836.

been under pressure from the Kansas college and instructed the publisher to change the title of the march to "Kansas Wildcats." Second, he could also have sent the publisher the march originally intended for the college together with "The Sword of San Jacinto" and perhaps the untitled march as well, and the publisher might have mixed them up. In any case, only one of the three marches was published — the one known today as "Kansas Wildcats."

What happened to the various manuscripts of the three marches is not clear. If they were indeed all sent to the publisher, it is possible that all might not have been returned. After Sousa's death, the manuscripts at the Sands Point home were stored in the basement archives uncatalogued and, for the most part, unsorted. Later, Sousa's daughters gave some manuscripts to the Library of Congress. In one package was found the first page of the band score of "The Wildcats" and the final fifteen pages of the untitled march. What became of the missing pages of either march is not known.

MSS: Pi 1pp; nd np [LC]
Pub: Presser
©: Bd; pi: Presser 19May1931; ren JPrS & HSA 16Jul1958
Orch: Presser 8Mar1932; ren Presser 24Feb1960
Pi duet: Presser 18May1932; not ren

KEEPING STEP WITH THE UNION (1921)

The inspiration for this march probably came from an 1855 address by the American congressman and raconteur Rufus Choate. This excerpt from the address is printed on the sheet music: "We join ourselves to no party that does not carry the flag and keep step to the music of the Union." The composition was dedicated to Mrs. Warren G. Harding, wife of the President, and Sousa added his own patriotic verses.

MSS: N/A
Pub: Presser
©: Bd: Presser 2May1921; ren JPrS & HSA 17Aug1948
Pi: Presser 18May1921; ren JPrS & HSA 17Aug1948

Orch; pi duet: Presser 10Jun1921; ren JPrS & HSA 17Aug1948
Pi six hands: Presser 10Jun1921; not ren
V/pi: Presser 27Jun1921; ren JPrS & HSA 17Aug1948
Two pi, eight hands: Presser 27Jun1921; not ren

KING COTTON (1895)

It is a curious fact of the music world that marches written for fairs and expositions almost always fade into oblivion. Two notable exceptions are Sousa's "King Cotton" and "The Fairest of the Fair." The former was written for the Cotton States Exposition of 1895, and the latter for the Boston Food Fair of 1908.

Sousa and his band had great drawing power at fairs and expositions and were much sought after. But officials of the Cotton States Exposition in Atlanta attempted to cancel their three-week contract with the Sousa Band because of serious financial difficulties. At Sousa's insistence they honored their contract, and at the first concert they became aware of their shortsightedness. Atlanta newspapers carried rave reviews of the band's performances. For example:

> ...The band is a mascot. It has pulled many expositions out of financial ruts. It actually saved the Midwinter Fair in San Francisco. Recently at the St. Louis and Dallas expositions Sousa's Band proved an extraordinary musical attraction, and played before enormous audiences. It is safe to predict that history will repeat itself in Atlanta, and that the band will do the Exposition immense good. A great many people in South Carolina, Alabama and Georgia have postponed their visit to the Exposition so as to be here during Sousa's engagement, and these people will now begin to pour in.
>
> Sousa's latest march, "King Cotton," has proved a winner. It has been heard from one end of Dixie to the other and has aroused great enthusiasm and proved a fine advertisement for the Exposition.[40]

The Sousa Band did indeed bring the exposition "out of the red," and the same officials who had tried to cancel Sousa's engagement pleaded with him to extend

---
[40] *Atlanta Commercial*, November 19, 1895.

it. "King Cotton" was named the official march of the exposition, and it has since become one of the perennial Sousa favorites.

MSS: a) Bd 9pp; 28July1895 Manhattan
        Beach, N.Y. [UI]
    b) Orch 2pp inc; nd np [LC]
    c) Orch 1pp inc; nd np [UI]
Pub: Church
©: Pi: Church 1Aug1895; ren JPS
    21Feb1923
    Orch: Church 26Aug1895; ren
    JPS 21Feb1923
    Bd: Church 5Sep1895; not ren
    Pi duet; banjo; banjo & pi; guitar;
    guitar duet; mandolin; mandolin &
    guitar: Church 12Sep1895; not ren
    Pi six hands; mandolin duet; mandolin
    & pi; mandolin & pi & guitar; two
    mandolins & guitar; two mandolins &
    pi; two mandolins & guitar: Church
    19Sep1895; no renewals of any
    Zither; zither duet: Church 12Oct1895;
    not ren

THE LAMBS' MARCH (1914)

For the 1914 gambol of the celebrated Lambs Club of New York, Sousa composed this march and "The Lambs' Gambol" overture. He also accompanied a group of club members on a fund-raising tour of the major eastern cities. In each city he led a parade and apparently acted as musical director for their stage presentations.

Once again Sousa lived up to his reputation of not letting his music go to waste; much of "The Lambs' March" was taken from his unsuccessful 1882 operetta, "The Smugglers."

MSS: a) Orch 10pp; 20Apr1914 Phila. [LC]
    b) Bd 8pp; 23Apr1914 New York City
    [LC]
    c) Pi 2pp; nd np [LC]
Pub: Church
©: Pi: Church 18May1914; ren JvMS
    13Feb1942
    Bd; orch: Church 26May1914; ren
    JvMS 13Feb1942

THE LAND OF THE GOLDEN FLEECE
(See THE FEDERAL)
(Also see Suites: TALES OF A TRAVELER)

LEGION OF HONOR
(See COMRADES OF THE LEGION)

THE LEGIONNAIRES (1930)

On December 5, 1930, Sousa told a newspaper reporter that he was anxiously awaiting the inspiration for this march.[41] Later that day he sketched it out from start to finish.[42] The march was written at the request of the French government for the 1931 International Colonial and Overseas Exposition in Paris.[43] The only known manuscript does not reveal the identity of those to whom Sousa referred as legionnaires, but perhaps the frontispiece of the sheet music provides a clue. It depicts Washington and Lafayette and the dates 1776-1931. This would infer that these two pillars of democracy, who fought together in the American Revolution, were Sousa's "legionnaires."

MSS: Pi 1pp; 5Dec1930 np [LC]
Pub: Presser
©: Bd: Presser 2Jul1931; ren JPrS & HSA
    16Jul1958
    Pi: Presser 17Jul1931; ren JPrS & HSA
    21Jul1958
    Orch: Presser 16Feb1932; ren HSA
    31Aug1959

THE LIBERTY BELL (1893)

For $500 more, this march probably would have been named "The Devil's Deputy." Sousa was composing music for an operetta of that name at the request of the celebrated comedian Francis Wilson. Sousa asked $1,500 for the work, but Wilson offered $1,000. When they could not come to an agreement, Sousa withdrew with his partially completed manuscript, which included a lively march.

Sousa and George Frederick Hinton, one of the band's managers, were in Chicago witnessing a spectacle called *America* when a backdrop, with a huge painting of the Liberty Bell, was lowered. Hinton suggested that "The Liberty Bell" would be a good title for Sousa's new march. By coincidence, the next morning Sousa received

---

[41] *New York Times,* December 6, 1930.
[42] The piano sketch is dated December 5, 1930. The fact that the march was written in one day was confirmed in an interview printed in the *New York Evening Journal,* December 17, 1930.
[43] *Philadelphia Sunday News,* July 22, 1934.

a letter from his wife in which she told how their son had marched in his first parade in Philadelphia — a parade honoring the return of the Liberty Bell, which had been on tour. The new march was then christened "The Liberty Bell."[44] It was one of the first marches Sousa sold to the John Church Company and was the first composition to bring Sousa a substantial financial reward.

According to a story told by the Sousa Band's first soprano, Marcella Lindh, she contributed one of the themes of the march. Sousa had heard her whistling a catchy tune of her own and had asked her permission to incorporate it into one of his marches. Several years later she heard "The Liberty Bell" march being performed by a band in Europe and recognized her own melody in the march.[45]

MSS: Bd 7pp; 14Nov1893 Chicago [USMC]
Pub: Church
©: Pi: Church 25Nov1893; ren JPS 16May1921
Pi duet: Church 4Jan1894; not ren
Orch: Church 11Jan1894; ren JPS 14Nov1921
Bd: Church 18Jan1894; ren JPS 14Nov1921
Banjo; banjo duet; banjo & pi; guitar; mandolin & pi; mandolin & guitar; mandolin & pi & guitar: Church 18Jan1894; not ren
Pi six hands: Church 15Feb1894; not ren
Zither; zither duet; Church 15Mar1894; not ren
Two mandolins & guitar: Church 5Apr1894; not ren

LIBERTY LOAN (1917)

At the request of William J. McAdoo, secretary of the treasury, and Charles H. Schweppe, one of the Liberty Loan direc-

tors, this march was written for the Fourth Liberty Loan campaign of World War I. It was later dedicated to the officers and men of the 40th United States Infantry. Its temporary popularity was partially dependent upon the "U.S. Field Artillery" march, with which it was paired on a Victor record. This record sold over 400,000 copies. The *Chicago Examiner* printed the march with a request for verses. Dozens poured in, but as far as can be determined none was ever endorsed by Sousa.

Sousa struggled for some time before hitting upon suitable melodies for this march. The flash of inspiration came one night at a dinner in Kansas City, and he jotted the notes on his cuff. In a test of his endurance he developed the march by working in his hotel room until dawn for two nights and then on the train from Kansas City to Chicago.[46]

MSS: N/A
Pub: Harms
©: Pi: JPS 7Oct1917 (in newspaper) again Harms 28Feb1918; ren JPrS & HSA 9Oct1944
Bd: Harms 19Nov1917; ren JPrS & HSA 1Dec1944

THE LIBERTY MARCH
(See LIBERTY LOAN)

THE LION TAMER
(See ON PARADE)

THE LOYAL LEGION (1890)

This march was written to commemorate the twenty-fifth anniversary of the Military Order of the Loyal Legion of the United States, an organization composed primarily of American Civil War officers and their descendants. The anniversary celebration was held in Philadelphia on April 15 and 16, 1890, and the U.S. Marine Band was ordered by the secretary of the navy to participate.[47]

The piece is seldom played today, but the Loyal Legion uses it occasionally at its

---

[44] Sousa often told this story to newspaper reporters, so it was widely circulated. It was reprinted in programs of the 1925 Sousa Band tour, when the march was featured with the addition of massive chimes. This program incorrectly states that the march was played at the first Sousa Band concert in 1892; this was a full year before the march was arranged for band.

[45] This story was told to the author by Marcella Lindh Jellinek in an interview at her Detroit home on September 5, 1965.

[46] *Chicago Examiner,* October 10, 1917.

[47] U.S. Marine Band Log, entry for February 25, 1890. The log states that the Loyal Legion was to pay expenses.

meetings.[48] Much of the march appeared in Sousa's operetta, *The Queen of Hearts* (1885).[49]

MSS: Opa 4pp inc: nd np [LC]
Pub: Coleman (bd; pi); Fischer (bd; pi duet)
©:   Pi: Coleman 11Apr1890 again 4May1894; ren JPS 6Feb1922
Also pub for bd and for pi duet but not ©

MAGNA CHARTA (1927)

This march was composed as a tribute to one of the most important documents in the history of English-speaking nations. Sousa was honoring a request of the International Magna Charta Day Association, which was urging the annual observance of Magna Charta Day on June 15.

MSS: Bd 9pp; 21Mar1927 Sands Pt. [LC]
Pub: Presser
©:   Pi: Presser 22Jun1927; ren JPrS & HSA 3Sep1954
     Pi duet: Presser 21Sep1927; ren JPrS & HSA 1Sep1955
     Bd: Presser 16Mar1928; ren JPrS & HSA 7Apr1955

THE MAN BEHIND THE GUN (1899)

In telling a reporter how this march was inspired, Sousa also gave his explanation of why his marches have been more successful than those of the master composers:

"A composition in march tempo must have the military instinct, and that is one reason why so few of the great composers have written successful marches. They lived in an atmosphere of peace. The roll of musketry had no meaning for them, so that quality is entirely absent from their work. The Spanish War was an inspiration to me. The 'Man Behind the Gun' was a musical echo of it."[50]

The march first appeared in the operetta *Chris and the Wonderful Lamp* (1899).

MSS: Pi 3pp; nd np [UI]
Pub: Church
©:   Pi: Church 9Dec1899; ren JPS 15Oct1927
     Orch: Church 26Dec1899; ren JPS 28Oct1927
     Guitar duet; two mandolins & pi; two mandolins & guitar: Church 15Jan1900; ren JPS 10Dec1927
     Bd: Church 3Feb1900; ren JPS 14Dec1927
     Pi duet; banjo; banjo duet; banjo & pi: Church 26Feb1900; ren JPS 14Dec1927

MANHATTAN BEACH (1893)

Following in the footsteps of Patrick Gilmore, Sousa became a popular figure at Manhattan Beach, the famous New York summer resort. One of his most lavish medals was presented to him in 1894 by the proprietor, Austin Corbin, and other shareholders. The previous season, Sousa had dedicated this march to Corbin, and one of his manuscripts is inscribed to him.

Sousa once told a reporter that the march had been derived from an earlier composition, probably "The Phoenix March" (1875): "I wrote 'Manhattan Beach' while playing a summer engagement at that once-popular resort, using as the basis an old march I had composed when I was with Milton Nobles."[51]

"Manhattan Beach" became a staple of bands all over the world, but the Sousa Band performed it differently by playing the trio and last section as a short descriptive piece. In this interpretation, soft clarinet arpeggios suggest the rolling ocean waves as one strolls along the beach. A band is heard in the distance. It grows louder and then fades away as the stroller continues along the beach.

MSS: a) Pi 2pp; nd np [Curtis Institute of Music]
     b) Pi 1pp inc; nd np [LC]
Pub: Church
©:   Pi: Church 10Sep1893; ren JPS 7Mar1921
     Banjo; banjo duet; banjo & pi; guitar; guitar duet; mandolin; mandolin & pi; mandolin & guitar; mandolin & pi

---

[48] Correspondence between H. Durston Saylor II, recorder, and the author, February, 1968. In this exchange I also learned that Sousa never held membership in the Loyal Legion.

[49] Interview in the *Boston Post*, October 1, 1922.

[50] *Wheeling* (W.Va.) *News*, February 11, 1916.

---

[51] *Grand Island* (Nebr.) *Daily Independent*, October 31, 1927.

& guitar; two mandolins & pi; two mandolins & guitar; zither; zither duet: Church 1Mar1894; not ren
Bd: Church 8Mar1894; ren JPS 14Nov1921
Pi duet: Church 8Mar1894; not ren
Orch: Church 15Mar1894; ren JPS 10Feb1922
Pi six hands: Church 29Mar1894; not ren

MARCH OF THE BLUES
(See Arrangements and Transcriptions: Marches)

MARCH OF THE MITTEN MEN (1923)
(POWER AND GLORY)

Thomas E. Mitten was top executive of the Philadelphia Rapid Transit Company, whose trolleys transported throngs of visitors to and from Willow Grove Park. This march was dedicated to both Mitten and his employees; hence the title. Mitten's favorite hymn, "Onward Christian Soldiers," is the basis of the march's trio, and a second edition was published as "Power and Glory," "a fraternal march."[52]

MSS: a) Bd 15pp 28Jun1923 Sands Pt. [LC]
b) Pi 2pp; 28Jun1923 Sands Pt. [LC]
c) Pi 6pp; 28Jun1923 np [LC]
d) Orch 17pp; 30May1924 Sands Pt. [Free Library of Phila.]
e) Pi 3pp; nd np [LC]
Pub: Presser
©: Pi: Presser 27Aug1923 again 11Dec1923; ren JPrS & HSA 24Nov1950 again 2Jan1951
Pi duet: Presser 11Dec1923; ren JPrS & HSA 2Jan1951
Bd: Presser 19Dec1923; ren JPrS & HSA 2Jan1951
Orch: Presser 15Oct1924; ren HSA 9Jul1952

MARCH OF THE PAN-AMERICANS
(1916)

It is odd that this, Sousa's longest march,

[52] There was a story circulated among Sousa Band members that the march was renamed because Sousa and Mitten had broken off relations, but this is probably inaccurate because the sheet music of "Power and Glory" also bears a dedication to Mitten. Too, Willow Grove Park was owned by the Philadelphia Rapid Transit Company, and Sousa's Band continued to play there for several more seasons.

had about the shortest life. It was written at the request of John Barrett, director general of the second Pan-American Scientific Congress, held in Washington, D.C., and was named the official march. The piece embraced national anthems of Argentina, Bolivia, Brazil, Chile, Colombia, Costa Rica, Cuba, San Domingo, Ecuador, Guatemala, Haiti, Honduras, Mexico, Nicaragua, Panama, Paraguay, Peru, Salvador, Uruguay, Venezuela, and the United States. The finale is "The Star Spangled Banner" played with woodwind variations in the style of Wagner's *Tannhauser* Overture.

MSS: N/A
Pub: Fischer
©: Bd: Fischer 7Oct1916; ren JvMS 30Dec1943
Also pub for orch but not ©

MARCH OF THE ROYAL TRUMPETS
(1892)

Six Egyptian trumpets, nearly five feet long, were used by the Sousa Band in featuring this composition on the first tour in 1892. There is no record of the piece being performed by the band after that season. However, in 1904 Sousa appropriated some of the themes for "Her Majesty the Queen," a movement of his *At the King's Court* suite. Band parts of the original "March of the Royal Trumpets" found their way to the Detroit Concert Band in 1966, and the piece was revived for a radio broadcast. This was the first performance in seventy-four years, and the march was never published in the original form.

MSS: a) Bd 4pp inc; nd np [LC]
b) Additions to several bd parts in Sousa's hand; nd np [USMC]
Not pub or ©

MARCH OF THE STATES
(See AMERICA FIRST)
(Also see Incidental Music: HIP HIP HOORAY)

MARCH OF THE SUN
(See PRINCE CHARMING)

THE MARCH PAST OF THE CORCORAN CADETS
(See CORCORAN CADETS)

THE MARCH PAST OF THE NATIONAL FENCIBLES
(See NATIONAL FENCIBLES)

THE MARCH PAST OF THE RIFLE REGIMENT
(See THE RIFLE REGIMENT)

MARCH PAST OF THE 40th INFANTRY
(See LIBERTY LOAN)

MARCH-SONG OF THE CHICAGO SCHOOLS
(See Other Vocal Works: WE MARCH, WE MARCH TO VICTORY)

MARQUETTE UNIVERSITY MARCH
(1924)

On November 16, 1923, in recognition of what Sousa had done for his country in both peace and war, Marquette University bestowed upon him an honorary Doctor of Music degree. It was the first such degree given by that university. Sousa composed this march as an expression of his appreciation and presented the piano manuscript to the university.

MSS: a) Pi 1pp inc; May1924 np [LC]
      b) Pi 2pp; nd np [Marquette Univ.
         Archives]
Pub: Church
©:   Bd: Church 4Nov1924; ren JPrS &
         HSA 9Jan1952
      Pi: Church 6Nov1924; ren JPrS & HSA
         9Jan1952
      Orch: Church 23Dec1924; not ren

MIKADO MARCH (1885)

The popularity of Sousa's medley marches, which were based on themes of other composers, never approached that of his original compositions. Such was the case with the "Mikado March," which utilized themes from the celebrated Gilbert and Sullivan operetta.

MSS: N/A

Pub: Coleman
©:   Bd: Coleman 29Oct1885; not ren

THE MINNESOTA MARCH (1927)

It seems incredible that an institution would refuse a composition by a composer of Sousa's stature, but this happened in the summer of 1927 in Minneapolis. Clarence W. Spears, coach of the University of Minnesota football team, had verbally requested the march for his school in 1926; the following year the march was formally requested by the alumni organization. When the time came for the dedication of the march at the Minnesota State Fair on September 3, 1927, the delegated alumni representative was out of town, and Lotus D. Coffman, president of the university, was asked to accept Sousa's manuscript of the march on behalf of the university. He refused, however, because he felt the march should be presented at a university function, not at the state fair, and he was wary of commercial implications. Nevertheless, the dedication ceremony was held, and the Sousa manuscript was accepted by the state fair president.

Sousa used Indian themes in the march, though sparingly, because he had been impressed by the number of Indian names in Minnesota. He later added field drum and bugle parts upon the request of Colonel Frederick G. Stutz, commanding officer of the 206th National Guard Infantry Regiment of Minnesota. The march's title was chosen in a campus contest, and words were written by student Michael J. Jalma.

MSS: a) Bd 15pp; 24Feb1927 Sands Pt. [UI]
      b) Pi 4pp; 24Aug1927 np [present
         location unknown]
Pub: Fox
©:   Bd: Fox 26Sep1927; ren JPrS & HSA
         13Jun1955
Also pub for pi but not ©

MOTHER GOOSE (1883)

One of the seldom-used marches in the Sousa Band repertoire was this medley of nursery tunes. Reflecting his sense of humor, Sousa used it in a sly manner. On one occasion, a matinee audience seemed unresponsive. He quietly uttered to the band, "If they're going to act like children, we'll give them children's music! Get up 'Mother Goose,' gentlemen." This got to be a joke with the bandsmen, and when Sousa appeared to be perturbed with a matinee audience, they would nudge one another and say, "The Old Man's about ready to give 'em 'Mother Goose'!"

The nursery tunes included are "Come All Ye Young Maids," "I'se Come to See Miss Jennie Jones," "Little Jack Horner," "There Is a Man in Our Town," "Our Dear Doctor," and "Down in the Meadow."

MSS: N/A
Pub: Pepper
©: Bd: Pepper 8Jun1883 again 4Jun1889; not ren
Pi: Pepper 1Feb1897; not ren

MOTHER HUBBARD MARCH (1885)

A companion piece to "Mother Goose," this medley march was also based on nursery rhymes. Included are "Three Blind Mice," "Thus the Farmer Sows His Seed," "Old Mother Hubbard," "Hey Diddle Diddle," "Little Redbird in the Tree," "London Bridge Is Falling Down," and "The Minstrel Boy."

MSS: Bd 5pp inc; nd np [LC]
Pub: Coleman
©: Orch: Coleman 20Oct1885 again 4May1894; ren JPS 6Feb1922
Pi: Coleman 3Apr1894 again 22Dec1894; ren JPS 6Feb1922
Also pub for bd but not ©

NATIONAL DEFENSE
(See UNIVERSAL PEACE and THE GRIDIRON CLUB)

NATIONAL FENCIBLES (1888)
(THE MARCH PAST OF THE NATIONAL FENCIBLES)

The National Fencibles of this march's title were a popular drill team of Washington, D.C. The words to the trio of the march reflect their esprit de corps:

"Forward to battle, the trumpet is sounding;
'Come if you dare!' We loudly sing.
Shoulder to shoulder, with hearts rebounding;

Onward we march with the Fencibles' swing."

MSS: N/A
Pub: Coleman
©: Pi: Coleman 13Jun1888 again 4May1894; ren JPS 19Jan1916 again 6Feb1922
Orch: Coleman 29Dec1888; ren JPS 19Jan1916
Guitar: Coleman 27Jun1894; ren JPS 6Feb1922
Mandolin & pi: Coleman 14Jul1894; ren JPS 6Feb1922
Also pub for bd but not ©

THE NATIONAL GAME (1925)

Judge Kenesaw Mountain Landis, baseball's high commissioner, asked Sousa to compose this march on the occasion of the National League's fiftieth anniversary. Earlier the two had met in Havana. No doubt Sousa told him of his enthusiasm for the game and of the Sousa Band's own team.

MSS: Bd 12pp; 31Mar1925 Sands Pt. [UI]
Pub: Fox
©: Pi: Fox 6Jul1925; ren JPrS & HSA 6Aug1952
Also pub for bd but not ©

THE NAVAL RESERVE (1917)

"The Boys in Navy Blue" was the alternate title of this march, which Sousa wrote while in charge of the Navy band program at Great Lakes during World War I. It was dedicated to the officers and men of the Naval Reserve. The second half of the march was based on his then current song, "Blue Ridge, I'm Coming Back to You."

MSS: N/A
Pub: Harms
©: Pi: Harms 28Jun1917; ren JPrS & HSA 28Jun1944
Bd: Harms 17Dec1940; ren Warner Brothers-Seven Arts 8Aug1968

NEW MEXICO (1928)

This march was originally called "The Queen of the Plateau" before being given its present title. It was dedicated to Governor R. C. Dillon and the people of the state and was reportedly written at the Governor's request. Sousa adapted several Spanish, Indian, and American songs of

New Mexico. One of them was the state song, "O, Fair New Mexico," by Elizabeth Garrett. Others were "La Desgracia," "Peña," and "Recuerdas de Amistad."

MSS: Bd 18pp; 30Jun1928 Sands Pt. [UI]
Pub: Fox
©:   Bd: Fox 16Nov1928; ren JPrS & HSA
       16Dec1955
     Pi: Fox 26Nov1928; ren JPrS & HSA
       16Dec1955

THE NEW YORK HIPPODROME (1915)

The Sousa Band's longest single engagement, from September 30, 1915, to June 4, 1916, was when it was featured in the *Hip Hip Hooray* extravaganza at the New York Hippodrome. Sousa wrote this march in commemoration of that engagement, and it was dedicated to Charles B. Dillingham, manager of the famous old theater. In a salute to Sousa on his sixty-first birthday, Dillingham arranged to have over two hundred theater orchestras around the country play the march at precisely the same time.

MSS: Pi 2 pp; 31Jul1915 Seattle [LC]
Pub: Harms
©:   Pi: Harms 28Sep1915; ren JvMS
       30Sep1942
     Bd: Harms 18Dec1940; ren Warner
       Brothers-Seven Arts 8Aug1968

NO SURRENDER
(See THE WASHINGTON POST)

NOBLES OF THE MYSTIC SHRINE
(1923)

Sousa became a member of the Ancient Arabic Order of Nobles of the Mystic Shrine in Washington in April, 1922, and was promptly named the first honorary director of the Almas Temple Shrine Band. His nephew, A. R. Varela, who sponsored him, asked him to compose this march. The new march saluted Shriners in general but was dedicated specifically to the Almas Temple and Imperial Council, A. A. O. N. M. S.

The Shriners' national convention was held in Washington in June, 1923, and Sousa was called upon to lead a huge band of 6,200 Shriners in Griffith Stadium. This,

incidentally, was the largest band Sousa ever conducted, and a new association with Shriners had just begun. Several Shrine bands accompanied the Sousa Band in performances of the new march as it toured the United States, and many additional appearances of the Sousa Band were arranged by Shriners. It is also noteworthy that in the last years of the Sousa Band approximately half the members were Shriners.

MSS: Pi 2pp inc; nd np [LC]
Pub: Fox
©:   Bd: Fox 14Mar1923; ren JPrS & HSA
       17Mar1950
     Pi: Fox 20Jun1923; ren JPrS & HSA
       28Jun1950

THE NORTHERN PINES (1931)

"So much is said from the negative side about the youth that it indeed restores one's faith to find here, year after year, hundreds of boys and girls with such ideals, such marked ability and evident industry."[53] Many times in the 1920's Sousa expressed optimism about the future of music in America. The country's potential was in the hands of youthful musicians whose capabilities inspired him on countless occasions. Perhaps his greatest inspiration in this vein came in July, 1930, when he was guest conductor at the National Music Camp at Interlochen. After this memorable occasion, he was invited to return the following year.

The camp at Interlochen was founded by Dr. Joseph E. Maddy among beautiful pines of Northern Michigan in Indian country. Just prior to Sousa's second visit, he composed "The Northern Pines" and dedicated it to Dr. Maddy and the camp. He conducted the National High School Band in the first performance at a Sousa Day program on Sunday afternoon, July 26, 1931, at which time the faculty and students presented him with a medal. Sousa signed over royalties of the new march, which had not yet been printed, to the camp. A Sousa scholarship was founded,

---

[53] Quoted in the American Bandmasters Association convention program of August 6-9, 1936.

and one or more outstanding music students were brought to Interlochen each year for several seasons. Today the walkway which circumnavigates the principal stage and audience area is known as the John Philip Sousa Walk.

MSS: a) Bd 2pp inc; nd np [LC]
     b) Pi 3pp; nd np [LC]
     c) Pi 3pp; nd np [LC]
     d) Pi 2pp inc; nd np [LC]
     e) Pi 1pp inc; nd np [LC]
Pub: Schirmer
©: Pi (unpub): Schirmer 14Jul1931; ren
    JPrS & HSA 21Jul1958
    Bd: Schirmer 12Oct1931; ren HSA
    16Feb1959
    Pi: Schirmer 6Nov1931; ren HSA
    16Feb1959
    Orch: Schirmer 23Nov1931; ren HSA
    16Feb1959

NURSERY RHYMES
(See MOTHER GOOSE
and MOTHER HUBBARD)

THE OCCIDENTAL (1887)

With important manuscripts unaccounted for, no dedication specified on the printed music, and no mention in Sousa's memoirs, it is not known why this march was given its odd title. It was not published until four years after it was written.

MSS: Pi 1pp; 27Aug1887; np [LC]
Pub: Coleman
©: Bd: Coleman 22Jul1891; not ren
    Pi: Coleman 22Jul1891 again
    4May1894; ren JPS 6Feb1922
    Orch: Coleman 29Dec1891; not ren

OLD IRONSIDES (1926)

In 1926, patriotic citizens noted the deterioration of the historic old frigate *Constitution,* better known as "Old Ironsides," and waged a vigorous campaign to have it restored. At a rally held in Madison Square Garden, enough money was raised to insure success of the movement. For that occasion, Sousa composed this march. He led the massed bands of the U.S. Navy, Marine Corps, and Army, but whether or not the new march was played is not certain. Oddly, the march was never published, and

only a manuscript sketch is known to exist today.

MSS: Pi 2pp; nd np [LC]
Not pub or ©

ON PARADE (1892)
(THE LION TAMER)

Sousa inserted this original march when he orchestrated Goodwin and Stahl's operetta, *The Lion Tamer.* The march was later published as a separate composition under two titles, "On Parade" and "The Lion Tamer."

MSS: N/A
Pub: Grasmuk & Schott (bd; orch); Harms
    (pi)
©: Pi: Harms 20Apr1892 again 14Feb1895;
    not ren
    Orch: J. Charles Grasmuk 29Apr1893;
    ren JPS 7Mar1921
    Banjo: Harms 17Jun1893; ren JPS
    7Mar1921
    Bd: Grasmuk & Schott 26Jun1895; ren
    JPS 8Feb1923

ON THE CAMPUS (1920)

Sousa's daughter, Helen Sousa Abert, stated that her father had written this march at the request of the publisher. It was dedicated "To collegians, past, present, and future." One of two sets of words Mrs. Abert wrote for the march appeared on the sheet music, and she was of the opinion that the rejected version was not as "corny" as the printed version.[54]

MSS: Bd 14pp; 25Dec1920 Sands Pt. [UI]
Pub: Fox
©: V/pi: Fox 18Apr1921; ren JPrS & HSA
    10Oct1948
    Bd: Fox 11May1921; ren JPrS & HSA
    28May1948
    Pi: Fox 18May1921; ren JPrS & HSA
    28May1948

ON THE TRAMP (1879)

"On the Tramp" — that is, "on the march" — was the first of Sousa's marches to have the characteristic "Sousa swing" in the final section. Ironically, he got little

---

[54] Interview with the author, September, 1963.

for his efforts, and the conversation with his publisher went something like this:

"We won't give you twenty-five dollars for it."

"Will you give me fifteen dollars for it?"

"We wouldn't give you fifteen cents for it."

"Would you give me one of your new dictionaries for it?"

"Yes."[55]

MSS: N/A
Pub: Grasmuk & Schott (bd); Stoddart (pi);
          Hitchcock (pi)
©:   Pi: Stoddart 14Jul1879; not ren
          Bd: Grasmuk & Schott 11Oct1895; ren
          JPS 8Feb1923

ON TO VICTORY
(See THE FREE LANCE)

ONWARD WE MARCH WITH THE FENCIBLES' SWING
(See NATIONAL FENCIBLES)

OUR FLIRTATION (1880)
(OUR FLIRTATIONS)

Our Flirtations was a musical comedy first produced in Philadelphia in 1880. Sousa was responsible for the incidental music, which included this original march. It was dedicated to Henry L. West, a newspaperman of the *Washington Post* staff.

MSS: N/A
Pub: Coleman
©:   Pi: Coleman 20Feb1890 again
          4May1894; ren JPS 26Nov1917 again
          6Feb1922
          Two banjos: Coleman 1Jul1895; ren
          JPS 8Feb1923
Also pub for bd but not ©

PAN-AMERICAN MARCH
(See MARCH OF THE PAN-AMERICANS)

PARIS EXPOSITION
(See THE TRITON and HAIL TO THE SPIRIT OF LIBERTY)

THE PATHFINDER OF PANAMA (1915)

One of twelve marches Sousa composed for various expositions or fairs, "The Pathfinder of Panama" was dedicated to the Panama Canal and the Panama-Pacific Exposition, held in San Francisco in 1915. Sousa's Band played a nine-week engagement at the exposition. The march was composed at the request of Walter Anthony, a reporter for the *San Francisco Call*. The Panama Canal was the pathfinder of Sousa's title; it shortened the ocean voyage between San Francisco and New York by 8,000 miles.

MSS: N/A
Pub: Church
©:   Bd: Church 19Apr1915; ren JvMS
          8Jan1943
          Orch: Church 3May1915; ren JvMS
          22Mar1943
          Pi: Church 22May1915; ren JvMS
          22Mar1943

THE PENNSYLVANIA MILITARY COLLEGE MARCH
(THE PENNSYLVANIA MILITARY MARCH)
(See THE DAUNTLESS BATTALION)

PET OF THE PETTICOATS (1883)

Discussions of this obscure composition are not to be found among Sousa's writings. The printed music offers no clue to the origin of the title.

MSS: N/A
Pub: Pepper
©:   Bd: Pepper 8Jun1883 again 15Nov1883;
          not ren

THE PHOENIX MARCH (1875)
(THE BLUDSO MARCH)

Early in his career, Sousa was musical director for a traveling company which produced the play *Bohemians and Detectives* (later called *The Phoenix*, at Sousa's suggestion), starring Milton Nobles. Sousa composed incidental music for the production. He also composed this march and dedicated it to Nobles, but evidently it was not intended for use in the play. Nearly half a century afterward, Nobles told how Sousa had composed the march en route to Memphis.[56] It was first called "The

---

[55] *New York Herald,* September 6, 1912.

[56] *Memphis Commercial Appeal,* October 18, 1924.

Bludso March," Jim Bludso being the principal character of the play.

The only remnant of the march is a fragment given as the May 10 entry in Sousa's musical almanac, *Through the Year with Sousa*. Part of the march was used later as basis for his "Manhattan Beach" march.[57]

MSS: N/A
Not pub or ©

THE PICADOR (1889)

"The Picador" was one of several marches sold outright to the publisher, Harry Coleman, for $35 each. That sum included arrangements for band, orchestra, and piano. The origin of the march's title is unknown.

MSS: N/A
Pub: Coleman
©:   E-flat cornet: Coleman 1Nov1889;
        ren JPS 18Aug1917
      Pi: Coleman 30Dec1889 again
        4May1894; ren JPS 18Aug1917
        again 6Feb1922
      Guitar: Coleman 27Jun1894; ren JPS
        6Feb1922
      Mandolin & pi: Coleman 14Jul1894;
        ren JPS 6Feb1922
      Banjo: Coleman 1Jul1895; ren JPS
        8Feb1923
Also pub for bd and for pi duet but not ©

POWER AND GLORY
(See MARCH OF THE MITTEN MEN)

POWHATAN'S DAUGHTER (1907)

This was the march that first endeared Sousa to the Indians of America. It was a salute to Pocahontas, daughter of Chief Powhatan, and was written for the Jamestown Exposition of 1907. This exposition marked the three hundredth anniversary of the first English settlement in America.

MSS: N/A
Pub: Church
©:   Bd; orch: Church 7Aug1907; ren JvMS
        10Jan1935

---

[57] "Sousa's First March," an interview with Milton Nobles. (Clipping in the 1898 Sousa Band press book.) Nobles referred to his ownership of the manuscript in another interview, "A Modern Columbus," in *Dramatic Mirror*, June 5, 1909.

Pi; pi duet: Church 8Aug1907; ren JvMS 10Jan1935

PRESIDENT GARFIELD'S FUNERAL MARCH
(See IN MEMORIAM)

PRESIDENT GARFIELD'S INAUGURATION MARCH (1881)

The only two marches Sousa dedicated to presidents of the United States were composed for James A. Garfield, and they marked the beginning and end of his short tenure of office. The first was the stately "President Garfield's Inauguration March," which bears the inscription Opus 131. It was first performed by the U.S. Marine Band, with Sousa conducting, at the inauguration ceremonies on March 4, 1881. The second march honoring President Garfield was "In Memoriam."

MSS: N/A
Pub: Pond
©:   Pi: Pond 25Feb1881; not ren

THE PRIDE OF PITTSBURGH (1901)

The title of this composition was selected in a contest sponsored by Pittsburgh newspapers, but inasmuch as the march was never published Sousa subsequently used at least three other titles when programming it with the Sousa Band. These were "The Belle of Pittsburgh," "Homage to Pittsburgh," and "Homage to Nevin and Foster." The march was written for the dedication of Music Hall at the Western Pennsylvania Exposition (Pittsburgh Exposition) and included melodies by two Pittsburgh composers, Stephen Foster and Ethelbert Nevin. Foster's "Come Where My Love Lies Dreaming" and Nevin's "Narcissus" were the melodies used.

MSS: N/A
Not pub or ©

THE PRIDE OF THE WOLVERINES
(1926)

Mayor John W. Smith of Detroit publicly requested this march at a Sousa Band concert in that city in 1925. Sousa responded by composing this, one of his most vigorous marches, and dedicating it to Mayor Smith and the people of Detroit. It was later declared the official march of Detroit at a brief concert in the Detroit council chambers given by the Cass Technical High School Band, directed by former Sousa Band clarinetist Roy Miller.[58]

MSS: a) Bd 14pp; 10Jun1926 Sands Pt. [UI]
         b) Pi 1pp inc; nd np [LC]
Pub: Fox
©:   Bd: Fox 19Oct1926; ren JPrS & HSA
         6May1954
         Duet or two-part chorus: Fox
         26Nov1927; ren JPrS & HSA
         13Jun1955
Also pub for pi but not ©

PRINCE CHARMING (1928)

Given the opportunity, Sousa would willingly conduct youth bands or orchestras, because youthful musicians were always close to his heart. In January, 1926, he directed a select orchestra of Los Angeles elementary school children. This so inspired him that he composed this march and dedicated it to the orchestra and its organizer, Jennie L. Jones. Two years later the orchestra had grown to 425 members, and they came on stage at a Sousa Band concert to serenade Sousa with their new march.

The identity of Prince Charming was never made public. Also, one Los Angeles newspaper referred to the composition as "March of the Sun," another title yet to be explained.

MSS: Pi 4pp; 5Jul1928 np [LC]
Pub: Fischer
©:   Orch: Fischer 8Nov1928; ren JPrS &
         HSA 9Nov1955
         Bd: Fischer 14Feb1929; ren JPrS &
         HSA 24May1956 again 10Oct1956

PUSHING ON
(See Songs — Music by Sousa
and Words by Others)

THE QUEEN OF THE PLATEAU
(See NEW MEXICO)

------

[58] "The Pride of the Wolverines" has since been replaced as the official march of Detroit by "Hail, Detroit," composed by Leonard B. Smith.

THE QUILTING PARTY MARCH (1889)

"The Quilting Party," or "Aunt Dinah's Quilting Party," was a popular song in the United States in the late 1880's. Sousa capitalized on its popularity by using it in the trio of this march, written while he was leader of the U.S. Marine Band.

MSS: Bd 1pp inc; nd np [LC]
Not pub or ©

RECOGNITION MARCH (circa 1880)

For many years the only suggestion of this composition's existence was an eleven-measure excerpt which constituted the January 17 entry in Sousa's musical almanac of 1910, *Through the Year with Sousa*. Then in 1970, when Sousa's heirs presented the Library of Congress with manuscripts they had held in storage since 1932, one of the surprises was the discovery of a full set of band parts of an untitled Sousa march. Comparison with the excerpt from *Through the Year with Sousa* showed the march to be none other than the long-lost "Recognition March." The parts were in a copyist's hand.

An analysis of the march's form shows it to be of 1880 vintage. It bears no similarity to any of the published Sousa marches of that era, and this gives rise to an interesting speculation. It is entirely possible that "Recognition March" is a revised version of an unpublished march known as "Salutation" (1873). Sousa had written "Salutation" at the age of nineteen for a ceremony in which a new leader of the U.S. Marine Band took command. The new leader had belittled him for his effort. Seven years later, Sousa replaced this same man as leader of the Marine Band. Not being of the inclination to waste music, Sousa may have revised "Salutation" and given it the new name. Thus "Salutation" would then have finally received its "recognition."

MSS: N/A
Not pub or ©

RESUMPTION MARCH (1879)

The derivation of this march's title was the resumption of the use of gold and silver coins in the United States after the post–Civil War inflation and depression.

MSS: N/A
Pub: Pepper (bd) ; Shaw (others)
©:   Pi: Shaw 25May1879; not ren
       Vi or flute with pi: Shaw
          26May1879; not ren
       Bd: Pepper 14Sep1882; not ren
Also pub by Shaw in collection for vi or flute
  with pi, *Evening Pastimes*

REVIEW (1873)

This was Sousa's first published march, and it was sold outright to the publisher for 100 copies of the sheet music. It was called Opus 5 and was dedicated to Colonel William G. Moore of the Washington Light Infantry. In later years, Sousa did not have a very high opinion of the march. To wit: "... Happily for me and for the general public it never became at all popular, and the echoes of the strains have long ago died away. I suppose it is now so deeply buried in oblivion that a 1,000 foot pole could not reach it. It is such a long time since I wrote it that I have no recollection whatever of the air. I did not preserve the manuscript...."[59]

MSS: N/A
Pub: Lee & Walker
©:   Pi: Lee & Walker 31Jul1873; not ren

REVIVAL MARCH (1876)
(THE GREAT REVIVAL MARCH AND SALVATION ARMY RALLY)

This march incorporated the hymn "[In the] Sweet Bye and Bye" and was probably written at the suggestion of Simon Hassler, the Philadelphia composer and orchestra leader. It was one of Sousa's earliest marches and was written for orchestra, not band. His former music teacher, John Esputa, Jr., made note of the march and correctly predicted Sousa's future in music. He wrote in the September 30, 1876, issue of his weekly newspaper, the *Musical Monitor:* "We have now on hand the 'Grand Revival March' composed by J. P. Sousa of this city, and which was played with immense success by Hassler's orchestra at

[59] *Sioux City* (Iowa) *Journal,* November 11, 1898.

the Chestnut St. Theater, Phila. The march is deserving of credit. We are glad to see such proficiency in one so young, and predict for him a brilliant future."

MSS: N/A
Pub: Ditson (pi) ; Coleman (bd; orch) ;
       Andre (orch)
©:   Pi: JPS & Simon Hassler 25Sep1876
          again Ditson 3Nov1876; not ren
       Orch: Coleman 14Jul1894; ren JPS
          6Feb1922
       Bd: Coleman 18Dec1894; not ren

RIDERS FOR THE FLAG (1927)
(RIDERS OF THE FLAG)

This march was composed at the request of Colonel Osmun Latrobe, Regimental Commander of the 4th U.S. Cavalry, and was dedicated to Colonel Latrobe, his officers, and men. It is unusual in construction in that it is the only Sousa march with a coda.

MSS: Bd 10pp; 8Apr1927 Brooklyn, N.Y. [UI]
Pub: Fox
©:   Bd: Fox 12Aug1927; ren JPrS & HSA
          13Jun1955
Also pub for pi but not ©

THE RIFLE REGIMENT (1886)
(THE MARCH PAST OF THE RIFLE REGIMENT)

According to an inscription on the printed music, this march was dedicated to the officers and men of the 3rd U.S. Infantry. Although different from Sousa's other marches in musical format, it is regarded as one of his better efforts.

MSS: a) Pi 1pp inc; nd np [LC]
       b) Pi 1pp inc; nd np [UI]
Pub: Fischer
©:   Pi: Fischer 31Dec1886; ren JPS
          12Dec1914
       Orch: Fischer 2Nov1893; ren JPS
          7Mar1921
Also pub for bd and for vi but not ©

RIGHT FORWARD (1881)

"Guide Right" and "Right Forward," a pair of parade marches composed in 1881, have marching commands for their titles. Both were dedicated to a Marine Captain R. S. Collum, presumably a friend of Sousa's in Washington, D.C.

MSS: N/A
Pub: Pond (pi); Coleman (bd); Pepper (bd);
       Fischer (orch; bd)
©:   Pi: Pond 28Feb1881; not ren
     Bd: Coleman 7Dec1885 again Pepper
       3Apr1895; not ren
     Orch: Fischer 31Dec1912; not ren

RIGHT — LEFT (1883)

This unusual march calls for shouts of
"Right! Left!" at regular intervals in the
trio. Perhaps it was used in this manner by
the Marine Band on the drill field.

MSS: Pi 3pp; nd np [UI]
Pub: Pepper (bd; orch); Barnes (pi;
       mandolins & guitar & pi); Chappell
       (bd)
©:   Bd: Pepper 8Jun1883 again 17Dec1883
       again 13Aug1896; not ren
     Orch: Pepper 17Oct1894; not ren
     Pi: Barnes 17Nov1894; not ren
     Three mandolins & guitar & pi: Barnes
       29Mar1895; not ren

THE ROYAL WELCH FUSILIERS
(No. 1) (1929)
THE ROYAL WELCH FUSILIERS
(No. 2) (1930)

These two marches were composed in
memory of the association of U.S. Marines
with the 2nd Battalion of the Royal Welch
Fusiliers in 1900 during the Boxer Rebellion in China. The occasion was the
thirtieth anniversary of the battle of Tientsin. General Wendelle C. Neville, commandant of the Marine Corps, asked Sousa
to compose a march, and the fact that two
separate marches were composed was revealed in an exchange of letters between
Sousa and Neville. Late in 1929, Sousa
composed a medley-march which included
"World Turned Upside Down," "Hymn of
the Marines," "Men of Harlech," and
"God Bless the Prince of Wales." When he
asked Neville's opinion, Neville replied that
he would prefer an original Sousa composition. So Sousa composed a second march,
and this is the one known today.

"The Royal Welch Fusiliers" (No. 2)
was given its premiere in the presence of
President Hoover. This took place at the
annual Gridiron Club dinner in Washington at the Willard Hotel on April 26, 1930.

Sousa conducted members of the Marine
Band in the new march, and President
Hoover spoke, giving his own personal account of the Boxer Rebellion. He had been
a mining engineer in China at the time and
was besieged at Tientsin, where he was in
charge of civil defense. The march was
given a public premiere on the White
House lawn on May 12 for the benefit of
newsreel companies. These newsreels provided one of the few motion pictures of
Sousa which have survived, and they show
Sousa conducting the Marine Band with
President Hoover, the British ambassador,
and other dignitaries looking on.

Sousa was asked to travel to Wales with
Marine Corps officers so that he could
personally present his manuscript to the
Fusiliers. He obliged, and on June 25 at
Tidworth he conducted the band of the
2nd Battalion, Royal Welch Fusiliers, in the
march's first performance in Britain. He
presented his original manuscript, handsomely bound, to General Charles M. Do-
belle, commandant of the Fusiliers. Today
this manuscript is preserved at Caernarvon
Castle.

MSS: a) (*No. 1*) Bd, 2 versions 24pp, both
       inc; 11Nov1929 Sands Pt. [LC]
     b) (*No. 2*) Bd 11pp; 7Feb1930 Sands
       Pt. [Regimental Museum, Caernarvon
       Castle, Wales]
     c) (*No. 2*) Orch 10pp; 2May1930 Sands
       Pt. [USMC]
     d) (*No. 2*) Bd 3pp inc; nd np [LC]
     e) (*No. 2*) Pi 2pp; nd np [LC]
Pub: Presser
©:   Pi: Presser 24Apr1930; ren JPrS & HSA
       10May1957 again 19Jul1957
     Bd: Presser 28Apr1930; ren JPrS &
       HSA 10May1957 again 19Jul1957
     Orch: Presser 2Jul1930; ren JPrS &
       HSA 19Jul1957
     Pi duet: Presser 8Oct1930; ren JPrS &
       HSA 19Nov1957

SABRE AND SPURS (1918)

According to the inscription on the sheet
music and on both of Sousa's known manuscripts, this was to be the "March of the
American Cavalry." It was dedicated to
the officers and men of the 311th Cavalry,
commanded by Colonel George W. K.
Kirkpatrick. It is another of Sousa's World

War I efforts which retained its popularity after the war.

Today it may seem amusing that a scroll of appreciation designated Sousa "honorary life member of the Officers' Mess of the 311th Cavalry." But in Army terminology of the day this meant that he was made an honorary life member of the regiment, the highest honor they could bestow.

MSS: a) Pi 3pp; 25May1918 np [UI]
b) Bd 14pp; nd np [UI]
Pub: Fox
©: Pi: Fox 6Jul1918 again 22Aug1918; ren JPrS & HSA 24Jan1946 again 5Aug1946
Also pub for bd but not ©

SAINT LOUIS EXPOSITION
(See THE DIRECTORATE)

SALUTATION (1873)

This was apparently Sousa's second march, written while he was a musician in the Marine Band. It was intended as a salute to the new leader, Louis Schneider. Schneider gruffly ordered the march off the stands, alienating the young Sousa. Schneider was amply repaid for his deed, however: it was none other than Sousa who replaced him as leader of the band five years later.

MSS: N/A
Not pub or ©

THE SALVATION ARMY (1930)

Commander Evangeline Booth, daughter of William Booth, founder of the Salvation Army, asked Sousa to compose this march, and it was to her that he dedicated it. It received its premiere on May 16, 1930, at a pageant in New York celebrating the fiftieth anniversary of the Salvation Army in the United States. Sousa conducted the massed bands. In this march he had incorporated the Salvationists' favorite hymn, "O Boundless Salvation," and when these strains were played the surprised audience broke into enthusiastic applause.

Shortly after Sousa's death, the story of how he had sought advice on what approach to take in this composition was told in the Salvationists' own newspaper, the

War Cry. Colonel William H. Barrett, who wrote the heart-warming story, told of several interviews in Sousa's New York office. To get the Salvationists' slant on "O Boundless Salvation," Sousa asked Colonel Barrett to sing it. He asked to hear it again, and this time he joined in. He was profoundly moved and remarked that the composer — William Booth — had been inspired. Colonel Barrett may not have realized it, but that was the most sincere compliment Sousa could have made. In his article, Colonel Barrett was discerning in his observation that Sousa "saw the bright side of everything and the good in everybody." He closed in this manner: "My dear friend has gone to his Eternal Home having been promoted suddenly. I expect to meet him when my life journey is ended."[60]

MSS: a) Bd 9pp inc; nd np [LC]
b) Pi 2pp; nd np [LC]
Pub: Presser
©: Bd; pi: Presser 7Apr1930; ren JPrS & HSA 10May1957 again 19Jul1957

SEMPER FIDELIS (1888)

It is unfortunate that President Chester A. Arthur, the man responsible for this march, did not live to hear it. In a conversation with Sousa, then leader of the U.S. Marine Band, he expressed his displeasure at the official use of the song "Hail to the Chief." When Sousa stated that it was actually an old Scottish boating song, the President suggested that he compose more appropriate music. Sousa responded with two pieces, not one. First he composed "Presidential Polonaise" (1886). Then, two years after Arthur's death, he wrote "Semper Fidelis."

The march takes its title from the motto of the U.S. Marine Corps: "Semper Fidelis" — "Always Faithful." The trio is an extension of an earlier Sousa composition, "With Steady Step," one of eight brief trumpet and drum pieces he wrote for *The Trumpet and Drum* (1886). It was dedicated to those who inspired it — the officers and men of the U.S. Marine Corps. In Sousa's own words: "I wrote 'Semper Fidelis' one night while in tears, after my

---

[60] *War Cry,* April 2, 1932.

comrades of the Marine Corps had sung their famous hymn at Quantico."[61]

For the first performance, Sousa demonstrated his flair for theatrics:

"We were marching down Pennsylvania Avenue, and had turned the corner at the Treasury Building. On the reviewing stand were President Harrison, many members of the diplomatic corps, a large part of the House and Senate, and an immense number of invited guests besides. I had so timed our playing of the march that the 'trumpet' theme would be heard for the first time, just as we got to the front of the reviewing stand. Suddenly ten extra trumpets were shot in the air, and the 'theme' was pealed out in unison. Nothing like it had ever been heard there before — when the great throng on the stand had recovered its surprise, it rose in a body, and led by the President himself, showed its pleasure in a mighty swell of applause. It was a proud moment for us all."[62]

"Semper Fidelis" subsequently gained recognition as the official march of the U.S. Marine Corps. Sousa regarded it as his best march, musically speaking. It became one of his most popular marches, and he once stated that it was the favorite march of Kaiser Wilhelm II of Germany — before World War I, of course.[63] It was played by the Sousa Band in many foreign countries and always received acclaim as a well-known composition. Few knew that it had been sold outright to the publisher for the unbelievably low sum of $35.

MSS: a) Bd 1pp inc; nd np [UI]
      b) Pi 1pp inc; nd np [USMC]
      c) Flute part 1pp; nd np [USMC]
Pub: Coleman
©: Orch: Coleman 29Dec1888; ren JPS 19Jan1916
    Pi: Coleman 4May1894; ren JPS 6Feb1922
    Two mandolins & guitar & pi: Coleman 1Apr1898; not ren
Also pub for bd but not ©

SEN-SEN
(See YORKTOWN CENTENNIAL)

---

[61] *Grand Island* (Nebr.) *Daily Independent,* October 31, 1927.
[62] "Sidelights on Sousa's Personality," *Musical America,* July 9, 1910.
[63] *Boston Post,* September 17, 1922.

SESQUICENTENNIAL EXPOSITION MARCH (1926)

The Sesquicentennial Exposition of 1926 was held in Philadelphia, the occasion being the hundred and fiftieth anniversary of American independence. Sousa composed this march at the request of exposition officials and dedicated it to the mayor of Philadelphia, W. Freeland Kendrick.

MSS: Pi 1pp inc; 23Mar1926 np [LC]
Pub: Fox
©: Bd: Fox 18Jun1926; ren JPrS & HSA 25Aug1953
    Pi: Fox 26Jul1926; ren JPrS & HSA 25Aug1953

SISTERHOOD OF THE STATES
(See Incidental Music: HIP HIP HOORAY)

(Reference) THE SMUGGLERS (THE SMUGGLERS' MARCH)

The march from the operetta *The Smugglers* (1882) is not classified as a separate composition because there is no evidence that it was ever extracted and arranged as a quickstep march by that name. However, Sousa did make further use of most of it when he composed "The Lambs' March" in 1914.

SOLID MEN TO THE FRONT (1918)

Although this World War I march has not been as popular as several other Sousa compositions of that era, it is regarded by scholars as one of his better efforts. The title first appeared on the manuscript of the march known as "Wisconsin Forward Forever" but was subsequently used for this march.

MSS: Pi 2pp; nd np [LC]
Pub: Schirmer
©: Pi: Schirmer 14Mar1918; ren JPrS & HSA 25Apr1945
Also pub for bd but not ©

SOUND OFF (1885)

As leader of the U.S. Marine Band, Sousa came under the command of Major George Porter Houston. In Sousa's eyes, Houston was a stern but fair officer, and this march was dedicated to him. As in the case of "Guide Right," "Right Forward," and "Right-Left," the title was derived from a marching command.

MSS: Pi 1pp inc; nd np [LC]
Pub: Coleman
©: Bd: Coleman 7Nov1885; not ren
Pi: Coleman 7Dec1885 again 4May1894; ren JPS 6Feb1922

SOUVENIR MARCH
(See THE TRITON)

THE SPIRIT OF LIBERTY
(See HAIL TO THE SPIRIT OF LIBERTY)

SPIRIT OF NIAGARA
(See THE INVINCIBLE EAGLE)

THE STARS AND STRIPES FOREVER
(1896)

With the possible exception of "The Star Spangled Banner," no musical composition has done more to arouse the patriotic spirit of America than this, John Philip Sousa's most beloved composition. It is sometimes taken to be the national march of the United States, although it has never officially been so designated. Symbolic of flag-waving in general, it has been used with considerable effectiveness to generate patriotic feeling ever since its introduction in Philadelphia on May 14, 1897, when the staid *Public Ledger* reported: "... It is stirring enough to rouse the American eagle from his crag, and set him to shriek exultantly while he hurls his arrows at the aurora borealis."[64]

Aside from this flowery review, the march's reception was only slightly above average for a new Sousa march. It grew gradually in public acceptance, and with the advent of the Spanish-American War the nation suddenly needed such patriotic music. Capitalizing on this situation, Sousa used it with maximum effect to climax his moving pageant, *The Trooping of the Colors.*

"The Stars and Stripes Forever" had found its place in history. There was a vigorous response wherever it was performed, and audiences began to rise as though it were the national anthem. This became traditional at Sousa Band concerts. It was his practice to have the cornets, trumpets, trombones, and piccolos line up at the front of the stage for the final trio, and this added to the excitement. Many bands still perform the piece this way.

With the passing years the march has endeared itself to the American people. The sight of Sousa conducting his own great band in this his most glorious composition always triggered an emotional response. The piece was expected — and sometimes openly demanded — at every concert of the Sousa Band. Usually it was played unannounced as an encore. Many former Sousa Band members have stated that they could not recall a concert in which it was not played, and that they too were inspired by looking into the misty eyes of those in the audience. That the players never tired of it is surely a measure of its greatness.

Sousa was very emotional in speaking of his own patriotism. When asked why he composed this march, he would insist that its strains were divinely inspired. In a Sousa Band program at Willow Grove we find this account:

Someone asked, "Who influenced you to compose 'Stars and Stripes Forever,'" and before the question was hardly asked, Sousa replied, "God — and I say this in all reverence! I was in Europe and I got a cablegram that my manager was dead. I was in Italy and I wished to get home as soon as possible. I rushed to Genoa, then to Paris and to England and sailed for America. On board the steamer as I walked miles up and down the deck, back and forth, a mental band was playing 'Stars and Stripes Forever.' Day after day as I walked it persisted in crashing into my very soul. I wrote it on Christmas Day, 1896."[65]

---

[64] *Philadelphia Public Ledger,* May 15, 1897, referring to the concert of the Sousa Band the previous day at the Academy of Music. (Research done by Elizabeth Hartman, head of music department, Free Library of Philadelphia.)

[65] Program for week beginning August 19, 1923.

The march was not put to paper on board the ship. Presumably it was penned in Sousa's hotel suite in New York soon after docking.

The composition was actually born of homesickness, as Sousa freely told interviewers, and some of the melodic lines were conceived while he was still in Europe.[66] In one such interview he stated:

"In a kind of dreamy way I used to think over old days at Washington when I was leader of the Marine Band . . . when we played at all public official functions, and I could see the Stars and Stripes flying from the flagstaff in the grounds of the White House just as plainly as if I were back there again.

"Then I began to think of all the countries I had visited, of the foreign people I had met, of the vast difference between America and American people and other countries and other peoples, and that flag of ours became glorified . . . and to my imagination it seemed to be the biggest, grandest, flag in the world, and I could not get back under it quick enough.

"It was in this impatient, fretful state of mind that the inspiration to compose 'The Stars and Stripes Forever' came to me, and to my imagination it was a genuine inspiration, irresistible, complete, definite, and I could not rest until I had finished the composition.[67] Then I experienced a wonderful sense of relief and relaxation. I was satisfied, delighted, with my work after it was done. The feeling of impatience passed away, and I was content to rest peacefully until the ship had docked and I was once more under the folds of the grand old flag of our country."[68]

The interviewer then added this telling postlude: " 'Amen! to those sentiments,' I said. And as I looked at John Philip Sousa there were tears in his eyes."[69]

Sousa explained to the press that the

three themes of the final trio were meant to typify the three sections of the United States. The broad melody, or main theme, represents the North. The South is represented by the famous piccolo obbligato, and the West by the bold countermelody of the trombones.

By almost any musical standard, "The Stars and Stripes Forever" is a masterpiece, even without its patriotic significance. But by virtue of that patriotic significance it is by far the most popular march ever written, and its popularity is by no means limited to the United States. Abroad, it has always symbolized America. It has been recorded more often than practically any other composition ever written. Sales of the sheet music alone netted Sousa over $400,000 in his lifetime;[70] radio broadcasts, sheet music, and phonograph records brought his heirs tidy sums for many years. After the copyright expired in 1953, over fifty new arrangements appeared in the United States alone. Looking back at the march's astonishing success, it is difficult to believe that the publisher had shown little faith in it and that he had even suggested to Sousa that "Forever" be striken from the title.[71]

Sousa did not claim that his march title was original. He could have come by it in one of two ways. First, the favorite toast of bandmaster Patrick S. Gilmore's was "Here's to the stars and stripes forever!"[72] Also, one of Sousa's publishers had earlier printed a piece with the same title.[73]

Sousa wrote words for the march, evidently for use in *The Trooping of the Colors*, his pageant of 1898. These are printed below. One phrase ("Death to the enemy!") was curiously omitted, however

---

[66] In several interviews Sousa referred to the conception of at least part of the march in Europe. One such interview was printed in the *Sioux City* (Iowa) *Journal,* November 11, 1898.

[67] Mentally, that is.

[68] The ship referred to in the above accounts was a White Star liner, the *Teutonic*. On this voyage it sailed from England on December 16, 1896, and docked in New York on December 23.

[69] "Sousa a National Inspiration!" *New York Review,* October 30, 1915.

[70] As stated in Sousa's article, "Why the World Needs Bands," in the September, 1930, issue of *Etude.*

[71] Sousa made this statement in a 1919 interview. (Unidentified clipping in the Sousa Band press book of 1919.)

[72] *New York Herald,* July 17, 1910.

[73] "The Stars and Stripes Forever," a marching song by William J. Lemon, dedicated to Civil War volunteers. It was published by Lee and Walker in 1861. It is possible that Sousa saw the song, with its beautifully illuminated frontispiece, in Lee and Walker's Philadelphia office in 1872.

—one which he said came to him repeatedly while he was pacing the decks of the *Teutonic*.[74]

Let martial note in triumph float
And liberty extend its mighty hand;
A flag appears 'mid thunderous cheers,
The banner of the Western land.
The emblem of the brave and true.
Its folds protect no tyrant crew;
The red and white and starry blue
Is freedom's shield and hope.

Other nations may deem their flags the best
And cheer them with fervid elation
But the flag of the North, and South and West
Is the flag of flags, the flag of Freedom's nation.

Hurrah for the flag of the free!
May it wave as our standard forever,
The gem of the land and the sea,
The banner of the right.
Let despots remember the day
When our fathers with mighty endeavor
Proclaimed as they marched to the fray
That by their might and by their right it waves forever.

(Second time)
Let eagle shriek from lofty peak
The never-ending watchword of our land;
Let summer breeze waft through the trees
The echo of the chorus grand.
Sing out for liberty and light,
Sing out for freedom and the right.
Sing out for Union and its might,
O patriotic sons.

Other nations may deem their flags the best
(Etc.)

Hurrah for the flag of the free!
(Etc.)

MSS: a) Pi 2pp; 25Dec1896 np [LC]
       b) Bd 8pp; 26Apr1897 Boston [LC]
Pub: Church
©:   Pi; pi duet; pi six hands: Church 14May1897; ren JPS 11Apr1925
    Banjo; banjo & pi; mandolin; mandolin & pi; mandolin & guitar; two mandolins & guitar; two mandolins & pi; zither: Church 14May1897; not ren
    Banjo duet: Church 14May1897; ren W. Wessenberg (arranger) 11May1925
    Guitar: Church 14May1897; ren C. Henlein (arranger) 11May1925

Mandolin & pi & guitar: Church 14May1897; ren John N. Klohr (arranger) 11May1925
Zither duet: Church 14May1897; ren Joseph A. Koch (arranger) 11May1925
Bd: Church 5Jun1897; ren JPS 9May1925
Orch: Church 1Jul1897; ren JPS 9May1925
V/pi: Church 15Apr1898; ren JPS 12Mar1926
Mixed chorus: Church 13May1899; ren JPS 23Mar1927
Male quartette: Church 9Sep1899; ren JPS 7Sep1927

THE SWORD OF SAN JACINTO
(See KANSAS WILDCATS)

THE THUNDERER (1889)

Other than the fact that Sousa's "thunderer" was undoubtedly a Mason, his identity may never be revealed. "The Thunderer" march was dedicated to Columbia Commandery No. 2, Knights Templar, of Washington, D.C., and it was composed on the occasion of the Twenty-fourth Triennial Conclave of the Grand Encampment. The conclave was held in October, 1889, and was sponsored by Columbia Commandery No. 2. Sousa had been "knighted" in that organization three years earlier.

"The Thunderer" was Mrs. John Philip Sousa's favorite march. This was revealed by their daughter Helen, who also surmised that the "thunderer" might have been her father's salute to the *London Times*, which was known as "the thunderer."[75] It has since been determined that Sousa probably had no association with the newspaper at that time, however. The "thunderer" might have been one of the men in charge of making arrangements for the 1889 conclave — in particular, Myron M. Parker, who worked tirelessly to make the event the spectacular success that it was.[76]

---

[74] "According to Sousa," *Daily Express* (London), January 11, 1905.

[75] Interview with the author, September, 1963.

[76] 33,000 Knights Templar participated. The event, and Parker's efforts, are described on pp. 79-81 and 123-26 of *History of Columbia Commandery No. 2 Knights Templar, 1863-1963* (private publ.).

In the second section of the march, Sousa included an adaptation of an earlier trumpet and drum piece, "Here's Your Health, Sir!" which he had written for *The Trumpet and Drum* (1886).

MSS: N/A
Pub: Coleman
©:   E-flat cornet: Coleman 1Nov1889; ren
        JPS 18Aug1917
        Pi: Coleman 22Nov1889 again
        4May1894; ren JPS 18Aug1917
        again 6Feb1922
        Orch: Coleman 31Dec1889; ren JPS
        18Aug1917
Also pub for bd and for two pi but not ©

TRANSIT OF VENUS (1883)

It is not known whether or not Sousa witnessed either of the two transits of Venus that occurred in his lifetime, but the phenomenon was the basis for the title of this march and one of his three novels.

MSS: N/A
Pub: Pepper
©:   Bd: Pepper 8Jun1883 again 15Nov1883
        again 13Aug1896; not ren
        Orch: Pepper 19Nov1894; not ren
        Pi: Pepper 20Aug1896; not ren

THE TRITON (1892)

The musical revisions and the abundance of titles given this composition have resulted in much confusion. In spite of all efforts to make it popular, it was a multiple flop.

Included in *Evening Pastime*, the 1879 collection of solos arranged by Sousa for violin and piano, was a short march by J. Molloy called "The Triton." This was published by J. F. Shaw of Philadelphia.

The composition grew from a simple arrangement to a march in 1892 when a second Philadelphia publisher, J. W. Pepper, entered the scene. Sousa added two more melodies to his original arrangement, and the new version was published for band as "The Triton Medley March." Whether or not these two additional melodies are Sousa's is not known.

Pepper published an edition for piano as "Triton March" in 1896 and then confused the public by publishing the same composition under a different title, "Souvenir." "Souvenir" was distributed free at a music exposition; hence its new title.[77]

The confusion was compounded in 1900 when still another version was published as "Paris Exposition." It was in the first issue of Pepper's new periodical, the *Piano Music Magazine*. This version had been altered by an arranger who changed the last two sections from 6/8 to 2/4 rhythm and omitted a da capo repeat.

By this time, Sousa was publishing with a third Philadelphia firm, John Church, who apparently avoided the march. The persistent Pepper was not yet finished, however, for he republished the march for piano as "The Triton Two-Step" in 1906. After this failed, he capitulated.

MSS: Bd 1pp inc; nd np [LC]
Pub: Pepper (bd; pi); Shaw (in 1879
        collection for vi or flute with pi,
        Evening Pastime)
©:   Bd: Pepper 7Oct1892; not ren
        Pi: Pepper 30Dec1896; not ren

TRIUMPH OF TIME (1885)

Since Sousa did not discuss this march in any of his writings, the origin of the title must be left to speculation. Although the music was copyrighted in six different years, Time did indeed triumph over it — it was never popular.

MSS: Bd 1pp inc; nd np [LC]
Pub: Coleman (bd; pi); Fischer (in 1890
        all-Sousa album for pi entitled *Home
        Circle Music Series No. 30*)
©:   Bd: Coleman 30Dec1885; ren JPS
        13Dec1913
        Pi: Coleman 1Apr1893 again 4May1894;
        ren JPS 7Mar1921 again 6Feb1922

UNCHAIN THE DOGS OF WAR
(See THE BRIDE ELECT)

UNCLE SAM'S NAVY
(See THE GLORY OF THE
YANKEE NAVY)

[77] An inscription on the front cover reads, "Compliments of J. W. Pepper, Exhibit No. 656, West Arcade, Section 0-34."

UNIVERSAL PEACE (probably 1925 or 1926)
(See also THE GRIDIRON CLUB)

The manuscript of this unpublished march was discovered in the archives of Sousa's Sands Point home in 1965. An earlier title, "National Defense," had been crossed out. The first and episodic sections are identical to those of "The Gridiron Club" (1926).

MSS: Pi, 2 versions, 2pp each; nd np [LC]
Not pub or ©

UNIVERSITY OF ILLINOIS (1929)

Sousa considered the University of Illinois Band the finest college band in the world and had great admiration for its director, A. Austin Harding. Some of Sousa's musicians were graduates of Harding's band, and others had studied at the university in off-season.

This march was completed on June 6, 1929, and given its premiere at a Sousa Band broadcast on June 17. On March 20 of the following year Sousa visited the university and was given a royal welcome. He was made honorary conductor of the band, presented with a handsome gold medal, and named "Great Tribal Chief of the Illini." In typical Sousa humor, he filled out a freshman try-out sheet, stating that his instrument was a "low-pitched baton," and that although his tonguing was "triple-threat," his embouchure had been "lost in the war."

Before his death Sousa had promised Harding that the Sousa Band library would be willed to the university. The bulk of it was eventually presented by Sousa's widow and is now in the school's Sousa Library.

MSS: Bd 16pp; 6Jun1929 Sands Pt. [LC]
Pub: Church
©: Pi: Church 15Aug1929; ren JPrS & HSA 22Aug1956 again 10Oct1956
Bd: Church 7Oct1929; ren JPrS & HSA 3Oct1956

UNIVERSITY OF MINNESOTA MARCH
(See THE MINNESOTA MARCH)

UNIVERSITY OF NEBRASKA (1928)

Apparently Sousa had at one time con-

sidered using "The Cornhuskers" as the title of this march, because several newspapers made reference to that title. It was dedicated to the faculty and students of the University of Nebraska.

MSS: a) Pi 2pp; 2Feb1928 np [LC]
b) Bd 9pp; 9Feb1929 Sands Pt. [UI]
Pub: Fox
©: Bd: Fox 4Oct1928; ren JPrS & HSA 16Dec1955

USAAC MARCH (1918)

Volunteers of the U.S. Army Ambulance Corps, 80 percent of whom were decorated for bravery in World War I, quickly won Sousa's admiration. As president of the American Amateur Trapshooters' Association, Sousa persuaded members of that organization to donate twenty-four ambulances and other vehicles to the corps. When he paid an informal visit to the USAAC camp at Allentown, Pennsylvania, Colonel C. P. Franklin, the commanding officer, asked him to compose a march for them.[78] Sousa was pleased to be asked and promptly obliged. Some tragedy apparently befell the manuscript, however, precluding its use during the war.

The march was written on or about May 18, 1918.[79] It was a medley-type march, containing melodies from a musical called *Good-Bye Bill*, which had been composed by two USAACs, William B. Kernell and Richard Fechheimer. Sousa sent a copy of the march to Colonel Franklin, who was then in Italy. In a letter to Colonel Franklin dated September 7, 1918, he stated that he planned to make an orchestration of the march and then have it published. Nothing more is known of the march except that the piano sheet music was published by Chappell of London and that Sousa's original sketch somehow made its way to the Library of Congress.[80] It is

[78] Research done by John R. Smucker of Wynnewood, Pennsylvania, trustee of the USAAC Association.
[79] Correspondence between the author and James A. Friberg of New Port Richey, Florida. Friberg was Sousa's copyist at the Great Lakes Naval Training Center. He made a copy of the march for Sousa shortly after it was written.
[80] This was apparently Friberg's copy.

possible that Sousa's orchestration — if it was made — was lost at sea either en route to Colonel Franklin in Italy or perhaps on the way to the publisher in London. Chappell has no record of receiving the march, because their records were destroyed in a fire.[81]

The story of the "USAAC March" has a happy ending, however. The USAACs finally heard their march played by a band — five decades after it was written. The USAAC Association held its fiftieth anniversary reunion in 1967 at Allentown, site of Camp Crane, where members had received their training during the war. At a concert by the Allentown Band, directed by former Sousa cornetist Albertus Meyers, the "USAAC March" was performed in an arrangement for band by R. C. Wetherhold.

MSS: Pi 2pp; nd np [LC]
Pub: Chappell
©:   Pi: Chappell 1Dec1919; ren JPrS &
       HSA 4Dec1946

U.S. FIELD ARTILLERY (1917)

During Sousa's brief wartime service in the navy, he was invited to a luncheon meeting in New York with Secretary of the Navy Josephus Daniels and Army Lieutenant George Friedlander. Friedlander, of the 306th Field Artillery, asked Sousa to compose a march for that regiment, suggesting that the march be built around an artillery song then known by such names as "The Caisson Song," "The Caissons Go Rolling Along," and "The Field Artillery Song."[82] The song was believed to be quite old, perhaps of Civil War origin, and had not been published; the composer was believed dead.

Sousa liked the song and agreed to use it. He set it in a different key, changed the harmonic structure, refined the melody, gave it a more snappy rhythm, and added this to his own original material. The complete composition was then published as the "U.S. Field Artillery" march.

Sousa's touch added the spark necessary to transform the little-known artillery song into the army's most popular melody. The new march was eagerly adopted by the army's artillery units and later by the army as a whole. The Victor Talking Machine Company promptly issued a recording of the march with Sousa personally conducting former members of his own band, and the piece became the best known of all Sousa's World War I compositions. On the record it was paired with another Sousa composition also dedicated to the U.S. Army: the "Liberty Loan" march. In a year's time, the recording sold over 400,000 copies.

Sheet music of the march also sold well. Its attractive cover was the copy of a work by the sculptor James E. Kelly, well known for his portrayal of military subjects. Kelly set aside other work on a $200,000 piece of sculpture in Delaware to complete the clay bas-relief model for the cover. The march was also published in an outstanding band arrangement by Mayhew L. Lake.

It came as quite a surprise to Sousa and Lieutenant Friedlander to learn that the composer of "The Caisson Song" was still very much alive and that the song was less than ten years old. It had been written in March, 1908, by Lieutenant Edmund L. Gruber of the U.S. Army Field Artillery at Camp Stotsenburg, Philippine Islands. The piece was composed in the presence of at least two fellow officers who assisted in writing the lyrics.[83] No doubt Lieutenant Gruber was even more surprised to find that his song, much revised, had skyrocketed to fame. He raised no objections to Sousa's use of the song, which was serving the army's purpose so admirably.

Gruber's song had a peculiar history after the Sousa march was published. Sousa's treatment of the melody had made it so attractive to several publishers that

---

[81] Correspondence between the author and Chappell and Co., Ltd., February and March, 1965.

[82] *New York Eagle*, January 31, 1918.

[83] Gruber's own account of the composition was published in the *Field Artillery Journal*, July, 1926. This account was confirmed by Major General Robert M. Danford, one of those present, in a letter to the author dated July 25, 1965. Further confirmation was provided by Mrs. Gruber in a letter to the author, January 5, 1966.

they fought over it. Shortly after the publication of the "U.S. Field Artillery" march, the melody found its way into several song collections and became exceptionally popular during the 1920's. It is not known whether or not Gruber gave written permission for the use of his song in any of these publications, but he did permit its incorporation into a volume of West Point songs in 1921.

The melody became even more popular when the Hoover Vacuum Cleaner Company adopted it as its sales song. The company added its own words and used it in radio advertising. Unaware of the song's origin, a Hoover salesman called on Mrs. Gruber in 1929 and attempted to sell her a sweeper. Mrs. Gruber informed him of the origin of Hoover's sales song and suggested that this entitled her to a sweeper, gratis. She received one, and her husband endorsed Hoover sweepers. This did not please certain artillery officers, who later asked Hoover to refrain from the use of what they considered their own exclusive song.[84]

When Gruber's personal application for a copyright of the song was denied in 1930, he gave up hope of ever claiming royalties. However, in 1942 the sponsors of the West Point publication reestablished their claim and brought suit against the E. C. Schirmer Company, another of the song's publishers. The court ruled that the melody had in effect been dedicated to public use and that its widespread use for over thirty years with no substantial objection by the composer constituted a practical abandonment by the composer. This judgment was upheld in an appeal the following year.[85]

Gruber rose to the rank of brigadier general and died in active service in 1941. He had composed over a hundred songs for his own enjoyment and had not expected any of them to reach Tin Pan Alley. But the one paraphrased by John

Philip Sousa achieved a popularity beyond his wildest dreams. It glorified the U.S. Army Field Artillery, so it mattered little to him that many users of his melody made money while he received nothing. The time-honored manuscript of his original song now hangs in the library of the U.S. Army Artillery and Missile School at Fort Sill, Oklahoma.

MSS: N/A
Pub: Fischer
©: Pi; bd; orch: JPS 22Jan1918; ren JPrS & HSA 5Feb1945
Full mandolin orch: JPS 10Jul1918; ren JPrS & HSA 29Jul1945

VENUS
(See THE TRANSIT OF VENUS)

THE VICTORY CHEST (1918)

Sousa came to Cleveland in 1918 with his navy "Jackie" band at the height of the Liberty Loan bond drive. In Cleveland, the fund was called the Victory Chest. While there, Sousa apparently penned part or all of this march. The sole clue to its existence is a photograph found among items of Sousa's personal library which were bequeathed to the U.S. Marine Corps Museum in 1969. This photograph shows Sousa seated at a piano playing what appears to be a three-page manuscript. Four measures of this march, evidently the introduction, are shown as an insert on the photograph. It is written in Sousa's hand, and he has dated it May 24, 1918.

MSS: N/A
Not pub or ©

THE VOLUNTEERS (1918)

The man who asked Sousa to compose this march (Robert D. Heinl, chief of the Department of Patriotic Service) also requested that he include sounds characteristic of a shipyard. Sousa thought this unusual for a march, but he complied. Sections of the march were named "The Call to March," "Getting Busy," and "Laying the Keel Blocks," and the score called for sirens, anvils, and a riveting machine.

---

[84] Letter to the Hoover Vacuum Cleaner Company from Major General U. Birnie, September 28, 1934.

[85] *Enger et al.* v. *E. C. Schirmer Music Company*, District Court, Massachusetts, December 28, 1942. Also same parties, Circuit Court of Appeals, First Circuit, December 29, 1943.

The march was given a stirring premiere at the New York Hippodrome on March 3, 1918, by the combined bands of the navy's Atlantic fleet, Sousa conducting. It was dedicated to Edward N. Hurley, chairman of the U.S. Shipping Board, and to the ship-builders who were constructing America's emergency fleet. Sousa was dissatisfied with a riveting machine made to his specifications by a Chicago instrument manufacturer and called upon the Hippodrome sound effects man. A huge noise-maker was devised and used with ear-shattering effectiveness. Many people were puzzled at the departure from Sousa's usual march style, but he was merely fulfilling a request.

MSS: Pi 2pp; 13Feb1918 np [LC]
Pub: Fischer
©:   Bd; orch; pi: JPS 10May1918; ren
      JPrS & HSA 17May1945
      Full mandolin orch: JPS 28Aug1918;
      ren JPrS & HSA 10Sep1945

WASHINGTON BICENTENNIAL
(WASHINGTON'S BICENTENNIAL)
(See GEORGE WASHINGTON
BICENTENNIAL)

THE WASHINGTON POST (1889)

During the 1880's, several Washington, D.C., newspapers competed vigorously for public favor. One of these, the *Washington Post,* organized what was known as the *Washington Post* Amateur Authors' Association and sponsored an essay contest for school children. Frank Hatton and Beriah Wilkins, owners of the newspaper, asked Sousa, then leader of the Marine Band, to compose a march for the award ceremony.

The ceremony was held on the Smithsonian grounds on June 15, 1889. President Harrison and other dignitaries were among the huge crowd. When the new march was played by Sousa and the Marine Band, it was enthusiastically received, and within days it became exceptionally popular in Washington.

The march happened to be admirably suited to the two-step dance, which was just being introduced. A dancemasters' organization adopted it at their yearly convention, and soon the march was vaulted into international fame. The two-step gradually replaced the waltz as a popular dance, and variations of the basic two-step insured the march's popularity all through the 1890's and into the twentieth century. Sousa's march became identified with the two-step, and it was as famous abroad as it was in the United States. In some European countries, all two-steps were called "Washington posts." Pirated editions of the music appeared in many foreign countries. In Britain, for example, it was known by such names as "No Surrender" and "Washington Greys."

Next to "The Stars and Stripes Forever," "The Washington Post" has been Sousa's most widely known march. He delighted in telling how he had heard it in so many different countries, played in so many ways — and often accredited to native composers. It was a standard at Sousa Band performances and was often openly demanded when not scheduled for a program. It was painful for Sousa to relate that, like "Semper Fidelis" and other marches of that period, he received only $35 for it, while the publisher made a fortune. Of that sum, $25 was for a piano arrangement, $5 for a band arrangement, and $5 for an orchestra arrangement.

Today, at a community room in Washington, a spotlight illuminates a life-sized color portrait of the black-bearded Sousa, resplendent in his scarlet Marine Band uniform. This is the John Philip Sousa Community Room in the Washington Post Building. It is the newspaper's tribute to the man who first gave it worldwide fame.

MSS: a) Bd 4pp inc: 3Jul1889 Washington,
          D.C. [LC]
       b) Pi 1pp; nd np [LC]
Pub: Coleman
©:   Bd: Coleman 14Aug1889; not ren
      Pi: Coleman 23Sep1889 again
          4May1894; ren JPS 18Aug1917 again
          6Feb1922
      Orch: Coleman 23Sep1889; ren JPS
          18Aug1917
      Pi six hands: Coleman 12Aug1893; ren
          JPS 7Mar1921
      Three zithers: Coleman 28Aug1893; not
          ren
      Banjo: Coleman 28Dec1893; ren JPS
          7Mar1921

Cornet & pi: Coleman 4May1894; ren
JPS 6Feb1922
Also pub for pi duet but not ©

WE ARE COMING
(See Songs — Words by Others)

WEDDING MARCH (1918)
(THE AMERICAN WEDDING MARCH)

During World War I, when anti-German feelings were high, representatives of the American Relief Legion asked Sousa to compose a wedding march to replace the music of Wagner and Mendelssohn for American weddings. Sousa fulfilled their request, but his march was forgotten soon after the war ended.

MSS: Bd 17pp; 31Jul1918 Detroit [UI]
Pub: Fox
©: Pi: Fox 7Oct1918 again 19Dec1918; ren
JPrS & HSA 14Apr1946 again
12Jun1946
Bd: Fox 22Oct1918; ren JPrS & HSA
5Jun1946

THE WHITE PLUME (1884)

Sousa and Edward M. Taber collaborated on a song called "We'll Follow Where the White Plume Waves" to support the presidential election campaign of James Gillespie Blaine, affectionately known as the "plumed knight." Sousa rearranged the song as a military march, added new sections, and called it "The White Plume."

MSS: N/A
Pub: Ellis (bd; pi); Church (orch)
©: Pi: Ellis 15Jul1884; not ren
Bd. Ellis 25Jul1884; ren JPS 11May1912
Orch: Church 5May1909; ren JvMS
4Jan1937

THE WHITE ROSE (1917)

At a concert by the Sousa Band in York, Pennsylvania, a civic committee requested this Sousa march. The march was to be used at the York Flower Festival, commemorating White Rose Day. The white rose is the emblem of the House of York, in England, from which York, Pennsylvania, took its name. The White Rose Day celebration was canceled, owing to priorities of

World War I. Nevertheless, Sousa's march was played at a public concert by combined bands and given some measure of publicity in a recording by the Victor Talking Machine Company. It never became popular, however. By request, Sousa incorporated several themes from the opera *Nittaunis,* composed by York banker C. C. Frick.

MSS: N/A
Pub: Harms
©: Pi: Harms 10May1917; ren JPrS &
HSA 2 Jun1944
Bd: Harms 23Dec1940; ren Warner
Brothers-Seven Arts 8Jan1968

WHO'S WHO IN NAVY BLUE (1920)

It is not often that a composer dedicates music to a wooden Indian. Sousa did just that by dedicating this march to Tecumseh, whose stern figurehead adorns Bancroft Hall at the U.S. Naval Academy at Annapolis. Clippings in the Sousa Band press books of 1920 refer to this march as having been written at the midshipmen's request, although school records do not bear this out. In recognition of Sousa's contribution to the navy during World War I, he reportedly was presented a miniature class ring and made an honorary member of the graduating class of 1921. A Sousa Band recording of the march, paired with "Comrades of the Legion," sold over 500,000 copies.

MSS: Bd 9pp; 14Feb1920 Sands Pt. [UI]
Pub: Church
©: Pi: Church 25May1920; ren JPrS &
HSA 4Sep1947
Also pub for bd and for orch but not ©

THE WILDCATS (1930 or 1931)
(THE WILDCATS OF KANSAS MARCH)
(See also UNTITLED MARCH, KANSAS
WILDCATS, and THE GRIDIRON CLUB)

After Sousa's death his two daughters presented a number of his manuscripts to the Library of Congress. The first page of one of the manuscripts is entitled "The Wildcats," and a note in Priscilla Sousa's hand refers to it as her father's "Kansas Wildcats" march. However, a study of the manuscript showed that the first page belonged

John Philip Sousa

not to "Kansas Wildcats" but to an entirely different march called "The Wildcats," and that the remaining pages belonged to yet another march — one still without a title. Neither piece was ever published. A second manuscript of "The Wildcats" is entitled "The Wildcats of Kansas," leaving no question that this was the composition originally intended for the Kansas State College of Agriculture and Applied Science at Manhattan. However, the college received a totally different march — one originally entitled "The Sword of San Jacinto."

Parts of "The Wildcats" were written as early as 1926, as evidenced by one of the manuscripts which consists mostly of this march but also has sections of "The Gridiron Club" (1926), as well as one other section which was never used.

MSS: a) Bd, entitled "The Wildcats," 1pp inc; nd np [LC]
b) Pi, entitled "The Wildcats of Kansas," 2 pp inc; nd np [LC]
c) Pi, two untitled versions, 1pp each, both inc; nd np [LC]
d) Pi, untitled, with sections of "The Gridiron Club," 1pp inc; nd np [LC]
Not pub or ©

WILLOW BLOSSOMS
(See Various Dance Forms)

WISCONSIN FORWARD FOREVER
(1917)

Sousa crossed out the title "Solid Men to the Front" on his manuscript of this march and substituted the present title. It may originally have been intended to salute Wisconsin's contribution to the war effort, because in press reports it was also referred to as "Wisconsin to the Front" and "Wisconsin at the Front." "Forward" apparently took precedence as a title word, because that was the Wisconsin state motto.

Words to the march were written by the poet Berton Braley, a member of the University of Wisconsin's class of 1905, and the march was dedicated to the faculty, students, and alumni of the university. Maxson F. Juddell, a senior at the university, was responsible for the march's pro-

motion, and he persuaded the celebrated artist Howard Chandler Christy to do the artwork for the frontispiece of the sheet music.

MSS: Pi 4 pp; 2May1917 Sands Pt. [LC]
Pub: Harms
©: Pi: Harms 11Jun1917; ren JPrS & HSA 12Jun1944
Bd: Harms 6Dec1940; ren Warner Brothers-Seven Arts 8Aug1968

THE WOLVERINE MARCH (1881)

Little is known about the circumstances which gave rise to the composition of this march. It was "Respectfully dedicated to His Excellency Hon. David H. Jerome, Governor of Michigan, and Staff." According to an inscription on the sheet music, it was first performed by the U.S. Marine Band at a reception given by the Michigan State Association in Washington on March 2, 1881.

MSS: N/A
Pub: Pond (pi); Coleman (bd); Pepper (bd; orch)
©: Pi: Pond 2Mar1881; not ren
Bd: Coleman 7Dec1885 again Pepper 16Jan1895; not ren
Orch: Pepper 3Apr1895; not ren

THE YANKEE GIRL
(See THE GLORY OF THE YANKEE NAVY)

YORKTOWN CENTENNIAL (1881)
(YORKTOWN'S CENTENNIAL)

The Yorktown (Virginia) Centennial was held to commemorate the hundredth anniversary of the last important battle of the Revolutionary War: the surrender at Yorktown. Sousa, then leader of the U.S. Marine Band, composed this march for the event and dedicated it to Colonel H. C. Corbin, master of ceremonies of the centennial.

Another printing of the same march was issued in 1900 as "Sen Sen." This was part of a promotion scheme of the T. B. Dunn Company of Rochester, New York, a subsidiary of the Sen Sen Chiclet Company. It is not known whether or not Sousa was a part of this business venture.

MSS: Pi 2pp; 9Sep1881 np [LC]
Pub: Ellis (pi); Coleman (bd); Church
      (orch)
©: Pi: Ellis 20Feb1882; not ren
      Bd: Coleman 31Dec1885; ren JPS
      13Dec1913
      Orch: Church 5May1909; ren JvMS
      4Jan1937

(UNTITLED MARCH) (1930)
(See also THE WILDCATS
and KANSAS WILDCATS)

All but the title page of Sousa's band score of this unpublished march has been on file at the Library of Congress for many years. Sousa's daughter Priscilla had placed it in a folder with the first page of "The Wildcats," thinking the manuscripts belonged together and that they were the march called "Kansas Wildcats." Such was not the case, however. Later, a complete piano score of the untitled march turned up, but this manuscript, too, bore no title. Thus the intended recipient of the march may never be known.

The colossal mix-up involving this untitled march and various marches called "The Wildcats," "Kansas Wildcats," "The Sword of San Jacinto," "Universal Peace," and "The Gridiron Club" is evidence of the fact that the titles of Sousa's marches were sometimes changed before the marches were published.

MSS: a) Bd 15pp inc; 8[?]Feb1930 Sands Pt.
      [LC]
      b) Pi 3pp; nd np [LC]
Not pub or ©

SUITES

The Sousa suites are unique among compositions written for band. Composed over a period of thirty-two years, they coincided with the years of Sousa's most extensive travels, and the inspiration for most of them came from these travels. They are descriptive in nature and picturesque in their instrumental effects.

Inasmuch as all were conceived for band, it is understandable that they have never been adopted by symphony orchestras. They have never been ranked with the orchestral suites of the major composers, but some scholars insist that some of Sousa's serious suites are brilliant compositions and do not deserve to be forgotten. Those most familiar with them — members of Sousa's Band — differed widely in their evaluations. However, they realized that Sousa was proud of his suites and gave their utmost in performances.

There are perhaps two main reasons why the Sousa suites are seldom heard today. First, they are considered period music. Second, they are difficult to perform and therefore require considerable preparation. Reviewers were seldom critical when Sousa conducted them himself, and they were often generous in their praise. Still, the suites have not lived on. It is odd that a group of compositions should depend on the composer-conductor for survival, but such was the case with Sousa's suites. This, of course, attests to his unusual skill as a conductor.

(Reference) **THE AMERICAN MAID**

I Rondo, "You Do Not Need a Doctor"

II Dream picture, "The Sleeping Soldiers" ("The Sleepers on the Ground")
III Dance hilarious, "With Pleasure" (1912)

In 1913 Sousa pieced together this suite from existing compositions. "You Do Not Need a Doctor" and "The Sleeping Soldiers" were borrowed from his operetta *The American Maid* (1909), and the dance "With Pleasure" had been written the previous year.

AT THE KING'S COURT (1904)

I "Her Ladyship, the Countess"
II "Her Grace, the Duchess"
III "Her Majesty, the Queen"

This suite was probably inspired by one of the two command performances of the Sousa Band before King Edward VII of England. Of the three movements, only the last saw wide use by bands. This was constructed largely from an earlier composition, "March of the Royal Trumpets" (1892). The march was among other compositions forfeited to heirs of the deceased Sousa Band manager David Blakely in litigation following his death. Later, Sousa rewrote the march, set it in a different key, added new material, and entitled it "Her Majesty, the Queen."

MSS: (Complete suite) bd 66pp; 20Sep1904 Wooster, Ohio [LC]
Pub: Church
©: (Complete suite) pi: Church 13Mar1905; ren JvMS 28Jan1933
(Complete suite) bd: Church 14Dec1912; ren Chappell 14Dec1939

AT THE MOVIES
(See IMPRESSIONS AT THE MOVIES)

CAMERA STUDIES (1920)

I "The Flashing Eyes of Andalusia"
II "Drifting to Loveland"
III "The Children's Ball"

Sousa left nothing among his memoirs to indicate the source of inspiration for this suite — perhaps because of its relatively short life. Despite many published editions, the work never became popular.

MSS: a) (Complete suite) Bd 20pp; "The
Flashing Eyes of Andalusia" dated
15Jun1920 Sands Pt. and 1Sep1920
Noble, Pa.; "The Children's Ball"
dated 25Aug1920 Noble, Pa. [LC]
b) ("The Flashing Eyes of Andalusia")
pi 2pp; nd np [LC]
c) ("Drifting to Loveland") bd 1pp inc;
17Jun1920 Sands Pt. [LC]
Pub: Fox
©: ("The Children's Ball" and "The
Flashing Eyes of Andalusia") orch:
Fox 27Jul1921; ren JPrS & HSA
18Jan1949
("Drifting to Loveland") orch: Fox
27Jul1921; ren JPrS & HSA
10Oct1948
(Complete suite) orch: Fox 11Nov1921;
ren JPrS & HSA 18Jan1949
("The Children's Ball" and "The
Flashing Eyes of Andalusia") pi: Fox
11Nov1921; ren JPrS & HSA
18Jan1949
("Drifting to Loveland") pi: Fox
11Nov1921; ren JPrS & HSA
27Sep1949
(Complete suite) bd: Fox 11Nov1921;
not ren

(Reference) EL CAPITAN AND HIS FRIENDS

I "El Capitan" (1895)
II "The Charlatan" (1898)
III "The Bride Elect" (1897)

To make up this suite, Sousa used selections from three of his operettas.

CUBALAND (1925)
(CUBA UNDER THREE FLAGS)

I "Under the Spanish Flag"
II "Under the American Flag"
III "Under the Cuban Flag"

This suite depicts the rule of Cuba under three different governments in the years 1875, 1898, and 1925. The inspiration came during Sousa's vacation in Havana in the winter of 1924. Strangely, Sousa mentioned neither this vacation nor the band's brief 1922 visit to Cuba in his autobiography. Each movement of the suite included melodies characteristic of the ruling country. Excerpts from "The Spanish Constitution" and "Andalusian Dances" are found in the first movement. The second movement has suggestions of several American songs and ends with "Hot Time in the Old Town." "La Bayamesa," a Cuban traditional song, is interwoven into the third movement.

MSS: a) ("Under the American Flag") bd
19pp; May1925 Sands Pt. [LC]
b) ("Under the Cuban Flag") bd 25pp;
21May1925 Sands Pt. [LC]
Pub: Fischer
©: (Complete suite) bd: Fischer 16Jul1927;
ren JPrS & HSA 12Nov1954

DWELLERS OF THE WESTERN WORLD
(1910)

I "The Red Man"
II "The White Man"
III "The Black Man"

The titles of the three movements of this suite reflect the order in which the three races came to inhabit the Western World. It was written just before the world tour of 1910-11 and was well received in every country in which it was played. Sousa is at his descriptive best in the characteristic music of each race. As a grand finale, his grandiose "The Messiah of Nations" (1902) was incorporated into "The White Man."

MSS: ("The White Man") bd 29pp inc; nd np
[LC]
Pub: Church
©: ("The Black Man"; "The Red Man")
pi: Church 1Nov1910 again
31Dec1910 again 14Sep1921; ren
JvMS 6Jan1938
(Complete suite) bd: Church 5Apr1911
again Chappell 18May1911; ren
Chappell 18May1938 again JvMS
25Feb1939
(Complete suite) orch: Church
11Mar1916; ren Church 5Jan1944

IMPRESSIONS AT THE MOVIES (1922)
(AT THE MOVIES)

I "The Serenaders" ("The Musical Mokes") ("The Jazz Band in Action")
II "The Crafty Villain and the Timid Maid"
III "Balance All and Swing Partners"

There is little doubt about Sousa's inspiration for this suite. He provided the publisher with "Scenarios for Cinematographers" describing the episodes he had in mind. In the opening movement, coeds are being serenaded in a neighborhood university. In the second movement, the timid maid pleads for her safety while being pursued by a clever and relentless villain. The third movement depicts a dance on the village green. While critics agreed that the suite was interesting and original, it met with the same fate as most other movie music of the era.

MSS: N/A
Pub: Fischer
©:   (Complete suite) bd: Fischer 28Aug1922; not ren

(Reference) THE INTERNATIONALS
(THE THREE S's)

I "Morning Journals" (Johann Strauss, Jr.)
II "The Lost Chord" (Arthur Sullivan)
III "Mars and Venus" (John Philip Sousa)

Three well-known composers of lighter works were represented in this grouping of existing works. The third selection is from the suite *Looking Upward* (1902).

THE LAST DAYS OF POMPEII (1893)

I "In the House of Burbo and Stratonice"
II "Nydia" ("Nydia the Blind Girl")
III "The Destruction" ("The Destruction of Pompeii and Nydia's Death")

Sousa often referred to this as his finest composition and programmed it more often than any of his other suites. He was particularly proud of the original descriptive effects. Perhaps, in an effort to keep these effects exclusive with the Sousa Band, he did not release the work to a publisher until nineteen years after it was written.

MSS: (Complete suite) bd 34pp in bound volume; 18Jan1893 Washington, D.C. [LC]
Pub: Church
©:   (Complete suite) bd: Church 15Jul1912; ren JvMS 7May1940

LEAVES FROM MY NOTEBOOK (1922)

I "The Genial Hostess"
II "The Campfire Girls"
III "The Lively Flapper"

Three descriptive pictures are painted in this suite, which generally was not greeted by critics as a work of lasting quality. But it was popular with the Campfire Girls, who presented Sousa with many token gifts and honors in cities where his band performed it.

MSS: a) Pi sketches 3pp inc; 22Jun1922 np [LC]
     b) (Complete suite) bd 54pp; "The Lively Flapper" dated 27Jun1922 Sands Pt.; "The Campfire Girls" dated 4Jul1922 Sands Pt.; "The Genial Hostess" dated 22Jul1922 Montreal [LC]
Pub: Fox
©:   (Complete suite) pi: Fox 9Oct1923; ren JPrS & HSA 1Nov1950

LOOKING UPWARD (1902)

I "By the Light of the Polar Star"
II "Beneath the Southern Cross" ("Under the Southern Cross")
III "Mars and Venus"

The inspiration for the first movement of this suite came on a crisp South Dakota night while Sousa was looking at the heavens from the window of his train. The second was inspired by an advertisement about the steamship *Southern Cross*. The idea for the third movement, like the first, came while Sousa was gazing at the heavens on a clear evening. Several months later, when the suite was developed from his sketches, Sousa borrowed two melodies for the first movement from Act II of *Chris and the Wonderful Lamp,* his operetta of 1899.

MSS: (Complete suite) bd 66pp; 22Sep1902
   Peoria, Ill. [LC]
Pub: Church
©: (Complete suite) pi: Church
   16Dec1904; ren JPS 1Mar1932
   (Complete suite) bd: Church
   1Feb1905; ren JvMS 28Jan1933

(Reference) MAIDENS THREE

I "The Coquette" (1887)
II "The Summer Girl" (1901)
III "The Dancing Girl" (Tarantella from
   The Bride Elect) (1897)

This was another of the suites conveniently assembled from existing compositions.

PEOPLE WHO LIVE IN GLASS HOUSES
(1909)

I "The Champagnes"
II "The Rhine Wines" ("The Rhine-
   landers")
III "White Rock and Psyches"
IV "The Whiskies — Scotch, Irish, Bour-
   bon and Rye" ("The Whiskies —
   Scotch, Irish and Kentucky")
V "Convention of the Cordials, Wines,
   Whiskies, and White Rock" ("Con-
   vention of the Liqueurs, Wines and
   Whiskies") ("The Cordials")
   ("Pousse Cafe")

This music, which was never published as a suite, is characteristic of the countries in which the various drinks originated. It was later revised, arranged for orchestra, and used as ballet music in a revival of *The Bride Elect* in Philadelphia in 1923.

MSS: a) (Complete suite) bd 48pp;
   25May1909 New York City [LC]
   b) (Coda of "The Rhine Wines") bd
   2pp; 23Mar1916 np [UI]
   c) (Complete suite) orch 61pp;
   6Dec1920 Sands Pt. [LC]
Not pub or ©

TALES OF A TRAVELER (1911)

I "The Kaffir on the Karoo"
II "In the Land of the Golden Fleece"
III "Grand Promenade at the White
   House" ("New Year's Reception at
   the White House")

IV "Easter Monday on the White House
   Lawn"

This suite was conceived while the Sousa Band was on its world tour of 1910-11. With the exception of *The Last Days of Pompeii*, Sousa used it more often than any of his other suites. The first movement is descriptive of the dances of the Karoo, a native of South Africa. The second, a "valse romantique," was dedicated "To the Matrons and Maids of Australia." A change in the suite's order came in 1928 when "Easter Monday on the White House Lawn" was written to replace "Grand Promenade at the White House."

A bit of interesting history surrounds the third movement. Shortly after it was written, its name was changed from "Grand Promenade at the White House" to "Coronation March." This was done to fulfill a request made by British music publishers for a composition to be used at the coronation of King George V.[1] However, only music of British composers was used at the coronation ceremony.[2] This movement of the suite was then published as "Grand Festival March" and dedicated to British bands and bandmasters. But for reasons not understood its original title was soon restored and used thereafter.

MSS: a) ("Grand Promenade at the White
   House") pi 4pp; 7Mar1911 "On
   board the Tainui en route to South
   Africa" [LC]
   b) ("Grand Promenade at the White
   House") bd 11pp; 13Mar1911 "On
   board the Tainui en route to South
   Africa" [LC]
   c) ("Coronation March") orch 15pp;
   18Mar1911 "On board the Tainui
   en route to South Africa" [LC]
   d) ("The Kaffir on the Karoo") bd
   17pp; 21Mar1912 Hot Springs, Va.
   [LC]
   e) ("The Land of the Golden Fleece")
   bd 19pp; 18Apr1912 New Orleans
   [LC]
   f) ("Easter Monday on the White House
   Lawn") bd 14pp; 30May1928 Sands
   Pt. [LC]
Pub: Church

---

[1] *Wichita* (Kans.) *Eagle,* September 17, 1911.
[2] Research done by K. C. Harrison, city librarian of Westminster, England.

©:   ("Grand Festival March") pi: Church
      17May1911; ren JvMS 24Feb1939
      ("In the Land of the Golden Fleece")
      bd: Church 7Oct1912 again
      30Mar1914; ren JvMS 12Dec1941
      ("In the Land of the Golden Fleece")
      pi: Church 7Oct1912; ren JvMS
      7May1940
      ("Grand Promenade at the White
      House"; "The Kaffir on the Karoo")
      bd: Church 30Mar1914; ren JvMS
      12Dec1941
      ("Easter Monday on the White House
      Lawn") bd: Church 14Apr1929; ren
      JPrS & HSA 10Oct1956

THREE QUOTATIONS (1895)

I "The King of France" (marched up
   the hill
   With twenty thousand men;
   The King of France marched down
   the hill
   And ne'er went up again.)
II "I, Too, Was Born in Arcadia"
III "In Darkest Africa" ("Nigger in the
    Woodpile")

The quotations upon which this suite was
founded were more familiar when it was
written than they are today. The first two
can be traced to sixteenth-century writings,
and the third was a conversational phrase.
No doubt they are to be found somewhere
in the rare books of Sousa's personal library.

MSS: a) ("The King of France") pi 3pp;
         14Oct1895 np [UI]
      b) (Complete suite) bd 30pp;
         23Dec1895 New York City [LC]
Pub: Church
©:   ("I, Too, Was Born in Arcadia") pi:
      Church 3Feb1896; not ren
      ("In Darkest Africa"; "The King of
      France") pi: Church 3Feb1896; not
      ren
      ("I, Too, Was Born in Arcadia"; "In
      Darkest Africa") Church 3Sep1896;
      not ren
      ("The King of France") bd: Church
      3Sep1896; ren JPS 1Aug1924
      ("I, Too, Was Born in Arcadia"; "In
      Darkest Africa") orch: Church
      15Oct1896; not ren
      ("The King of France") orch: Church
      15Oct1896; ren JPS 20Sep1924

THE THREE S's
(See THE INTERNATIONALS)

DESCRIPTIVE PIECES

THE CHARIOT RACE (1890)
(BEN HUR CHARIOT RACE)

Hannah Harris, a Philadelphia educator, had heard the U.S. Marine Band in Washington and arranged to bring Sousa and the band to Philadelphia for concerts. In a later letter to Sousa she suggested that he write this descriptive piece, speculating that it would be a success because of the current popularity of *Ben Hur*. She was correct.

MSS: a) Bd 17pp in bound volume;
        19Dec1890 Washington, D.C. [LC]
     b) Bd 1pp inc; 18Sep1924 np [LC]
Pub: Ditson
©:   Pi: Ditson 25Aug1892; not ren

SHERIDAN'S RIDE (1891)

I "Waiting for the Bugle"
II "The Attack"
III "The Death of Thoburn"
IV "The Coming of Sheridan"
V "The Apothesis"

These "scenes historical" were inspired by Thomas B. Read's stirring Civil War poem, "Sheridan's Ride." Sousa well remembered General Sheridan's famous ride, because it took place near his native Washington when he was a boy of nine.

MSS: Bd 18pp in bound volume; 14Nov1891
      Washington, D.C. [LC]
Pub: Church
©:   Bd: Church 13Jul1908; ren JvMS
       2Jan1936

A STAG PARTY
(See Humoresques)

SONGS

As John Philip Sousa's marches reflected his manly bearing and military background, so did his songs reflect his most personal thoughts. They told of his compassion and love of all things beautiful. A study of these songs reveals a Sousa which the public never knew.

In general, the songs in this section are of a more delicate nature than those composed for his operettas. But some were written for situations and well illustrate his sense of humor. He was inspired by both tragedy and comedy and felt compelled to put each to song; his broad range of interests may be seen in the titles alone.

Sousa was sensitive to criticism of his songs because they were very dear to him. He preferred to discuss his songs rather than his marches, but seldom was he given the opportunity. He never seemed to adjust to the fact that they did not find their way into a circle of art songs, even though his public was exposed to them repeatedly by the sopranos of the Sousa Band — Sousa insisted that they add a few of his songs to their repertoires.

Although not popular, they were not what musicians would call inferior music. In fact, among those early pieces which have long been out of print one may find pleasant melodies — if he is willing to overlook an occasional lyric which may be considered outdated or even corny by today's standards. Sousa was often moved to set poetry to music, but these pieces, too, failed to make their mark. One factor not to be ignored in their present-day lack of acceptance is the fact that many scholars have a reluctance to study music composed by a bandsman. Sousa referred to this as "musical snobbery" and was deeply hurt by it. Another factor is that most people are actually unaware of the fact that Sousa composed anything but marches.

For the sake of clarity, the songs of Sousa's operettas are not discussed in this section. If all the individual songs of the operettas were to be added to those here, the total would be nearly four hundred.

The songs may be divided into three basic types: those for which Sousa wrote both the words and the music, those which he set to poems, and those in which he collaborated with another author.

AH ME! (1876)
Poem by Emma M. Swallow

But for the resistance of Emma Swallow's stepfather and Sousa's discovery of another suitor, Sousa would have married this young lady of Washington, D.C., in the fall of 1877. After a lover's quarrel, she sent him a poem entitled "Ah Me!" He set it to music and gave it the designation Opus 29. According to an inscription on the frontispiece of the sheet music, it is an "ancient ballad."

MSS: N/A
Pub: Meyer
Not ©

THE AMERICAN NATIONAL SONG
(See O MY COUNTRY)

ANNABEL LEE (1931)
Poem by Edgar Allan Poe

Sousa's injury, caused by his fall from a horse in 1921, plagued him thereafter. Ten years after the fall, he entered a hospital in Baltimore to determine if corrective surgery was necessary. Newspaper reporters thought the career of the seventy-six-year-old Sousa might be ending, but they met with his usual exclamation: "When you hear of Sousa retiring, you will hear of Sousa dead!" Jubilant upon learning that an operation was unnecessary, he was inclined toward composition and so informed the reporters. Recalling that Edgar Allan Poe had descended from a prominent Baltimore family and that he had died and was buried in Baltimore, Sousa set the poem "Annabel Lee" to music.

MSS: V/pi (2 versions) 6pp; nd np [LC]
Pub: Presser
©: V/pi: Presser 5May1931; ren JPrS & HSA 16Jul1958

THE BELLE OF BAYOU TECHE (1911)
Poem by O. E. Lynne

Sousa's younger daughter, Helen, gave a personal account of the background of this composition. While on his world tour, her father had been impressed by the poem, which he had read in a magazine, and he immediately set it to music.[1] Fond memories of both the poem and her father's music for it inspired Helen to name the favorite of her long line of pedigree poodles The Belle of Bayou Teche.

MSS: N/A
Pub: Church
©: V/pi: Church 11Dec1911; ren JvMS 25Feb1939

BLUE RIDGE, I'M COMING BACK TO YOU (1917)
Words by John Philip Sousa

In this wartime song a man responds to the call of his flag and nostalgically bids farewell to his mountain home, his family, friends, and bride-to-be. Sousa told of composing it for use with his navy band at a

New York Hippodrome concert given for the benefit of the Woman's Auxiliary Naval Recruiting Station.[2] The song was used under three other titles. He wrote a second set of words, and this version was published as "Great Lakes," or "The Boys in Navy Blue." Also, most of the music was incorporated into a march, "The Naval Reserve" (1917).

MSS: N/A
Pub: Harms
©: V/pi (as "Blue Ridge, I'm Coming Back to You"): Harms 27Jun1917; ren JPrS & HSA 27Jun1944. (As "Great Lakes"): Harms 2Feb1918; ren JPrS & HSA 2Feb1945
"Blue Ridge, I'm Coming Back to You" was also pub for bd and for orch but not ©

BOOTS (1916)
Poem by Rudyard Kipling

It is easy to understand why Kipling's poem appealed to Sousa; it is intense and martial in nature. The song was used by the Sousa Band only for a short period during and after World War I, but alumni of the Sousa Band appreciated its musical worth and programmed it with their own bands many years after Sousa's death.

MSS: a) Orch 16pp; 7Apr1916 New York City [UI]
      b) V/pi 11pp; nd np [UI]
Pub: Harms
©: V/pi: Harms 11May1916; ren JvMS 2Jun1943

THE BOYS ARE HOME AGAIN
(See WHEN THE BOYS COME SAILING HOME!)

THE BOYS IN NAVY BLUE
(See BLUE RIDGE, I'M COMING BACK TO YOU)

THE BROWN THRUSH
(See THERE'S A MERRY BROWN THRUSH)

COME LAUGH AND BE MERRY (1916)
Words by ?

Hurriedly scribbled in the upper left-hand

---

[1] As related to the author in an interview on September 15, 1963.

[2] *Marching Along*, p. 315.

corner of the manuscript of this song is a name beginning with "H," probably that of the author of the verse. The manuscript was apparently meant to be discarded and was found among unsorted music at Sousa's Sands Point estate in 1965.

MSS: V/pi 1pp; 8Mar1916 np [LC]
Not pub or ©

COTTAGE SCENE
(See 'DEED I HAS TO LAUGH)

CROSSING THE BAR (1926)
Poem by Alfred, Lord Tennyson

Sousa apparently felt this was not one of his better efforts, for he seldom performed it. When he did, the newspaper critics usually ignored it. One wrote that it was the worst Sousa composition he had ever heard.[3] Sousa did not indicate why he selected this poem to set to music, but perhaps the poem itself provides a clue: "... And may there be no sadness of farewell when I embark."

MSS: Bd 5pp; 26Jun1926 Sands Pt. [LC]
Pub: Witmark
©:   V/pi: Witmark 24Jun1926; ren JPrS & HSA 24Jun1953

DAY AND NIGHT (1873)
Words by Emma M. Swallow

Flowers are gold-hearted and gay in the laughter of the sun but sober and pale beneath the sorrowful stars, according to the words of this song by Sousa's youthful sweetheart Emma. It is found in his sketchbook of 1873-76.

MSS: V/pi 1pp; Oct1873 np [LC]
Not pub or ©

'DEED I HAS TO LAUGH (1877)
(COTTAGE SCENE)

This comical "plantation scene song and dance," as it was advertised, was composed for the Griffin and Rice Minstrel Company of Philadelphia. It is written in Negro dia-

lect and includes a short monologue at the end. It was first published in a series of period songs in *Stoddart's Musical Library* and later by Hitchcock as a separate song.

MSS: N/A
Pub: Stoddart; Hitchcock
©:   V/pi: Stoddart: 17Nov1877; not ren

DO WE? WE DO (1889)
Words by John Philip Sousa

The Gridiron Club of Washington, D.C., is not a club of football buffs; it is a social organization of Washington journalists. When Sousa was voted in as a limited member and named musical director in 1889, he composed this song. In "Do We? We Do," the "Griddies" heartily endorse wine, women, and song — especially the wine.

MSS: N/A
Pub: Ellis
©:   V/pi: Ellis 26Jan1889; ren JPS 13Jan1917

FALL TENDERLY, ROSES
(probably late 1860's)
Words by John Philip Sousa

The unpublished manuscript of this song, discovered in 1965 at Sousa's Sands Point estate, might well be the earliest existing Sousa work. In a very youthful hand, "par J. Philip Sousa," the verse is a gentle reminder of the end of summer.

MSS: V/pi 2pp; nd np [LC]
Not pub or ©

THE FIGHTING RACE (1919)
Poem by J. I. C. Clarke

Kelly, Burke, and Shea were the three Irishmen in Clarke's stirring poem who possessed "good honest fighting blood" and gave their lives for their country. The song was often programmed by the Sousa Band as "Kelly and Burke and Shea."

MSS: a) V/pi 4pp; nd np [LC]
     b) V/pi 5pp; nd np [LC]
     c) Bd 7pp with 2 additional pp in a copyist's hand; nd np [LC]
     d) V/bd with new ending 5pp; 21Aug1922 Willow Grove, Pa. [LC]
Pub: Flammer

---

[3] Unidentified clipping in the career scrapbook of former Sousa Band saxophonist Owen Kincaid. Probably November, 1926.

©:   V/pi: Flammer 29May1919; ren JPrS &
       HSA 11Jan1947

FOREVER AND A DAY (1927)
Words by Irving Bibo and John Philip Sousa

For an obscure composition from an obscure stage production, the heraldry of the sheet music to this song is impressive. It reads: "The Theme Song of Edward Knoblock and George Rosenener's Sensational Broadway Success 'Speakeasy'." The song was featured on the 1927 tour of the Sousa Band but never became popular. There were two sets of words; Sousa's appeared on an early manuscript, but Bibo's were used for the published version.

MSS: a) V/pi 4 pp of several versions, inc; nd
        np [LC]
     b) Several bd parts in Sousa's hand; nd
        np [UI]
Pub: Bibo
©:   V/pi: Bibo 27Oct1927; ren Stasny
       Music Co. 8Nov1954 and again by
       JPrS & HSA 1Sep1955

THE FREE LUNCH CADETS (1877)
Words by John Philip Sousa

Set in the style of early minstrel shows, this humorous song tells of a group of freeloading individuals who tour the town in search of snacks furnished by saloons. They call themselves "free lunch cadets" and continually seek new recruits. Members of this fraternity may expect sauerkraut, barley soup, corned beef, red herring, limburger cheese, mushroom pie, and hot corn.

MSS: N/A
Pub: Stoddart
©:   V/pi: Stoddart 17Nov1877; not ren
       Pi (as "march"): Stoddart 26Dec1877;
       not ren

GREAT LAKES
(See BLUE RIDGE, I'M COMING
BACK TO YOU)

HOPING (1877)
Poem by Jefferson H. Nones

There is no evidence that Jefferson Nones was related to Albert S. Nones, with whom Sousa collaborated on "Mavourneen As-

thore" (1878). To the music for "Hoping," Sousa assigned the notation Opus 39.

MSS: N/A
Pub: Stoddart
©:   V/pi: Stoddart 27Nov1877; not ren

I LOVE JIM (circa 1916)
Words by Helen Sousa Abert

The manuscript of this song, a collaboration between Sousa and his younger daughter Helen, was found among unsorted manuscripts at the Sands Point estate in 1965. The song is about a girl who surveys prospective husbands and then becomes the bride of a rich bootlegger who can provide many luxuries.

MSS: V/pi 3pp; nd np [LC]
Not pub or ©

I WONDER (1888)
Words by Edward M. Taber

Sousa considered "I Wonder," one of his few noncomical collaborations with Edward M. Taber, among the better ballads of the day. The verse asks whether life in the next world will be as peaceful and full of love and beauty as that known in one's youth. Both words and music are entirely different from the situation song of the same name in the operetta *Desiree* (1883), also a collaboration with Taber.

MSS: a) V/pi 2pp; nd np [LC]
     b) Several bd parts in Sousa's hand;
        baritone saxophone part dated
        2Mar1894 New York City [USMC]
     c) Bd 6pp; 29Aug1919 Willow Grove,
        Pa. [LC]
Pub: Ellis
©:   V/pi: Ellis 21Feb1888; not ren

IN FLANDERS FIELDS THE POPPIES GROW (1918)
Poem by John D. McCrae

The Canadian Army medical officer Colonel John McCrae penciled this poignant poem during the second battle of Ypres, and it became what is generally regarded as the greatest poem of World War I. Through a mutual friend, McCrae sent an autographed copy of the poem to Sousa with the request that he give it a musical setting. Sousa received it during the Sousa Band engagement in Montreal in July, 1917. His immediate impression was that the poem was magnificent, and he promised to comply. McCrae did not live to hear Sousa's music. In Sousa's own words: "I had just mailed the final proofs in my hotel and had picked up a paper from the bookstall when the first news I read was the death in battle of Col. McCrae."[4]

MSS: Orch 7pp; 8Mar1918 Sands Pt. [UI]
Pub: Schirmer
©: V/pi: Schirmer 27Feb1918; ren JPrS & HSA 25Apr1945

IT WAS REALLY VERY FORTUNATE FOR ME (1913)
Words by Charles Brown

This humorous song concerns a soldier who was selected to lead a charge. As he paused to tie his shoelaces, all his comrades died — and he lived to receive a medal for bravery.

MSS: a) V/pi 3pp; 7Jul1913 np [LC]
      b) Several orch parts in Sousa's hand; nd np [LC]
Not pub or ©

IT'S A THING WE ARE APT TO FORGET
(1900 or after)
Words by John Philip Sousa

In this "topical song," as Sousa called it, he elaborates on the grief caused by an umbrella borrowed but not returned, money loaned but not repaid, political promises not kept, and other common annoyances. The undated song was discovered in 1969 among other manuscripts kept in storage by Sousa's heirs.

MSS: V/pi 2pp; nd np [LC]
Not pub or ©

I'VE MADE MY PLANS FOR THE SUMMER (1907)
Words by John Philip Sousa

"I've made my plans for the summer." This is the maiden's reply to a marriage proposal in this humorous song. The lady dreams of happy days at Luna Park (Coney

Island) — "shooting the chutes" and listening to the band. She says she might reconsider at the end of the summer. The song was written at the request of one of the proprietors of the Coney Island amusement park in New York.

MSS: N/A
Pub: Church
©: V/pi: Church 10May1907; not ren
      V/orch: Church 15May1907; ren JvMS 10Jan1935
      Cornet, flugelhorn, trombone, or baritone with bd: Church 16May1907; ren JvMS 10Jan1935

THE JOURNAL (1924)
Words by John Philip Sousa

Sousa was a guest of the *Milwaukee Journal* staff when his band stopped in Milwaukee on its 1924 tour. He penned this very short marching song while in their office. The verse briefly compliments them on their efforts to get the news to the people.

MSS: V/pi 1pp; 8Nov1924 Milwaukee [in possession of *Milwaukee Journal* staff]
Pub: *Milwaukee Journal* (in newspaper only)
Not ©

KELLY AND BURKE AND SHAE
(See THE FIGHTING RACE)

LONELY (1877)
Poem by Jefferson H. Nones

In Nones's poem, a lonely soul reflects on the days of his youth and grieves over being in the twilight of his life. The music was designated Opus 32 and was published as part of a collection entitled *Stoddart's Musical Library*. It is one of a set of three compositions called "Number 19," which sold for ten cents.

MSS: N/A
Pub: Stoddart
©: V/pi: Stoddart (covered by © of *Stoddart's Musical Library*, 1877)

LOVE ME LITTLE, LOVE ME LONG (1877)
Words by John Philip Sousa

In this song, the imaginary (?) object of Sousa's affection is given his philosophy of

---

[4] *Morning Bulletin*, Edmonton, Alberta, Canada, July 7, 1919.

love. She is being told that he prefers a lasting love to a strong and spirited love which "burneth soon to waste."

MSS: N/A
Pub: Shaw
©: V/pi: Shaw 20Sep1878; not ren

LOVE THAT COMES WHEN MAY-ROSES BLOW (1889)
Words by John Philip Sousa

This "valse-aria" was another of the unknown Sousa works discovered among unpublished manuscripts at his Sands Point home in 1965. There are no verses on the manuscript.

MSS: Pi 2pp; 3Jul1889 np [LC]
Not pub or ©

THE LOVE THAT LIVES FOREVER (1917)
Words by George P. Wallihan

Found enclosed in the only known manuscript of this ballad was an undated letter from Wallihan requesting that Sousa find an air for his lyric. The song was used with the Sousa Band as a vocal or cornet solo, in an arrangement by bandsman Peter Buys.

MSS: V/pi 1pp; 27Dec1917 Chicago [LC]
Pub: Schirmer
©: V/pi: Schirmer 9Mar1918; ren JPrS & HSA 25Apr1945

LOVELY MARY DONNELLY (1918)
Poem by William Allingham

The prettiest and gayest girl at the dance in Allingham's poem is Mary Donnelly. As Miss Donnelly is described, Sousa weaves a pretty theme; as she dances a jig, Sousa supplies a jigtime melody.

MSS: a) V/pi 3pp; nd np [LC]
     b) V/pi 1pp inc; nd np [LC]
Pub: Schirmer
©: V/pi: Schirmer 9Mar1918; ren JPrS & HSA 25Apr1945

LOVE'S RADIANT HOUR (1928)
Words by Helen Boardman Knox

"Love's Sunrise" was the original title of this song before it was published. It was dedicated to and introduced by Marjorie Moody, whom Sousa respected and admired both as an artist and as a personal friend. Miss Moody sang more concerts with the Sousa Band than any other vocalist. After completing the band arrangement, Sousa penned another manuscript and presented Miss Moody with her own personal copy. Two years earlier, he had dedicated "There's a Merry Brown Thrush" to her.

MSS: a) Bd 23pp; 20Jun1928 Sands Pt. [LC]
     b) V/pi 5pp; 28Jun1928 np [in possession of Mrs. Everett Glines (Marjorie Moody), Albany, N.Y.]
Pub: Witmark
©: V/pi: Witmark 10Aug1928; ren JPrS & HSA & Rebecca Knox Freericks 10Aug1955

THE MAGIC GLASS (1877)
Poem by Charles Swain

The second of two musical settings Sousa gave to poems of the English poet Charles Swain was "The Magic Glass," which invites maidens to see the deep secrets of the future by looking into the crystal. There is no evidence that Sousa was ever personally acquainted with Swain. He was no doubt familiar with Swain's works, however, possibly by his contact in an informal literary society called the Vis-à-Vis.

MSS: N/A
Pub: North
©: V/pi: North 20Mar1877; not ren

MAID OF THE MEADOW (1897)
Words by John Philip Sousa

One of the songs most frequently sung by the sopranos of the Sousa Band was "Maid of the Meadow." It is possibly a song cut from the operetta *The Bride Elect* or else added as the production was revised. It was unpublished for over two decades before appearing as an independent song in a collection called *Book of Songs*.[5]

MSS: N/A
Pub: Church

---

[5] There is a remote possibility that "Maid of the Meadow" was extracted from *The Charlatan* rather than *The Bride Elect*. Its date of composition was estimated from its appearances in Sousa Band programs.

©:   V/pi: Church (covered by © of *Book of Songs,* 1920)

MALLIE (no date)
Words by J. W. Heysinger

Until 1965, the only clue to the existence of this song was that it was included in the list of compositions in Sousa's autobiography. At that time a manuscript was discovered in an uncatalogued section of the Sousa Band library at the University of Illinois. Sousa made no mention of the lyricist, J. W. Heysinger, in his writings.

MSS: V/pi 3pp; nd np [UI]
Not pub or ©

MAVOURNEEN ASTHORE (1878)
Words by Albert S. Nones

According to the inscription on the frontispiece, this music was "Written for and sung by J. L. Carncross, Esq., of Carncross and Dixie's Minstrels." When the young Sousa lived in Philadelphia, this minstrel company was performing burlesques on popular plays, operettas, songs, and the like. "Mavourneen Asthore" was probably a spoof of either the current play *Kathleen Mavourneen* or the Irish ballad of the same name. J. F. Carncross and E. F. Dixie had also played Washington theaters for several seasons before this, so Sousa may have had prior associations with their company.

MSS: N/A
Pub: Stoddart
©:   V/pi: Stoddart 16Feb1878; not ren

THE MESSIAH OF NATIONS
(See Other Vocal Works)

THE MILKMAID (1914)
Poem by Austin Dobson

At Sousa Band concerts, one of the songs used exclusively by the sopranos was "The Milkmaid." It was programmed mostly at outdoor concerts at places such as Willow Grove Park.

MSS: a) Bd 3pp; 12Aug1914 Sands Pt. [LC]
      b) V/pi 2pp; nd np [LC]
      c) V/pi 2pp inc; nd np [LC]

Pub: Church
©:   V/pi: Church 22Sep1914; ren JvMS 13Feb1942

MY OWN, MY GERALDINE (1887)
Poem by Francis C. Long

In an 1893 interview with a newspaper reporter, Sousa is quoted as saying that this song reflected the highest standard of his musical ability, adding that it was "of the better class of English ballads and in a vein with those of Sullivan."[6] It met with little success, but Sousa would not let it die, and in 1894 he made a band arrangement. It was used sparingly until 1900, at which time the music of the Sousa Band library was forfeited to the heirs of deceased band manager David Blakely in a court action. When the library was bought back from the Blakely heirs in 1924, Sousa put the song to use as a cornet solo.

MSS: Bd 7pp; 26Feb1894 New York City [USMC]
Pub: Ellis
©:   V/pi: Ellis 25Nov1887; not ren

MY SWEET SWEETHEART (no date)
Words by Jack Nilpon

This sentimental love song was another of the works discovered at Sousa's Sands Point home in 1965. He mentioned neither the composition nor the lyricist in his writings. There are two manuscripts, and the verses differ slightly.

MSS: a) V/pi 1pp; nd np [LC]
      b) V/pi 2pp; nd np [LC]
Not pub or ©

NAIL THE FLAG TO THE MAST (1890)
Poem by William Russell Frisbie

Although a notation on the frontispiece of the sheet music declares this to be a "sailor's song," Sousa's concept was broader. The words were his forte — patriotic in nature. Twenty-four years after the initial appearance of the song, he felt a need to express his feeling of nationalism. The

[6] *New York Advertiser,* August 27, 1893[?] (undated clipping in the Sousa Band press book of 1893).

song was then converted into a march, and two words were extracted from the chorus for the title: "Columbia's Pride."

MSS: a) V/pi 2pp; nd np [LC]
     b) V/pi 1pp inc; nd np [LC]
Pub: Ellis
©: V/pi: Ellis 17Mar1890; not ren

THE NAVY TOAST
(See THE TOAST)

O MY COUNTRY (1874)
Words by B. Lowlaws

The subtitle of this song seems pretentious: "The American National Song." The nine-teen-year-old Sousa copyrighted it himself, co-signing with B. Swallow — perhaps the Reverend Benjamin Swallow, the step-father of Sousa's sweetheart Emma. It is interesting that the name Lowlaws can be rearranged to read Swallow. The song was probably unpublished; the copyright division of the Library of Congress has no record of copies received.

MSS: N/A
Pub: ?
©: V/pi: JPS & B. Swallow 3Jan1874; not ren

O YE LILIES WHITE (1887)
Poem by Francis C. Long

One of two songs set to words of the rela-tively unknown poet Francis C. Long, this song was highly regarded by Sousa. He be-lieved that it belonged with the better bal-lads of the day and used it as a soprano solo with the band until at least the early 1900's, in an arrangement by cornetist Herbert L. Clarke.

MSS: N/A
Pub: Ellis
©: V/pi: Ellis 10Dec1887; not ren

ONLY A DREAM (1876)
Words by Mary A. Denison

Mary A. Denison was an early acquaint-ance for whom Sousa had high regard. This song was the first of three works in which she and Sousa collaborated; the other two were the song "When He Is Near" (1880) and the unfinished operetta *Florine* (1881).

MSS: V/pi 2pp; 2Mar1875 np [LC]
Pub: North
©: V/pi: North 29Jan1877; not ren

ONLY THEE (1876)
Poem by Charles Swain

This was the first of two musical settings given to verses of the nineteenth-century English poet Charles Swain. The song title is taken from lines of Swain's tender and touching love poem, "A Word of Thine."

MSS: N/A
Pub: North
©: V/pi: North 30Dec1876; not ren

O'REILLY'S KETTLEDRUM (1889)
Words by Edward M. Taber

This was one of two final collaborations with Edward M. Taber. It is a humorous ballad about a party in which a kettledrum was filled with punch. O'Reilly's social splash ended in a brawl.

MSS: V/pi 2pp; nd np [LC]
Pub: Coleman
©: V/pi: Coleman 13Dec1889; ren JPS 18Aug1917
Also pub for orch but not ©

OUR BOYS ARE HOME AGAIN
(See WHEN THE BOYS COME SAILING HOME!)

PRETTY PATTY HONEYWOOD (1881)
Poem by Cuthbert Bede

Sousa gave a lively, gay melody to this poem. He was doubtless reaching for the popular song market, because the poem he selected was not destined to be a classic. To wit:

> Pretty Patty Honeywood, fresh and fair and plump
> Into your affections I would like to jump . . .

MSS: N/A
Pub: Ellis
©: V/pi: Ellis 12Jul1881; not ren

THE PRIDE OF THE WOLVERINES
(See Marches)

PUSHING ON (1918)
Words by Guy F. Lee

While Sousa was supervising the U.S. Navy's band program at the Great Lakes Naval Training Center during World War I, he was asked by Guy F. Lee to put music to the words of his wartime lyric. The result was a piece of short-lived period music. Lee was a staff member of the *Chicago Tribune,* which introduced the song to its readers on September 29, 1918. He published sheet music for voice and piano, and then a band arrangement, with Sousa providing copyright protection on the former. The band arrangement was usually programmed as a march. Sousa hurriedly penned the music on September 26, 1918, in the presence of James A. Friberg, the navy musician who was assigned as his copyist, just before the "Jackie" band left for a tour to promote Liberty Bond sales.[7]

MSS: a) V/pi 2pp; 25 [sic] Sep1918 Chicago [in possession of James A. Friberg, New Port Richey, Fla.]
b) V/pi 2pp inc; nd np [LC]
c) V/pi 1pp inc; nd np [LC]
Pub: Guy F. Lee; also *Chicago Tribune* (in newspaper only)
©: V/pi: JPS 29Sep1918; not ren

A RARE OLD FELLOW (1881)
Poem by Barry Cornwall

The rare old fellow of this song is King Death, who pours out his cold black wine to welcome the distressed. Sousa's music is for baritone. It has a robust character, much different from his other songs. It was dedicated "To G. T. R. Knorr, of Philadelphia, Pa."

MSS: N/A
Pub: Balmer & Weber
©: V/pi: Balmer & Weber 27Apr1881; not ren

REVEILLE (1890)
Poem by Robert J. Burdette

Making use of the familiar bugle call, Sousa put music to Burdette's poem, which described dawn in an army camp. The

---

[7] Letters from Friberg to the author, December 31, 1965, and January 20, 1966.

song was dedicated "To the Army." A few years later the piece was used effectively in Sousa's operetta *The American Maid.*

MSS: N/A
Pub: Ellis
©: V/pi: Ellis 30Jan1890; ren JPS 31Dec1917

SEA NYMPH (no date)
Words by B. P. Wilmot

Neither B. P. Wilmot nor this song found its way into Sousa's writings. The manuscripts were discovered in the archives of the Sands Point estate in 1965.

MSS: V/pi 2pp (2 versions, both inc); nd np [LC]
Not pub or ©

A SERENADE IN SEVILLE (1924)
Words by James Francis Cooke

One of Sousa's closest friends in his later years was James Francis Cooke, editor of the highly regarded music periodical *Etude,* and it is surprising that this was their only joint musical effort. The composition was programmed frequently by the Sousa Band as a soprano solo. The sheet music carries the inscription "To Marie Sundelius."

MSS: Orch 8pp; 31Jul1924 Willow Grove, Pa. [LC]
Pub: Presser
©: V/pi: Presser 26Jul1924; ren HSA 9Jul1952

SMICK, SMACK, SMUCK (1878)
Words by John Philip Sousa

This hilarious — but gory — theater song needs explanation lest the reader misunderstand the young John Philip Sousa. It was written for a minstrel routine, with narration between the three verses and the trio. It is the story of a hapless young man who courted an unattractive girl who "... had a wart upon her nose and eyes that looked just like a crow's." She was seemingly bashful and retiring, but on the third date her beau discovered that she had an abnormal passion for kissing. A marathon began. Her lips became raw, her teeth came through her jaw, and her mouth became four feet wide. After a week, he took her to a "doctor shop" and had her cheek glued up.

MSS: N/A
Pub: Shaw
©: V/pi: Shaw 20Sep1878; not ren

THE SONG OF THE DAGGER (1916)
Words by John Philip Sousa

In 1916, Sousa was called upon to compose a short song as accompaniment for a singer in a scene called "The Weaker Strain" in Pathe's silent movie series, *Who's Guilty?* He responded with this simple song, which covered a range of only twelve tones and used single-syllable words with consonant sounds to make maximum use of lip expressiveness.

MSS: N/A
Not pub or ©

THE SONG OF THE SEA (1876)
Words by Emma M. Swallow

It would be interesting to know what inspired Emma Swallow to write the words to this song, which concerns a lover lost at sea. At the time, she was Sousa's fiance. Sousa referred to the song as Opus 27.

MSS: N/A
Pub: North
©: V/pi: North 29Jan1877; not ren

STAR OF LIGHT (1882)
Poem by Bessie Beach

Sousa made no mention of this song in his writings. It was uncovered in a search through copyright files at the Library of Congress. Bessie Beach's "star of light" was an angel. The inscription on the sheet music reads "To Ellen in Heaven," and the verse reads:

"Sweet guardian, like a blessed star of light,
That shines about my pathway pure and bright . . ."

MSS: N/A
Pub: Pond
©: V/pi: Mrs. M. D. Lincoln 21Aug1882 again by Bessie Beach 30Dec1882; not ren

STUFFED STORK (1894)
Words by John Philip Sousa

According to one of the manuscripts of this comical song, it was composed expressly for DeWolf Hopper to be sung in the production *Dr. Syntax*. A copyright of the song is recorded at the Copyright Division of the Library of Congress, but there is no record of copies received, indicating that it was probably unpublished. The Theodore Presser Company, successor to the publisher named in the copyright, has no record of it.

MSS: a) V/pi 2pp; nd np [LC]
b) V/pi 2pp inc; nd np [LC]
Pub: (If published) Church
©: V/pi: Church 24Aug1894; not ren

SWEET MISS INDUSTRY (1887)
Poem by S. Conant Foster

The demure maiden in Foster's poem is so busy cooking, washing, ironing, and raking hay that she cannot find time for play. However, she accepts a marriage proposal on the condition that she will then have leisure time.

MSS: Several bd parts in Sousa's hand; nd np [UI]
Pub: Ellis
©: V/pi: Ellis 4Jan1888; not ren

TALLY-HO! (1885)
Poem by Joaquin Miller

Sousa provided a lively setting for Miller's poem, which tells of a gentleman's exciting ride behind six horses, with his sweetheart by his side. The frontispiece of the sheet music states that the song was sung by R. L. Downing in Miller's play of the same name. Sousa also composed an overture for the play.

MSS: V/pi 8pp; nd np [LC]
Pub: Ellis
©: V/pi: Ellis 12Jan1885; not ren

THERE'S A MERRY BROWN THRUSH (1926)
Poem by Lucy Larcom

Although Sousa was seldom cast as a bird-lover, he had almost three dozen bird baths scattered about his Sands Point estate. Among his favorite birds was the one which inspired this song and also Lucy Larcom's poem, "The Brown Thrush." Sousa's song was composed specifically for Marjorie Moody, to be sung as an encore on the 1926 tour of the Sousa Band.[8]

MSS: Bd 4pp; 4Jun1926 Sands Pt. [LC]
Pub: Presser
©:   V/pi: Presser 22Jul1926; not ren

THERE'S SOMETHING MYSTERIOUS
(1889)
Words by Hunter MacCulloch

This piece is well-named, because the only suggestion of its existence is that it has a registered copyright. There is no record of copies received at the Copyright Division of the Library of Congress.

MSS: N/A
Pub: ?
©:   V/pi: Hunter MacCulloch 3Jun1889; not ren

THOUGH DOLLY IS MARRIED
(no date)
Words by M. E. W.

The only manuscript of this song known to exist is a fragment of the first page, and Sousa left nothing in his writings to indicate who M. E. W. might have been. The manuscript was discovered among other incomplete or unmarked manuscripts presented to the Library of Congress by Sousa's heirs in 1970.

MSS: V/pi 1pp inc; nd np [LC]
Not pub or ©

THE TOAST (1918)
(THE NAVY TOAST)
Words by R. H. Burnside

Two manuscripts of this song lay undiscovered for thirty-seven years after Sousa's death. One manuscript is entitled "The Navy Toast." A second, presumably done later, is called simply "The Toast" and has more verses.

In the song, navy men are toasting the

---

[8] Letter from Sousa to James Francis Cooke, editor of *Etude,* May 17, 1926.

flag, their comrades, their homes, their wives, and their sweethearts — and hoping that the wives and sweethearts will never meet. R. H. Burnside, the lyricist, was the producer of several extravaganzas at the old New York Hippodrome. The song might have been from one of the Hippodrome shows for which Sousa provided music, perhaps *Cheer Up* or *Everything.*

MSS: a) V/pi 2pp; 26May1918 np [LC]
         b) V/pi 4pp; nd np [LC]
Not pub or ©

2:15 (1889)
Words by Edward M. Taber

The humor of Edward M. Taber caught Sousa's fancy, as evidenced by their teamwork on two comic operettas and several humorous songs such as this. It is a burlesque on the figure 2:15. A ribbon clerk who makes $2.15 per week courts his sweetheart until 2:15 a.m. Her father, in a paternal rage, chases him in a 2.15-mile heat. He then learns the plumber's trade and makes $2.15 per hour, and the couple elopes on the 2:15 express.

MSS: N/A
Pub: Coleman
©:   V/pi: Coleman 13Dec1889; ren JPS 18Aug1917

WE ARE COMING (1918)
Poem by Edith Willis Linn

At the height of America's participation in World War I, the now defunct humor magazine *Life* sponsored a contest to find a poem suitable for use as a war song. A lady named Edith Willis Linn won the $500 prize. Sousa then composed the music and signed over the royalties to *Life*'s "Fresh Air Fund." He then arranged the song as a march, using the same title, so that it could be either sung or used for parades. For the premiere on March 10, 1918, the march version was performed at the New York Hippodrome by the combined bands of the Atlantic fleet, Lieutenant Sousa conducting.

MSS: N/A
Pub: Schirmer
©:   V/pi: Schirmer 16Feb1918; ren JPrS & HSA 25Apr1945

WE'LL FOLLOW WHERE THE WHITE PLUME WAVES (1884)
Words by Edward M. Taber

Sousa and his lyricist entered politics with this effort. It was a campaign song written to support James Gillespie Blaine, who ran for president against Grover Cleveland in 1884. Blaine was known in political circles as the "plumed knight." The enthusiastic song ends in the following manner:

> For victory and Blaine,
> From Oregon to Maine,
> We'll follow where the white plume waves.

Later, Sousa completely revised the song, converted it into a march, and called it "The White Plume." The song barely survived the election defeat, but the march was popular for many years.

MSS: N/A
Pub: Ellis
©: V/pi: JPS & Edward M. Taber 9Jun1884 again by Ellis 18Jun1884; not ren

WHEN HE IS NEAR (1880)
Words by Mary A. Denison

This is the second of two songs written with Mary A. Denison, the Washington author. Sousa did not list the song in the index of his works in his autobiography, as he did the other song, "Only a Dream" (1876). The identity of the near-perfect lover in Mrs. Denison's emotional verse may never be known.

MSS: N/A
Pub: Shaw
©: V/pi: Shaw 26May1880; not ren

WHEN THE BOYS COME SAILING HOME! (1918)
Words by Helen Sousa Abert

Sousa's younger daughter Helen supplied two sets of lyrics for this song. They were for editions printed as "When the Boys Come Sailing Home!" and "Our Boys Are Home Again." The music is the same for both editions.

MSS: N/A
Pub: Flammer

©: V/pi: Flammer 20Dec1918; ren JPrS & HSA 23Feb1946
Also pub for bd and for orch but not ©

WHILE NAVY SHIPS ARE COALING (1923)
Poem by Wells Hawks

In Sousa's hands, Hawks's patriotic poem was transformed into a sea chantey "with copious interpolations." The interpolations included "My Pretty Jane," "Listen to the Mocking Bird," "Ol' Carolina," and a fragment of Sousa's own march, "Keeping Step with the Union" (1921). It was dedicated to Rear Admiral William A. Moffett, to whom Sousa also dedicated "The Aviators" march (1931).

MSS: Bd 20pp; 13Jun1923 Sands Pt. [LC]
Pub: Presser
©: V/pi: Presser 23Feb1923; ren JPrS & HSA 24Aug1950

WILT THOU BE TRUE (1873)
Poem by E. Cook

From sketchy information given at the heading of this brief manuscript, one must conclude that the poem to which the music was set originally appeared in *Graham Magazine*.[9] The poem asks how long flowers will keep their festive character.

MSS: V/pi 1pp; Nov1873 np [LC]
Not pub or ©

THE WINDOW BLIND (1887)
Words by Edward M. Taber

Lyricist Taber sees the maiden of his dreams "across the way" and falls in love with her, but she does not know of his love. He is heartbroken when she is obscured by a "tantalizing green Venetian window blind."

MSS: V/pi 1pp inc; nd np [LC]
Pub: Ellis
©: V/pi: Ellis 3Dec1887; not ren

YALE MARCHING SONG (1920)
Words by Joseph Grant Ewing

This composition is another of those dis-

---

[9] There were several different "Graham" magazines in print in the early 1870's.

covered at Sousa's Sands Point estate in 1965, and one of the manuscripts is inscribed: "Words by Joseph Grant Ewing, '89." It was not Sousa's only effort on behalf of Yale; in 1897 he and DeWolf Hopper collaborated on a pep song by adding words to one of the themes from *El Capitan* (1895).

Sousa left little indication of a love for Yale in his writings, but several factors may have influenced him. He always seemed interested in the outcome of Yale football games. After Yale's victory over Princeton in 1915, his band was engaged to play an impromptu concert at the Yale Club in New York. Then too, the American composer Horatio Parker, who was head of Yale's music department, was among his personal friends.

MSS: a) V/pi 1pp; 21Jan1920 np [LC]
     b) V/pi 1pp inc; nd np [LC]
Not pub or ©

YOU'LL MISS LOTS OF FUN WHEN YOU'RE MARRIED (1890)
Words by Edward M. Taber

Taber satirically itemizes the advantages and blessings of married life, but at the end of each verse he suggests that "You'll miss lots of fun when you're married."

MSS: V/pi 1pp; nd np [LC]
Pub: Ellis
©:   V/pi: Ellis 19Apr1890; not ren

(UNTITLED SONG) (no date)
Words by James Adams

The untitled, undated manuscript of this song was presented to the Library of Congress in 1970 by Sousa's heirs. Two verses give a tender description of a sleeping baby girl.

MSS: V/pi 3pp inc; nd np [LC]
Not pub or ©

(UNTITLED SONG) (1874)
Words by Emma M. Swallow

Another piece recently discovered in Sousa's 1873-76 sketchbook was this short song which tells how nature falls silent at nightfall.

MSS: V/pi 2pp; Nov1874 np [LC]
Not pub or ©

OTHER VOCAL WORKS

THE LAST CRUSADE (1920)
Ballad

In a letter dated April 28, 1918, Anne Higginson Spicer asked Sousa to provide music for her religious poem, "The Last Crusade." Sousa responded with one of his most serious works, in a setting for mixed quartet and chorus. It bears some similarity to a cantata or oratorio but is shorter (thirty-four printed pages). It was dedicated to a Mrs. E. T. Stotesbury. Mrs. Spicer showed her appreciation in a touching poem which she later wrote to commemorate Sousa's seventieth birthday.[1]

MSS: a) V/pi 27pp; 5Feb1920 np [LC]
      b) V/orch 40pp; 13Mar1924 Sands Pt. [LC]
Pub: Church
©: Mixed quartet & chorus/pi: Church 15Sep1920; ren JPrS & HSA 30Oct1947

MARCH-SONG OF THE CHICAGO SCHOOLS
(See WE MARCH, WE MARCH TO VICTORY)

THE MESSIAH OF NATIONS (1902)
Based on poem by James Whitcomb Riley

In the exact center of Indianapolis stands the impressive Soldiers' and Sailors' Monument, symbolizing war and peace. It stands nearly twenty-six stories high and depicts the military services of the Civil War period. For the monument's dedication in 1902 the famed Hoosier poet James Whitcomb Riley wrote his stirring poem, "O Thou America, Messiah of Nations," and Sousa was asked to provide a musical setting for the poem. Sousa considered Riley's poem "the most beautiful patriotic words ever written in our country."[2] The two met three years later at a dinner given in Sousa's honor by the Bobbs-Merrill Company, the Indianapolis publishers of many of Riley's works. This firm had just published Sousa's second novel, *Pipetown Sandy*.

The first edition of "The Messiah of Nations" was issued in 1902 as a hymn, and complimentary copies were distributed at the dedication of the monument by the Bowen-Merrill (later Bobbs-Merrill) Company. Later Sousa incorporated the theme into "The White Man" movement of his suite, *Dwellers of the Western World* (1910). A second edition of "The Messiah of Nations," printed as a "patriotic anthem" in 1914, differed from the original in that the dynamics were changed and a new introduction was added. These changes were made by Sousa on a printed copy of the music now at the Library of Congress.

MSS: a) Bd 4pp; 26Feb1915 Sands Pt. [LC]
      b) Orch 4pp; 11Mar1915 Sands Pt. [LC]
      c) Orch 5pp; 8Dec1915 np [UI]
      d) Bd 5pp; 14Jul1924 Willow Grove, Pa. [UI]
Pub: Church
©: Mixed chorus/pi: Church 9May1902 again 20May1914; ren JPS 21Feb1930 again JvMS 13Feb1942

---

[1] This poem was found among Sousa's personal papers in 1965.

[2] John Philip Sousa, "The Force of Music," *American Legion Weekly*, September 1, 1922.

Women's trio/pi: Church 10Oct1918;
ren JPrS & HSA 4Apr1946
Male chorus/pi: Church 29Apr1919;
ren JPrS & HSA 3Jan1947

NON-COMMITTAL DECLARATIONS
(1920)
Vocal trio

This trio for women's voices might have
been extracted from one of Sousa's unpublished operettas, although his writings do
not indicate it. The piece was occasionally
performed at Willow Grove Park, where
Sousa sometimes engaged several vocalists
at one time. It was also performed on occasion as a cornet trio. The vocal parts of the
first manuscript are written in solfeggio.

MSS: a) V/pi 8pp; 31Mar1920 np [LC]
b) Bd 12pp; 15Jun1921 Sands Pt. [LC]
Pub: Church
©:   Women's trio/pi: Church 26Aug1920;
not ren

OH, WHY SHOULD THE SPIRIT OF
MORTAL BE PROUD (1899)
Hymn

Advertised as President Lincoln's favorite
hymn, this composition was given a new
musical setting by Sousa and scored for
mixed quartet. With words by William
Knox, it was composed on the occasion of
the ninetieth anniversary of Lincoln's birth.
A complimentary edition was distributed
by Klaw, Erlanger, and B. D. Stevens, the
managers of Sousa's operetta *Chris and the
Wonderful Lamp.*

MSS: Orch 22pp; 17Jan1899 New York City
[UI]
Pub: Church
©:   Mixed quartet/pi: Church 8Feb1899;
ren JPS 29Jan1927

TE DEUM IN B-FLAT (1874)

Although Sousa seldom mentioned this
early hymn of praise and thanksgiving, it
must have been used frequently, because
his conductor's score is well worn. It is inscribed "Opus 12" and is scored for mixed
quartet and organ.

MSS: a) Mixed quartet/organ 19pp; nd np
[LC]

b) Several vocal parts in Sousa's hand;
nd np [LC]
Not pub or ©

THE TROOPING OF THE COLORS
(1898)

Wild public reaction to this grandiose and
patriotic extravaganza illustrated Sousa's
extraordinary flair for showmanship. But
for the length of the work and the inclusion
of vocal parts, it could possibly be classified
as a fantasy for band. However, it is sub-
stantially different from any other Sousa
composition. Advertisements heralded is as
a "grand international spectacle" — seemingly a fitting description.

Some Americans of Spanish ancestry
might have had mixed emotions at the out-
break of the Spanish-American War, but
not John Philip Sousa. His military instinct
was aroused, and this work was a natural
expression of his patriotism. He organized
a tour of the larger cities and utilized local
choruses of several hundred voices to aug-
ment his sixty-piece band. In addition,
arrangements were made in each city for
participation by military units.

The pageantry began with the clatter of
drums and a trumpet fanfare which "proclaimed liberty throughout the world."
Fifes and drums played "The Spirit of '76"
and "Yankee Doodle," and nations friendly
to the United States were recognized. The
band played "British Grenadier" and a
quartet sang "God Save the Queen." "The
Marseillaise" was sung by a soloist and
chorus, and the chorus continued with
"Die Wacht am Rhine." After the band
played "The Wearing of the Green," "Der
Wasserfall" was sung by a trio. The excitement began in earnest as bagpipers entered
playing "The Campbells Are Coming." A
Cuban military attachment marched in to
the tune of "You'll Remember Me." Then
the band, chorus, and a soloist rang out
with stirring words to Sousa's newest
march: "The Stars and Stripes Forever."
Meanwhile, U.S. Army, Navy, and Marine
troops moved in with flags and banners flying. A pretty girl entered wearing the cos-
tume of Columbia, and all joined together
in the finale, "The Star Spangled Banner."

It is not difficult to imagine the profound effect on the audiences of a country which had just gone to war. Sousa was modest in referring to the "remarkable displays" of audiences. Newspapers reported everything from the waving of handkerchiefs to near bedlam. Repetition of "The Star Spangled Banner" was often demanded several times, and Sousa sometimes added to the enthusiasm by launching into "Dixie."

MSS: N/A
Pub: Church
©: Mixed chorus/pi: Church 28Mar1898; ren JPS 19Feb1926

WE MARCH, WE MARCH TO VICTORY
(1914)
Processional hymn

Several composers were numbered among the friends of Hobart Weed, a benefactor of St. Paul's Episcopal Church of Buffalo, New York. In 1904 Victor Herbert composed his Easter anthem, "Christ Is Risen," for the choir of St. Paul's at Weed's request. This composition of Sousa's was also dedicated to the choir and "To Hobart Weed, Esq." While attending church with Sousa in Buffalo on November 1, 1914, Weed asked Sousa to provide new music to the old hymn "We March, We March to Victory."[3] Sousa obliged two days later and added finishing touches on his sixtieth birthday, November 6.

Not only was the music to the original "We March, We March to Victory" revised; the words were also revised by another of Weed's friends, Gerard Moultrie. The work was published by the John Church Co. Several years later, this company was absorbed by the Theodore Presser Co., who printed the composition under another name. It was Moultrie who again paraphrased the words, and the new edition was entitled "March-Song of the Chicago Schools." This version was dedicated "To Hon. Wm. Hale Thompson, Mayor, and the school children of Chicago."

MSS: a) V/pi 1pp; 3Nov1914 Buffalo, N.Y. [UI]
b) Bd 3pp; 26Feb1915 Sands Pt. [UI]
Pub: Church; Presser
©: ("We March, We March to Victory") Soprano & unison chorus/pi: Church 23Mar1915; ren JvMS 6Jan1943
("March-Song of the Chicago Schools") Unison chorus/pi: Presser 28Nov1930; ren JPrS & HSA 2Dec1957

---

[3] *Binghamton* (N.Y.) *Press,* November 6, 1914.

WALTZES

THE BRIDE ELECT
(See Operettas)

EL CAPITAN
(See Operettas)

THE CHARLATAN
(See Operettas)

THE COEDS OF MICHIGAN (1925)

The extent of Sousa's association with the University of Michigan is not well known, but this composition may have been solicited when the Sousa Band played in Ann Arbor in November, 1924. It was dedicated "To the faculty and students of the University of Michigan." Shortly after its premiere, Sousa arranged it as an alto saxophone solo. It was used only once, however.

MSS: 1st alto saxophone part 2pp; Jul1925 np
[in possession of Harold B. Stephens, Long Beach, Calif.]
Pub: Church
©: Pi: Church 5May1925; ren JPrS & HSA 9Jun1952
Also pub for bd but not ©

THE COLONIAL DAMES WALTZES (1896)

In 1885, Sousa composed the "Wissahickon Waltz" for the proprietors of a Philadelphia department store, and it was published in their own magazine. Apparently dissatisfied with the limited distribution, he completely revised the composition, added new material, and renamed it "The Colonial Dames Waltzes." It was then dedicated to the National Society of Colonial Dames of America. The first edition of the composition with its new title appeared in the *Ladies' Home Journal* of April, 1896, marking the fifth anniversary of the Colonial Dames organization.

MSS: N/A
Pub: *Ladies' Home Journal* (in magazine only) pi; Church (bd; pi)
©: Pi: covered by © of Apr1896 issue of the magazine
Bd: Church 20Jan1898; ren JPS 28Dec1925

INTAGLIO WALTZES (1884)

This composition was dedicated "To Miss Dora M. Miller, California." Her father, Senator John F. Miller, was a friend of Sousa's. The composition was revised in 1897 and renamed "The Lady of the White House."

MSS: Bd 1pp inc; nd np [LC]
Pub: Eberbach
©: Pi: Eberbach 8Oct1884; not ren

THE LADY OF THE WHITE HOUSE (1897)

Mrs. William McKinley, wife of the President, gave permission for Sousa to dedicate this composition to her.[1] It was published in the January, 1898, issue of the *Ladies' Home Journal*. It saw no further publication; perhaps Mrs. McKinley objected to the fact the "The Lady of the

---

[1] *Washington Post,* December 6, 1897. It should be noted that while Sousa was leader of the U.S. Marine Band, he knew McKinley as a congressman.

White House" was actually a revision of "Intaglio Waltzes" (1884), which had been dedicated to another lady.

MSS: N/A
Pub: *Ladies' Home Journal* (in magazine only)
©: Pi: covered by © of the Jan1898 issue of the magazine

MOONLIGHT ON THE POTOMAC WALTZES (1872)

A gentleman named Albert Tabor, seeking to impress his lady friend, prevailed upon the eighteen-year-old Sousa to compose a set of waltzes in her honor. The result was Sousa's first published work, called Opus 3 and dedicated to Carrie E. Foote, but his writings do not reveal whether or not the lady was won.

MSS: N/A
Pub: Ellis
©: Pi: JPS 10Apr1901; not ren

PAROLES D'AMOUR VALSES (1880)

Several months before Sousa was appointed leader of the U.S. Marine Band in Washington, he dedicated this composition to Colonel C. G. McCawley, commandant of the Marine Corps.

MSS: Bd 14pp; 5May1880 Phila. [UI]
Pub: Shaw
©: Pi: Shaw 6Sep1880; not ren

LA REINE D'AMOUR VALSES (1874)

In a fancy script on the front cover of this early composition is the following curious inscription:

A M'd'lle Cawthorne Swallow
Washington D. C.
La Reine D'Amour
Valses
Par
J. Philip Sousa
Op. 9

The composition is not mentioned in Sousa's writings. Neither is Mademoiselle Swallow, but she was probably a relative of Emma Swallow, Sousa's sweetheart.

MSS: Pi 9pp; nd np [LC]
Not pub or ©

LA REINE DE LA MER VALSES (1886)

Chosen as one of the numbers for Sousa's farewell concert with the U.S. Marine Band in 1892 and programmed quite often by the Sousa Band, this was probably Sousa's favorite among his waltzes. It was dedicated to Mrs. W. C. Whitney, wife of the secretary of the navy.

MSS: a) Bd 1pp inc; 4Feb1886 Washington, D.C. [LC]
b) 1st cornet part in Sousa's hand; nd np [UI]
Pub: Coleman
©: Pi: Coleman 27Nov1886 again 27Jun1894; ren JPS 13Feb1914 again 6Feb1922
Orch: Coleman 27Dec1886; ren JPS 13Feb1914
Bd: Coleman 4Dec1888; ren JPS 19Jan1916

SANDALPHON WALTZES (1886)

Rose Cleveland, daughter of President Grover Cleveland, was the lovely young lady to whom this forgotten composition was dedicated. Sousa once remarked that if there ever lived a kinder or sweeter-mannered woman than Miss Cleveland, it had not been his lot to meet her.[2] He did not make known the origin of the title.

MSS: N/A
Not pub or ©

SARDANAPOLIS (1877)

Discovered among other unclassified manuscripts at the Sousa estate in 1965 was this waltz which Sousa neglected to make known to the world. The origin of his title could presumably be in Sardanapolus, a legendary Assyrian king. Sousa was deeply interested in history and mythology and could have found a fascination in written accounts of this ancient monarch.

MSS: Orch 56pp inc; 15Feb1877 Phila. [LC]
Not pub or ©

WISSAHICKON WALTZ (1885)

The U.S. Marine Band gave frequent con-

[2] John Philip Sousa, "Keeping Time" (Part 3), *Saturday Evening Post*, November 21, 1925.

certs in Philadelphia while Sousa was leader, and for one occasion he was commissioned to compose this waltz. It was published in 1885 in the spring issue of *Quarterly,* a magazine published by Strawbridge and Clothier, a prominent Philadelphia department store. "Wissahickon" refers to a creek in southeastern Pennsylvania, the largest part of which runs through Philadelphia in an area now known as Wissahickon Park. The composition was revised several years later and published as "The Colonial Dames Waltzes."

MSS: N/A
Pub: Strawbridge & Clothier (in magazine only)
©: Pi: Strawbridge & Clothier 18Apr1885; not ren

VARIOUS DANCE FORMS

ALEXANDER (1876 or 1877)
Gavotte

The existence of this composition was established by one of Sousa's former copyists, Louis Morris. He found it listed in programs of the Chestnut Street Theatre in Philadelphia, where Sousa was employed as a violinist in Simon Hassler's orchestra.[1]

MSS: N/A
Not pub or ©

THE COQUETTE (1887)
Caprice

In 1901, this short dance was one of three pieces integrated into a suite called *Maidens Three*. A verse found in Sousa Band programs described the maiden called "the coquette" as follows:

> I know a maiden fair to see,
> Take care! Take care!
> She can both false and friendly be,
> Beware! Beware!

MSS: a) Orch 3pp inc; nd np [LC]
     b) Violin/pi 1pp inc; nd np [LC]
Pub: Ellis (pi); Coleman (bd; orch; pi; violin/pi)
©: Pi: Ellis 10Dec1887 again Coleman 27Jun1894; ren JPS 6Feb1922
Orch: Coleman 28Dec1889; ren JPS 18Aug1917

CUCKOO (1873)
Galop

A few scattered notes suggest the sound of a cuckoo in this, one of Sousa's earliest

---

[1] Disclosed to the author in an interview on September 26, 1964.

compositions. It was sold to a Philadelphia publisher, together with "The Review" march, for a hundred printed copies of each piece.

MSS: N/A
Pub: Lee & Walker
©: Pi: Lee & Walker 31Jul1873; not ren

DANCE HILARIOUS
(See WITH PLEASURE)

THE GLIDING GIRL (1912)
Tango

According to a story circulated among former Sousa Band members, Sousa's daughter Priscilla gave him the idea for this composition. She had just returned from Europe, reporting that the tango was the rage there. She gave him a demonstration by gliding around the room, and he captured her graceful motions in music.

MSS: Bd 10pp; 7Aug1912 New York City [LC]
Pub: Church
©: Pi: Church 25Sep1912; ren JvMS 7May1940
Also pub for bd but not ©

IN ECHELON POLONAISE
(See PRESIDENTIAL POLONAISE)

LOVE'S BUT A DANCE, WHERE TIME PLAYS THE FIDDLE (1923)
Fox-trot

In 1971, when a staff member of the Library of Congress was cataloguing recently acquired Sousa manuscripts, he discovered this previously unknown composition. It was on the reverse side of the last page of a piano score of "March of the Mitten Men."

MSS: Pi 1pp inc; nd np [LC]
Not pub or ©

MYRRHA GAVOTTE (1876)

The piano sheet music of this composition bears the dedication "To Hon. William Hunter, Department of State, Washington, D.C." Sousa was showing his appreciation for Hunter's earlier generosity. It was Hunter who gave Sousa and three others regular employment as a string quartet in Washington and who tried to persuade him to seek a musical education in Europe.

MSS: Timpani part of bd arr in Sousa's hand; nd np [USMC]
Pub: Lee & Walker
©: Pi: JPS 27Jan1877; not ren

ON WINGS OF LIGHTNING (1876)
Galop

The inscription on the sheet music of this lively composition reads: "As played by Hassler's orchestra at the Chestnut Street Theatre, Phila."

MSS: N/A
Pub: Andre
©: Pi: JPS 12Dec1876; not ren

PEACHES AND CREAM (1924)
Fox-trot

This composition was introduced as an encore on the 1924 Sousa Band tour. According to one newspaper review, Sousa composed it ". . . after seeing his young granddaughter dance. . . ."[2]

MSS: Bd 10pp; 23Apr1924 Sands Pt. [LC]
Pub: Fischer
©: Orch; pi: Fischer 9Jan1925; ren JPrS & HSA 14Apr1952
Bd: Fischer 9Feb1925; ren JPrS & HSA 14Apr1952

PRESIDENTIAL POLONAISE (1886)

Toward the end of his term, President Arthur engaged Sousa in conversation con-

[2] *Decatur* (Ill.) *Herald,* November 6, 1924.

cerning the suitability of the presidential salutation "Hail to the Chief." When Sousa revealed that it was actually an old Scottish boating song, Arthur instructed him to replace it with a more suitable composition. Sousa's replacement consisted of two pieces, "Presidential Polonaise" and the march "Semper Fidelis" (1888). "Presidential Polonaise" was used for state affairs at the White House. Curiously, Sousa's band score is entitled "In Echelon Polonaise."

MSS: a) Bd 6pp; 25Nov1886 Washington, D.C. [LC]
b) Orch 7pp; 18Jan1889 Washington, D.C. [LC]
c) Pi 2pp inc; nd np [LC]
Pub: Coleman
©: Orch: Coleman 1Mar1889; ren JPS 17Feb1917
Pi: Coleman 1Mar1889 again 27Jun1894; ren JPS 17Feb1917 again 6Feb1922
Also pub for bd but not ©

QUEEN OF THE HARVEST (1889)
Quadrille

Sousa left no clues as to the origin of this composition's title, and it is listed only as a miscellaneous composition in his autobiography, *Marching Along.*

MSS: Orch 9pp inc; nd np [LC]
Pub: Coleman
©: Orch: Coleman 27Dec1889; ren JPS 18Aug1917
Pi: Coleman 30Dec1889 again 27Jun1894; ren JPS 18Aug1917 again 6Feb1922

LA REINE D'AMOUR
Polka
(See Instrumental Solos)
(Also see Waltzes)

SILVER SPRAY SCHOTTISCHE (1878)

American songs with "Silver Spray" or "Silver Fountain" in their titles were common in the late 1870's and early 1880's. Some of them were doubtless inspired by the award-winning fountain designed by Frederic Bartholdi for the Philadelphia Centennial Exposition of 1876. Sousa's schottische was dedicated to a Washington acquaintance, Charles F. Eaton.[3]

MSS: N/A
Pub: Shaw (pi) ; Coleman (orch)
©: Pi: Shaw 26Oct1878; not ren
Orch: Coleman 28Dec1889; ren JPS 18Aug1917

WITH PLEASURE (1912)
Dance hilarious

This short, syncopated composition was dedicated "to the members of the Huntingdon Valley Country Club" of Philadel-

---

[3] This is an assumption. The sheet music is inscribed: "To C. F. Eaton, Washington, D.C." Washington directories of the 1870's list a Charles F. Eaton, messenger/clerk in the U.S. Treasury Department. He lived in the southeastern section of the city, as did Sousa. Bartholdi's fountain, incidentally, is now located in Washington in a park near the Capitol.

phia. Sousa was a member of this organization and spent many of his leisure hours in athletic activities there while the Sousa Band was engaged in nearby Willow Grove Park. "With Pleasure" later became part of a suite which Sousa called *The American Maid* (1913), and it is possible that he used it in a revised edition of the operetta of the same name. In concerts by the Sousa Band it was sometimes programmed as "Dance Hilarious."

MSS: a) Bd 10pp; 8Sep1912 Willow Grove, Pa. [LC]
b) Orch 11pp; 12Nov1912 Great Barrington, Mass. [LC]
Pub: Church
©: Pi: Church 16Nov1912; ren JvMS 7May1940
Bd: Church 29Nov1912; ren JvMS 7May1940
Orch: Church 30Dec1912; ren JvMS 7May1940

HUMORESQUES

The humoresques prove dramatically that Sousa was a master showman. His perception of the musical tastes of his country is obvious in reading the titles of his humoresques and fantasies. In particular, the study of the humoresques gives considerable insight into the phenomenal success of the Sousa Band. Sousa saw great value in bringing popular melodies to the people in a humorous manner. Of the fourteen humoresques, none was published or copyrighted. In this way, they were kept exclusively for the Sousa Band.

Sousa did not compose all the humoresques used by his band. Some were written by Herman Bellstedt or another of the band's arrangers, but the most successful ones were written by Sousa himself. Because all the humoresques used by Sousa were either done by him or at his direction, it is reasonable to credit him with the development of the form. As developed by Sousa, the humoresque was in no way similar to forms used by classical composers. It was constructed in one of three ways, with sound effects and individual comedy added. First, it might be a series of humorous variations on a well-known melody, with fragments of other songs added where appropriate. Second, it might be a series of songs which had a common subject in their titles (such as "drinking" songs), or a series of unrelated songs collated in such a way that their titles would tell a story. Third, it might be a series of showpieces for various instruments to give the performers an opportunity to "ham it up." The most outstanding of all the Sousa humoresques "Showing Off before Company," was of this type.

Sousa used the humoresque more effectively than anyone else for two basic reasons. First, there were few musicians of Sousa's stature — and with his subtle wit — who were inclined to use humor in their music to any appreciable degree. Second, the Sousa Band was an aggregation of showmen. Sousa chose his band from a large number of fine musicians. All other talents being equal, showmanship made the difference.

It is tragic that these humoresques — masterfully and tastefully constructed — were not preserved for future generations. They represent a minor art form which is typically American and distinctively Sousa's. For these reasons, they are among his most important works.

AMONG MY SOUVENIRS (1928)

This humoresque was based upon the popular song of the same name by Horatio Nicholls and Edgar Leslie. It included several other popular songs interwoven with the Nicholls-Leslie song. Actually a humorous paraphrase, it relied more on program notes for wit than did most of the other Sousa humoresques. The 1928 programs described it as follows:

The Nicholls song, "Among My Souvenirs," is lengthened into a sketch. Among his souvenirs is a photograph, letters and a broken heart, and, as he meditates, he goes back before the broken hearted time and remembers when he and she were softly singing "Twinkling Stars Are Laughing at You and Me," and then his mind reverts to the time when he was "Seeing Her Home," recalling the songs of years gone by at "Aunt

110

Dinah's Quilting Party" — he was "Seeing Nellie Home," and then he travels to the Far East, and visions of "The Road to Mandalay" come to him — from that, he meditates on the "Sweet Mysteries of Life" and then comes the closing picture that he is once more "Among His Souvenirs."

MSS: Bd 32pp; 17May1928 Sands Pt. [LC]
Not pub or ©

THE BAND CAME BACK (1895)

Perhaps for lack of a better description at the time it was written, this piece was billed as a "fantastic episode." It was always programmed as the first number after intermission in order to catch the audience by surprise.

The house lights were turned off, revealing an empty stage. Slowly and deliberately, the musicians entered singly, in pairs, or in trios. Each played some popular tune upon entering, with the musicians onstage sometimes providing accompaniment for those coming on. After all were seated, Sousa made his appearance for the finale. The finale was originally "The Star Spangled Banner," but this was later changed to "Semper Fidelis" or one of the other popular Sousa marches.

In format, the piece was a reverse of the earlier humoresque "Good-Bye" (1892). It was so well received that it was completely revised in 1919 and called "Showing Off before Company." The musicians' parts amounted to sheets of paper with abbreviated instructions. They are to be found in the portion of the Sousa Band library which is now in the custody of the University of Illinois. The parts read as follows:

1. Flute plays "Listen to the Mocking Bird"
2. Country band
3. Horn quartet
4. Post Horn Galop
5. Baritone sax solo over bassi rhythm
6. Trumpet call
7. Ends up with "The Star Spangled Banner."

MSS: Bd 12pp; 28Feb1895 New York City [UI]
Not pub or ©

FOLLOW THE SWALLOW (1926)

Sousa used this humoresque on the 1926 and 1927 tours, primarily as an encore. It was based on the song "Follow the Swallow," which Eddie Cantor made popular in the Broadway show *Kid Boots*. The music was by Ray Henderson, and the words were by Billy Rose. The theme was played with jazz variations, introducing other melodies suggestive of the swallow's flight from north to south. Among these were "Linger Awhile," "The Flowers That Bloom in the Spring" (from *The Mikado*), a sketch from Offenbach's *Gaîté Parisienne,* and "Home Sweet Home."

MSS: Bd 28pp; 1Jun1926 Sands Pt. [LC]
Not pub or ©

GALLAGHER AND SHEAN (1923)

Gallagher and Shean were two well-known vaudeville comedians who had their own jolly theme song. To this theme Sousa added several other appropriately titled songs to paint a musical picture of their familiar comedy routines. The result was one of Sousa's funniest humoresques, enjoying great popularity during the 1923-24 season.

The additional songs were "Yes, We Have No Bananas," "Good-Night Ladies," "Three O'Clock in the Morning," "Carolina in the Morning," "We Won't Be Home until Morning," "Home Sweet Home," and "Drink to Me Only with Thine Eyes." Sousa's instrumentation was clever, especially in the imitation of the popular line, "Positively, Mr. Gallagher; absolutely, Mr. Shean." Several newspaper reviewers remarked that the instruments "literally talked."

MSS: a) Bd 21pp; 4Jul1923 Sands Pt. [LC]
b) Addenda to bd 7pp; nd np [LC]
Not pub or ©

GOOD-BYE (1892)

This piece was the Sousa Band's answer to Haydn's "Farewell Symphony." In "Good-Bye," the players go on strike because of the conductor's unjust criticism.

The rebellion starts as the oboe player

stands, plays "I'm Going Back to Dixie," and then strolls off stage. The others then leave singly or in groups, playing "The Soldier's Farewell," "Good-Bye Sweetheart," "The Last Rose of Summer," "Comrades," "Bye Bye My Honey I'm Gone," and "Then You'll Remember Me." Finally, the flutes and drums march out to "The Girl I Left Behind Me." All leave with solemn expressions, but the conductor ignores them and insolently keeps time with their melodies as they leave.

The musicians then remember that the next day is payday. A solitary player walks back playing "Annie Laurie." The others then come back in such a rush that they nearly stumble over each other, joining in on the same melody for the finale.

"Good-Bye" was a feature of the Sousa Band's first tour and was such a success that variations of it were used off and on until the late 1920's. On some occasions, local guest conductors would act Sousa's part.

MSS: Bd 36pp in bound volume; 5Feb1892
        Washington, D.C. [LC]
Not pub or ©

A LITTLE PEACH IN AN ORCHARD GREW (1885)

Of the fourteen known Sousa humoresques, this was the earliest. It would be totally unknown had he not mentioned it in occasional interviews.

MSS: N/A
Not pub or ©

LOOK FOR THE SILVER LINING (1922)

On the cover of the conductor's manuscript to this humoresque, Sousa wrote:

"Look for the Silver Lining (Kern)
and some extra wadding
Put together by John Philip Sousa"

Based on the song of the same name and other songs from the musical play *Sally*, by Jerome Kern, this work includes several melodic variations and appropriate sound effects. Also included are "There Is a Tavern in the Town" and "Stein Song."

MSS: Bd 38pp; 30May1922 Sands Pt. [LC]
Not pub or ©

THE MINGLING OF THE WETS AND THE DRYS (1926)

In 1922, Sousa had A. J. Garing, one of the band's arrangers, write a humoresque called "The Wets." Apparently it did not meet expectations. Sousa revised it, but in programming it that season he gave credit to Garing.

The intent of "The Wets" was to lampoon Prohibition, and it caused so much comment that Sousa revised it a second time in 1926, including more jazz rhythms. The new version was called "The Mingling of the Wets and the Drys." This year, a humorous story was added to the printed program. In this story, a "wet" and a "dry" go out together. They drink tea and water until early in the morning, longing for the good old days before Prohibition.

In addition to the melodies, some of which are spoofed by a small jazz ensemble, the percussion section adds the sounds of clinking glasses, popping corks, seltzer bottles, etc.

The songs used are: "Hail, Hail, the Gang's All Here," "Jingle Bells," "Hail to the Chief," "How Dry I Am," "Little Brown Jug," "Here's to No. 1 Drink Her Down," "Down Deep in the Cellar," "There'll Be a Hot Time in the Old Town," "Down Where the Wurtzberger Flows," "Comin' through the Rye," "Brown October Ale," "After the Ball," "Stumbling," "The Old Oaken Bucket," "We Won't Go Home until Morning," "The Storm" (from *William Tell* Overture), "Have a Little Drink," "Good Bye Forever," and "The Soldier's Chorus" (from *Faust*).

MSS: a) ("The Wets") Bd 36pp; nd np but
        presumably 1922 [LC]
      b) ("The Mingling of the Wets and the
        Drys") Bd 29pp; 1Jun1926 Sands Pt.
        [LC]
      c) (Addenda to "The Mingling of the
        Wets and the Drys") Bd 5pp;
        21Aug1926 Phila. [LC]
Not pub or ©

OH, HOW I'VE WAITED FOR YOU (1926)

Using a number of "waiting" songs, Sousa built this humoresque around the song

"Oh, How I've Waited for You," from the Broadway show *By the Way* by Nat Ayer and Harry Carlton. The additional songs were "Wait Til the Clouds Roll By," "Oh Boy," "Wait for the Wagon," and "Waiting at the Church." It was used sparingly in the late 1920's, usually as an encore.

MSS: Bd 27pp; 20May1926 Sands Pt. [LC] Not pub or ©

SALLY
(See LOOK FOR THE SILVER LINING)

SHOWING OFF BEFORE COMPANY
(1919)

If Sousa's Band could be remembered for one unique number, it would probably be "Showing Off before Company." This humoresque exemplified Sousa's superb showmanship and was one of his most sensational presentations.

The work was a revitalized version of Sousa's 1895 humoresque, "The Band Came Back," and was used extensively in the early 1920's. As with "The Band Came Back," it was offered just after intermission. After the house was darkened, the curtain was drawn to reveal an empty stage. The musicians came to the front of the stage alone or in groups, each playing a familiar selection in a manner which displayed individual and collective talents. The audience was kept in a stage of expectancy for a full twenty minutes until Sousa made his appearance in the finale.

The music and the order changed from year to year. Therefore no particular routine could be called "Showing Off before Company" exclusively. On a separate page enclosed in the conductor's score, however, are Sousa's own handwritten notes which outlined the preferred routine for one particular year, presumably 1919. Using accounts from newspaper reviews as a guide, it could be described as follows.

Backstage, the cornets, trumpets and drums play "I've Got Some Years to Do This In," and the remainder of the band joins in with "Keep the Home Fires Burning." The harpist makes the first entrance,

playing "Annie Laurie," and accompanies those to follow. The oboes make their appearance and play "The Cuckoo Song," giving an imitation of bagpipes. The first clarinets then enter and play a harmonized arrangement of "Pizzicato Polka." Next, the entire sousaphone section lumbers in, playing "In the Deep Cellar," and ending up with low notes at the bottom of their range. (When Indian John Kuhn was the soloist, he ended his contribution with a brilliant cadenza, descending note by note and laughing heartily before his final deep tone.) The flutes and piccolos then enter and play "The Golden Robin Polka." The trombones are next with "When the Clouds Roll By." Next, the cornet soloist makes a spectacular entrance with "The Post Horn Galop." (When Frank Simon was the solo cornetist, he used a specially made post horn. On the final chord, he would show his amazing breath control by holding a high note for a full minute.) The French horn quartet then makes its appearance with "Drink to Me Only with Thine Eyes." The next entrance is staggered; the double-bell euphoniums come in first, followed at four-measure intervals by three cornets. Four different melodies which harmonize with each other are played simultaneously. As the last cornet enters, they all break into "Hail, Hail, the Gang's All Here." The saxophone section then comes on and plays jazz arrangements of such songs as "Ja Da," "I Wish I Could," or "Hindoustan" for several minutes. The remainder of the clarinets and cornets, plus the trumpets, then come on the scene and play "I Want to Be Happy." The bassoons are next, rendering variations of "Yankee Doodle." The last to appear is the percussion section. While the xylophonist plays "I'll Say She Does," his partners add a lively and showy accompaniment in the background. With everyone thus received and in their seats, they all strike up the last strain of Sousa's "Semper Fidelis" march. The conductor marches to his podium and conducts the last few measures as the grand finale.

Sousa once explained his reasons for putting this humoresque together:

"I arranged that for two reasons. First of all, it gave all of my band members a chance for an individual appearance and a bit of individual applause, and then it gives them a certain amount of self-confidence too — it takes away that self-consciousness a soloist feels at first.

"And then I had another reason. People who do not know a great deal about the techniques of music, yet enjoy it greatly, are often very curious as to the tonal qualities of certain instruments, and the manner of playing them. When the band as a whole is playing, it is impossible to tell the lay listeners to distinguish the individual voices of the instruments, and often they cannot see how those in the rear rows are played. After they hear this musical mixture they will always be able to hunt through the medley of sounds that make up the whole and pick out the individual's work."[1]

MSS: Bd 46pp; 20May1919 np [LC]
Not pub or ©

SMILES (1919)

To construct this humoresque, Sousa made several clever and amusing variations of Roberts and Callahan's popular tune, "Smiles," and added fragments of many familiar airs. The piece was used as an encore, usually following "Showing Off before Company."

MSS: N/A
Not pub or ©

THE STAG PARTY (circa 1885)

In the absence of Sousa's manuscript, there is confusion concerning the date of this composition. It was written while he was conductor of the U.S. Marine Band and was later used occasionally by the Sousa Band between 1892 and 1896. One 1896 program at Manhattan Beach gave the date as 1885, but band parts in the Sousa Band library at the University of Illinois are dated 1890 by Marine Band copyists.

The piece features sound effects and is descriptive of a gay party of students on a night out, singing familiar refrains. The 1893 programs give a synopsis, as follows:

---

[1] *Cleveland Town Topics,* October 23, 1920.

"The good night to the ladies — Twelve o'clock — Around the festive board — The gentlemen persist in singing a well known air in a minor key — A young man, evidently engaged, softly sings 'Drink To Me Only With Thine Eyes.' As the fair one is not present, she is unable to grant the request. A member of the trombone family tells about a man in a cellar. The gentleman with the phenomenal bass voice continues the narrative — Moments of general hilarity follow — A Rhinelander hums a tune he loves. An American thinks 'Home, Sweet Home' will fit the same harmony. A Scotsman chimes in with 'Comin' Thro' the Rye,' bagpipe and all, while the representatives of the Clover Club insist that there is 'One More Bottle' — The guests join hands and sing 'Auld Lang Syne' — They are interrupted by a still, small voice — A convivial scion of the bassoon family murmurs something about somebody being his sweetheart — The guests announce their departure — The rolling home in the morning — A sleepy parent requests them 'not to make a noise or else they'll wake the baby.' They comply."

MSS: N/A
Not pub or ©

SWANEE (1920)

This humoresque was founded upon George Gershwin and Irving Caesar's song from the Broadway show *Sinbad*. Liberally sprinkled with unusual sound effects, it includes variations on the principal theme as well as "Hail, Hail, the Gang's All Here," "Listen to the Mocking Bird," "Dixie," and "Old Folks at Home." It was originally written in 1920, but Sousa revised it in 1928, using "Lassus Trombone" for the finale.

MSS: Bd 33pp; 10Jul1920 Sands Pt. [LC]
Not pub or ©

WAITING
(See OH, HOW I'VE WAITED FOR YOU)

THE WETS
(See THE MINGLING OF THE WETS AND THE DRYS)

WHAT DO YOU DO SUNDAY, MARY?
(1924)

This little-used humoresque featured copious sound effects and appropriately titled songs suggestive of how Mary might spend her Sunday. It is based on the song of the same name from the Broadway show *Poppy* by Stephen Jones and Irving Caesar.

MSS: a) Bd 31pp; 10May1924 Sands Pt. [LC]
　　　b) Addenda to bd 12pp; nd np [LC]
Not pub or ©

FANTASIES

Sousa's fantasies are divided into three groups, according to their instrumentation. Some are little more than medleys, but all received original treatment, from variations on one or more themes to the processing of several compositions, as was done in the humoresques. (But unlike the humoresques, they do not have the element of humor.) Some are highly imaginative and were usually well received by audiences.

A few additional fantasies performed by the Sousa Band cannot be considered Sousa compositions because they were not written out in full for the musicians. (These are distinguished by the word "Reference" beside the titles.) They were "head arrangements," or medleys in which the musicians made smooth transitions from one piece of printed music to another.

Fantasies for Band

(Reference) AN APPLICATION OF JAZZ TUNES (1924)

Prior to the more elaborate and refined "Jazz America" (1925), Sousa tested the public's reaction to a fantasy comprised entirely of jazz by stringing together this medley of syncopated melodies. It saw brief use at Willow Grove Park in 1924. It was also programmed as "Collocation, 'Limehouse Blues,' and others."

MSS: (If any) N/A
Not pub or ©

ASSEMBLY OF THE ARTISANS (1925)

The motif of this work is readily seen from the titles of the music used: "The Tinker's Song" from *Robin Hood* (De-Koven), "The Anvil Chorus" from *Il Trovatore* (Verdi), "The Armourer's Song" from *Robin Hood,* and "Theme" from *Polovstian Dances* (Borodin). It was apparently a revision of an earlier medley-fantasy, "The Workman's Compensation."

MSS: Inserts to several bd parts in Sousa's hand; nd np [UI]
Not pub or ©

THE BLENDING OF THE BLUE AND THE GRAY (1887)

"Dedicated to THE MARYLAND LINE on their return to Virginia twenty-six years after (1861-1887)" is the inscription on the sheet music of this fantasy, which bears no publisher's name. Apparently some patron or perhaps Sousa himself subsidized the printing. It was recorded in 1890 by the U.S. Marine Band when Sousa was leader, but it is not the same as the composition known as "The Blue and Gray Patrol," which was recorded by Sousa's Band in 1902 and 1903. A Sousa Band program of July 4, 1894, refers to it as a patrol, and it included: "The Reveille," "Maryland, My Maryland," "Carry Me Back to Ole Virginny," "Gay and Happy," "The Star Spangled Banner," "Dixie," and "Yankee Doodle."

MSS: N/A
Pub: ? (for pi)
Not ©

(Reference) A BOUQUET OF BELOVED INSPIRATIONS (1921)

This was a medley of orchestral masterpieces which were transcribed for band by various arrangers and pieced together by Sousa. The fact that the sequence varied suggests that is was given very little if any original treatment. The original medley included excerpts from *Carmen* (Bizet), *Invitation to the Dance* (Weber), *Spring Song* (Mendelssohn), *William Tell* Overture (Rossini), and at least one other. Some were deleted and others were added later, including excerpts from *Semiramide* Overture (Rossini) and *Poet and Peasant* Overture (Suppe). The conductor's score consisted merely of a melody outline.

MSS: Bd 8pp; nd np [LC]
Not pub or ©

THE CHARIOT RACE
(See Descriptive Pieces)

(Reference) A DAY AT GREAT LAKES (1917)

Similar in form to "A Bouquet of Beloved Inspirations," this was a medley of songs by several composers which was not written out in full. With sound effects, it suggested the various activities taking place at the U.S. Naval Training Station at Great Lakes, Illinois, during the course of a day. It was usually listed as a descriptive piece and was put together for and used by the Great Lakes "Jackie" Band when Sousa was musical director. The band made good use of it on Liberty Loan promotion tours. One of the selections was a currently popular song, "Throw Me a Rose," sung by one of the sailors in the band, and it usually brought a shower of roses from girls in the audience.

MSS: (if any) N/A
Not pub or ©

THE FANCY OF THE TOWN (1921)

A decade of popular songs was represented in this collection, ending with a march Sousa had proudly written for the newly formed American Legion. The inscription on the lengthy conductor's score reads: "The Fancy of the Town (1911-1920)" and included are the following compositions: "I Love a Lassie," "A Little Love, a Little Kiss," "Tango Argentino" ("Come, Le Va"), "Tipperary," "Poor Butterfly," "Over There," "Missouri Waltz," "Dardanella," "Me-Ow," and Sousa's "Comrades of the Legion."

MSS: Bd 69pp; 17Mar1921 Sands Pt. [LC]
Not pub or ©

(Reference) FIVE LEAVES FROM THE HYMNAL (1919)

This was a medley of five hymns used on only a few occasions during the 1919 tour of the Sousa Band. Since no manuscripts or band parts are known to exist, it is assumed that several stock hymn arrangements were used with little if any original treatment by Sousa.

MSS: (if any) N/A
Not pub or ©

THE HIGHBROWS AND THE LOWBROWS
(See A STUDY IN RHYTHMS)

IN PARLOR AND STREET (1880)

This was one of the first Sousa compositions written after he assumed leadership of the U.S. Marine Band in October, 1880. It is a cleverly arranged medley which was intended to bring the Marine Band concerts up to date with well-known opera and operetta excerpts and popular songs of the day. As the title suggests, the fantasy includes music heard both in the parlor and on the street. One of the pieces used was Sousa's own comical song, "Smick, Smack, Smuck" (1878). One holograph dating 1888 indicates that the fantasy might have been revised at that time.

MSS: a) Several bd parts in Sousa's hand; one dated 4Oct1888 St. Louis [UI]
     b) Insert to 4th clarinet part in Sousa's hand; nd np [Morton]
Not pub or ©

IN PULPIT AND PEW (1917)

Similar to "Five Leaves from the Hymnal" and "Songs of Grace and Songs of Glory," this was a mélange of hymns which Sousa used almost exclusively on Sunday. It included "Onward, Christian Soldiers," "There Is a Green Hill Far Away," "Jesus, Lover of My Soul," "Sun of My Soul," "Abide with Me," and "Adeste Fideles."

MSS: N/A
Not pub or ©

IN THE REALM OF THE DANCE (1902)
(IN THE REALM OF THE WALTZ)

Several waltzes of Linke, Bosc, and Danne were united in this fantasy, which was well received for many seasons. In his autobiography, Sousa tells of a coincidence in which all three of those composers happened to be in Paris sitting together in the front row of a Sousa Band concert when the number was programmed. Sousa observed their unusual interest but did not learn their identities until after the concert.

MSS: N/A
Not pub or ©

JAZZ AMERICA (1925)

The significance of this composition, approximately thirty minutes long, is that Sousa was recognizing jazz as an acceptable and original American musical form. In its various revisions, he employed twelve or more syncopated tunes and welded them into an interesting selection. In 1924 he had experimented with a brief collocation called "An Application of Jazz Tunes," and its success undoubtedly led to "Jazz America."

MSS: Bd 38pp; 9Jun1925 Sands Pt. [LC]
Not pub or ©

LIMEHOUSE BLUES
(See AN APPLICATION OF JAZZ TUNES)

THE MERRY-MERRY CHORUS (1923)

From interviews with reporters, as described in articles pasted in the Sousa Band press books, it was learned that Sousa was championing the opera and operetta chorus in this collection. He made remarks to the effect that operas and operettas were written primarily for the exploitation of star performers, and he created this selection to spotlight the often-neglected choruses.

MSS: Bd 9pp; 10Apr1923 New York City [LC]
Not pub or ©

MUSIC OF THE MINUTE (1922)

This fantasy was construed by the press as being jazz, but it could more accurately be described as a medley of popular songs, many of them syncopated. It was used until 1925, at which time it was replaced by "Jazz America."

Sousa was certainly up to date in the programming of this type of music for band concerts, catching audiences by surprise. From one newspaper account:

> ...Gone was the solemnity inspired by classical members. The first measure of the fantasy, "Music of the Minute," arranged by Sousa caused raised eyebrows and intensive listening among the conservative persons in the audience. As the number continued, the entire air of the concert changed. Sousa was playing jazz! That syncopated rhythm which has invaded the precincts of the purely classical was being presented to quarter of a century admirers by the ever-adaptable Sousa. Someone has said that the true test of the ability to withstand age is the faculty of appreciating and understanding the present. That John Philip Sousa has survived the discrepancies of the years is evidenced by his presentation of modern jazz as well as by the vigor of his personality.[1]

MSS: Bd 41pp; 2May1922 Sands Pt. [LC]
Not pub or ©

A MUSICAL PANORAMA OF THE NATIONS
(See THE SALUTE OF THE NATIONS)

AN OLD-FASHIONED GIRL (1922)

Not among Sousa's more successful fan-

---

[1] Undated clipping in the career scrapbook of soprano Nora Fauchald. Probably the *Bloomington* (Ind.) *Pantagraph,* November 4, 1924.

tasies, this one was utilized as an encore on the 1922 tour and infrequently thereafter. The music used by Sousa and the Sousa Band has not been located for study, but it was probably a series of variations on the popular song of the same name.

MSS: N/A
Not pub or ©

ON THE 5:15 (1916)

With appropriate changes of tempo and the addition of sound effects, this fantasy was constructed around the Tin Pan Alley song of the same name. It was little used, even during the year of its introduction.

MSS: Bd 15pp; 14Mar1916 New York City
   [UI]
Not pub or ©

ON WITH THE DANCE (1923)

Sousa Band programs state that this was a fantasy of familiar dance melodies "strung together by Sousa." It included "The Torchlight Dance" (Meyerbeer), "Until My Luck Comes Rolling Along" (George M. Cohan), "La Cinquantaine" (Marie), "Rigaudon de Dardanus" (Rameau), and "Aboriginal Indian Theme" (traditional).

MSS: Bd 6pp inc; nd np [LC]
Not pub or ©

(Reference) OVER THE FOOTLIGHTS IN NEW YORK (1897)

Sousa hurriedly pieced together this fantasy with a minimum of work, but it became one of his most popular numbers for several seasons. His unusual conductor's score consisted of one bar of music followed by the names of several songs. Apparently a copyist or arranger used this as a guide and wrote out the band parts, which are at the University of Illinois. Notes given in Sousa Band programs of 1898 explained the composition in this manner:

  Paderewski at Carnegie Hall; "El Capitan" at the Broadway Theatre; "Lucia" at the Metropolitan Opera House; "The Belle of New York" at the Casino; "The Girl

from Paris" at the Herald Square Theatre; "Faust" ballet at Koster & Bial's; "Trovatore" at the Academy of Music; and "Sousa's Band at Manhattan Beach."

MSS: Bd sketch 1pp; 13Nov1897 np [LC]
Not pub or ©

PATROL OF THE UNITED KINGDOM
(See ROSE, THISTLE AND SHAMROCK)

ROSE, THISTLE AND SHAMROCK
(1901)
(ROSE, SHAMROCK AND THISTLE)

Composed expressly for the Sousa Band's tour of Britain in 1901, this composition was also known as "Patrol of the United Kingdom." The rose was in honor of Canada, the thistle for Scotland, and the shamrock for Ireland.

MSS: a) Bd 9pp; 7Sep1901 np [UI]
   b) Pi 3pp; 10Oct1901 Glasgow, Scotland
   [UI]
Pub: Church (for bd)
Not ©

THE SALUTE OF THE NATIONS (1893)

This is a compilation of patriotic or typical melodies of countries represented at the Columbian Exposition, or Chicago World's Fair, of 1893. It commences with a fanfare and ends with "The Star Spangled Banner" ("The Star Spangled Banner" has variations à la Wagner's *Tannhauser* Overture). The countries portrayed are Italy, Switzerland, Germany, Russia, France, England, Scotland, and the United States, in that order.

Although the original manuscript is entitled "The Salute of the Nations to the Columbian Exposition," the piece saw further use. At the St. Louis Exposition in October, 1893, it was programmed as "The Salute of the Nations to the St. Louis Exposition." The following year it was programmed simply as a "grand mélange" and called "The Salute of the Nations" and also "A Musical Panorama of the Nations." It was seldom (if ever) used after that.

MSS: Bd 34pp; 30Mar1893 Washington, D.C.
   [LC]
Not pub or ©

SHERIDAN'S RIDE
(See Descriptive Pieces)

(Reference) SONGS AND MARCHES THAT LIVE IN THE HEARTS OF AMERICA (1919)

In all likelihood, this was a series of compositions played from stock arrangements in a given sequence without the necessity of arranging. Among other melodies, it included "Keep the Home Fires Burning" and Sousa's march, "Semper Fidelis."

MSS: (if any) N/A
Not pub or ©

SONGS OF GRACE AND SONGS OF GLORY (1892)
(SONGS OF GRACE AND GLORY)

No Sunday concerts were scheduled on the first two tours of the U.S. Marine Band in 1891 and 1892. When the Sousa Band was organized later in 1892, however, it was agreed by all parties concerned that Sunday concerts were necessary to insure financial success. Probably because of church opposition to Sabbath business at that time, Sousa arranged this group of hymns to be used as the opening number on Sunday concerts. It included: "Rock of Ages," "Beulah Land," "Chant of the Greek Church," "Steal Away," "Mary and Martha," "Lead, Kindly Light," "Glory E. Laudamus" (later omitted), "Oh Day of God" (later omitted), "The Palms," "Nearer My God to Thee," and "The Sevenfold Amen."

MSS: a) Bd 24pp in bound volume;
30Dec1892 Washington, D.C. [LC]
b) ("Lead, Kindly Light") inserts to bd parts in Sousa's hand; nd np [Morton]
Not pub or ©

SOUNDS FROM THE REVIVALS (1876)

Shortly after playing in the Offenbach Orchestra at the Centennial Exhibition in Philadelphia, Sousa may have been commissioned to compose this mélange of hymns for the centennial. Although he scored it for band, he was not to conduct a band for another four years. However,

one of the music contractors for whom he worked was Simon Hassler, and Hassler conducted band concerts regularly at the centennial. Therefore, "Sounds from the Revivals" might have been written for Hassler. It included: "Jesus, Lover of My Soul," "Nearer My God to Thee," "Come Holy Spirit," "Hold the Fort," and "[In the] Sweet Bye and Bye." The band parts are in the Sousa Library at the University of Illinois, but the work was rarely if ever performed by the Sousa Band.

MSS: Bd 16pp; 20Jul1876 Phila. [UI]
Not pub or ©

A STUDY IN RHYTHMS (1920)

The original version of this fantasy was a potpourri of classics, but it was later expanded to include popular songs which Sousa considered interesting rhythmically. Among the selections were: "Largo" (Handel), Sousa's variations on "Largo" in waltz tempo and called "Tempo di Valse," "Allegretto Scherzando" from *Symphony No. 8* (Beethoven), "Hungarian Rhapsody No. 2" (Liszt), "Sextet" from *Lucia* (Donizetti) played in ragtime, "Old Folks at Home" (Stephen Foster), and "Humoresque" (Dvorak).

MSS: Bd 50pp inc; nd np [LC]
Not pub or ©

TIPPERARY (1915)

An excellent description of this fantasy appeared in the *Seattle* (Wash.) *Post Intelligencer* of July 31, 1915.

What a great musician will do with a simple theme when it appeals to him Sousa demonstrates in his humoresque "Tipperary," which he played at the Metropolitan last night for an encore. The song is, in our minds, connected with the English and French armies. Sousa makes it a universal story. While the rhythm beats through the mingling sounds of instruments, you can hear the chants of the Hindus, the "Marseillaise," the tender songs of England, or Ireland, the wild, piercing tenor of Wales, the beat of drums, the whistle of fifes, the snatches of religious tunes. You see a lone Mulvaney sitting on a broken gun in the moonlight singing softly, "It's a Long Way to Tipperary." You hear a rollicking chorus in the distance curling out the same song. A Frenchman croons it above a wounded comrade. Afar off a big Highlander burrs the words in a mellow bass. The different Shires of England cry the song boldly. You can almost recognize the dialects. In a word, you get a complete picture of the war, with its attendant emotions. Sousa has done this with a simple ballad. It is a stroke of genius. Perhaps no other band could get out of it what he does, but it will always be effective, even commonly played.

MSS: N/A
Not pub or ©

THE TROOPING OF THE COLORS
(See Other Vocal Works)

TYROLIENNE

Various instruments of the band, particularly the cornets and clarinets, are featured in this work. It is a succession of variations on the traditional French theme of the same name. The only known manuscripts, the work of copyists, are in the library of the U.S. Marine Band. Sousa presumably wrote it as a showpiece for some of his better musicians when he was leader of the Marine Band, so the date may be affixed broadly as 1880-92.

MSS: N/A
Not pub or ©

WHEN MY DREAMS COME TRUE (1929)

One of Sousa's rarely played fantasies, this featured several variations on the popular song of the same name. It also included two other popular melodies: "I'll Always Be in Love with You" and "He's Going to Marry Yum Yum" (from *The Mikado*).

MSS: Bd 28pp; "8Aug" Sands Pt. [LC]
Not pub or ©

(Reference) THE WORKMAN'S COMPENSATION

An early fantasy from which "Assembly of the Artisans" (1925) probably evolved, this was a medley of songs suggestive of several crafts. The peculiar conductor's score consisted only of three printed parts glued together: "The Jolly Coppersmith" (Peters), "Boccaccio Selection" (Suppe), and "The Clock Store" (Orth). With the score, now at the University of Illinois Sousa library, is a sack of band parts labeled " 'Workman's Compensation' and extra parts." In addition to the parts for the above songs, parts to "The Anvil Chorus" (from Verdi's *Il Trovatore*) and selections from *Robin Hood* (DeKoven) are in the sack, suggesting that these were also part of the medley at one time.

MSS: Bd consists only of sequence of published selections pasted together in folio; nd np [UI]
Not pub or ©

Fantasies for Orchestra

IN THE SWEET BYE AND BYE (1876)

The following is quoted from an 1898 newspaper interview with Milton Nobles, the noted American actor. Sousa had been musical director of Nobles's touring stage production, *Bohemians and Detectives (The Phoenix)*, in 1875.

"At the close of the 1875 season Sousa returned to Washington and I came to Philadelphia. During the following year — the Centennial season — Simon Hassler came into my room in the Continental Hotel one

day, and some of Sousa's music was scattered over the bed. Picking it up he became interested with the fine arrangement, and as a result sent for Sousa to come to Philadelphia. He secured for him a place for two weeks as second violinist in the Offenbach concerts in the Centennial grounds.

"About that time Lotta was enjoying intense popularity and had made a big hit singing 'In the Sweet Bye and Bye.' Hassler wanted an arrangement for the song for his orchestra, and sending for Sousa asked him if he could in a couple of weeks make an arrangement. Sousa took the song to his room on Tuesday, and the following Monday brought it to Hassler, and in it had arranged a solo for every one of the twenty-two pieces of the orchestra, including the bass drum."[1]

MSS: N/A
Not pub or ©

THE INTERNATIONAL CONGRESS
(1876)

At the request of Jacques Offenbach, in whose orchestra Sousa played at the Centennial Exhibition in Philadelphia, Sousa based this fantasy on national airs. It commences with a fugue on "Yankee Doodle" and ended with "The Star Spangled Banner," arranged in the style of Wagner's *Tannhauser* Overture. The remaining airs are: "Hail Columbia," "God Save the Queen," "The Marseillaise," "The Wearing of the Green," "The Watch on the Rhine," "Russian Hymn," "Finland Folk Song," "Australian Hymn," "Polish Song,"

---

[1] *Philadelphia Times,* February, 1898. (Loose clipping in the Sousa Band press book of 1897-98.)

"Cossack's Lullaby," "Danish Hymn," "Italian Song," "Italian Patriotic March," "Greek National Air," and "National Dance of Poland."

Sousa made a band arrangement in 1882 for use at U.S. Marine Band concerts. When it was published in 1887 he refined the arrangement, and the manuscript of the later arrangement was discovered in a trunk at his Sands Point estate in 1965.

MSS: Bd 65pp in bound volume; 19Jan1887
     Washington, D.C. [LC]
Pub: Coleman
©: Bd: Coleman 7Oct1887 again Fischer
     15Jul1913; ren JvMS 14Aug1940

MEDLEY (1877)

An incomplete conductor's score of this fantasy was discovered in 1965. It is a medley of popular songs of the day, and at the top of the first page is the inscription "First performed at the Chestnut Street Theatre on the 27th of February, 1877."

MSS: Orch 2pp inc; 23Feb1877 Phila. [LC]
Not pub or ©

Fantasies for Individual Instruments

ADAMSONIA (1879)

Four popular songs by the contemporary composer Adams are included in this piece. It was published as sheet music and also in the 1879 collection *Evening Pastime.*

MSS: N/A (for vi or flute with pi)
Pub: Shaw
©: Covered by © of the collection

HOME SWEET HOME (1879)

These variations on the familiar song by Bishop and Payne were published as sheet music and also in the collection *Evening Pastime.*

MSS: N/A (for vi or flute with pi)
Pub: Shaw
©: Vi or flute with pi: Shaw
    29May1879; not ren

OUT OF WORK (1880)

This fantasy is of the "theme with variations" category. "Out of Work" was a popular song of the day.

MSS: N/A (for vi or flute with pi)
Pub: Stoddart
©: Vi or flute with pi: Stoddart
    5Feb1880; not ren

UNDER THE EAVES (1880)

Like "Out of Work," this fantasy was based on a currently popular tune and was published as a companion piece.

MSS: N/A (for vi or flute with pi)
Pub: Stoddart
©: Vi or flute with pi: Stoddart
    5Feb1880; not ren

INCIDENTAL MUSIC

BOHEMIANS AND DETECTIVES
(See THE PHOENIX)

CHEER UP (1916)

The musical review *Cheer Up* was the second of three New York Hippodrome extravaganzas for which Sousa composed some of the music. The producers were successful in surpassing *Hip Hip Hooray* of the previous year. An actual locomotive drew several railroad cars across the stage, elephants and teams of horses were used, and hundreds of performers were featured. The show was in the three acts, appropriately called Cheer One, Two, and Three. At times several attractions were playing simultaneously.

The *Land of Liberty,* a historical pageant, climaxed Cheer Two. Sousa composed and arranged this part of the music, and R. H. "Bunny" Burnside was responsible for the stage play. Originally, the pageant was to be called *The Making of a Nation.* It was, as one manuscript indicates, "an allegory," and countries whose immigrants helped mold the United States were recognized. The nations saluted were: Spain, France, England, Ireland, Scotland, Holland, Denmark, Sweden, Italy, Germany, Hungary, Russia, Poland, and Finland. Fifty-nine historical figures, from Christopher Columbus to Woodrow Wilson, were portrayed.

Although the first manuscript is dated 1916, the show was not staged until the fall of 1917. Sousa was present at only a few performances because of navy duties and commitments with the Sousa Band at Willow Grove Park. He was represented in Cheer One, however, in a scene which depicted a New York Hippodrome workshop. The actor portraying Sousa was Joseph Frohoff.

MSS: a) Orch 80pp; 26Sep1916 Sands Pt. [LC]
b) (Prelude) 9pp; 8Aug1917 Rochester, N.Y. [LC]
c) (Prelude to Scene) v/orch 3pp; 9Aug1917 Attica, N.Y. "en route" [LC]
d) ("Battle Cry of Freedom") orch 3pp; 14Aug1917 New York City [LC]
Not pub or ©

EVERYTHING (1918)

The twelfth act of the lavish fourteen-act New York Hippodrome review *Everything* was the colorful pageant, "In Lampland." Sousa arranged and composed music for the act, which depicted a wedding scene based on the theme "Lamps of the World." Exotic dances of Greece, France, India, Japan, Egypt, Burma, and Denmark were featured.

MSS: N/A
Not pub or ©

HIP HIP HOORAY (1915)

In the summer of 1915, while Sousa and his band were performing at the Panama-Pacific Exposition in San Francisco, they were engaged by the impresario Charles Dillingham for a New York Hippodrome extravaganza to be known as *Hip Hip Hooray.* Dillingham and his producer, R. H. Burnside, gave New York the most elaborate stage production it had ever seen. The newly built Hippodrome was the world's largest playhouse, and reviewers almost ran out of superlatives describing the show. With its elaborate staging, *Hip Hip Hooray* was an extravaganza in the truest sense of the word.

The Sousa Band played a double role in the show. As one act it stood in concert formation on the stage and played a short concert. Then, instead of the usual orchestra, it played in the pit to accompany most of the remaining acts. For this thirty to forty bandsmen were used.

Sousa's extracurricular salute was his march, "The New York Hippodrome," and his contribution to *Hip Hip Hooray* was his "Ballet of the States" (also called "March of the States" and "Sisterhood of the States"). This was used to accompany a ballet in which each of the forty-eight states was represented by a sextet of dancing girls. Sousa arranged and composed characteristic tunes for each state. The act was climaxed with "The Stars and Stripes Forever"; this usually resulted in unrestrained shouts of approval.

The show brought many happy moments to Sousa and his band. It was their longest single engagement, spread out over two seasons. The show ran from September, 1915, to June, 1916, in New York, and then from October, 1916, to March, 1917, on a tour of major eastern and midwestern cities. Sousa was held in high esteem by the 1,200 employees, and on his sixty-second birthday they presented him with a loving cup made from 1,200 dimes. One of the sidelights of the show was the hug and kiss traditionally bestowed on Sousa by the featured sopranos.

MSS: a) ("Sisterhood of the States") bd 40pp; 3Sep1915 Willow Grove, Pa. [UI]
b) (Addenda to "Sisterhood of the States") 4 pp; 13Jan1916 Boston [UI]
Not pub or ©

MATT MORGAN'S LIVING PICTURES
(1876)

In the spring of 1876 Sousa became conductor of Matt Morgan's unusual show which featured scenes posed by twenty girls, at least seven of whom were nude. It was billed as a "grand art exhibit of historical and mythological tableaux." Morgan, an artist for *Frank Leslie's Weekly*, directed the show and also painted the scenery. Sousa composed the short musical pieces that accompanied the poses. The scenes portrayed were "Choral Gatherers," "The Christian Martyr," "Cleopatra before Caesar," "The Destruction of Pompeii," "The Judgment of Paris," "Old Age," "Phryne before the Tribunal," "The Slave Market" ("The New Slave," or "The Slave Girl"), "The Shower of Gold," "Temptation of St. Anthony," and perhaps several others.

The show was probably the first of its kind in America, and it raised eyebrows wherever it played. Sousa joined the show in Washington and stayed with it for about nine weeks, traveling as far west as St. Louis.

MSS: a) ("Choral Gatherers") 1st vi/ conductor and French horn parts in Sousa's hand; nd np [UI]
b) ("Christian Martyr") viola and 2nd vi parts in Sousa's hand; nd np [UI]
c) ("Cleopatra before Caesar") several orch parts in Sousa's hand; nd np [UI]
d) ("The New Slave") French horn part in Sousa's hand; nd np [UI]
e) ("Old Age") 2nd vi part in Sousa's hand; nd np [UI]
f) ("Phryne before the Tribunal") several orch parts in Sousa's hand; nd np [UI]
Not pub or ©

OUR FLIRTATIONS (1880)

Our Flirtations, a three-act "society comedy," was one of the forerunners of the American musical comedy. Based on a play by James Bird Wilson, the plot revolved around the multitudinous flirtations of a merry party of picnickers and was interspersed with songs and dancing. Sousa composed and arranged the music, which included several popular songs of the day. *Our Flirtations* probably bore some similarity to an earlier "society comedy" called *Flirtation,* which played in Philadelphia late in 1876.[1]

---

[1] F. F. Mackay, a well-known Philadelphia comedian, was the principal character and man-

The most noteworthy remnant of this musical comedy is Sousa's march "Our Flirtation," although several other songs were published separately. Of these, Sousa wrote the words to "Oh My! De Sight." Wilson J. Vance, with whom Sousa collaborated on two operettas, wrote the words to "Love's Beguiling." And of more than passing interest is the song "The Lily Bells," with words by Sousa's former — and supposedly alienated — sweetheart, Emma (Swallow) Bartlett.

MSS: a) Orch 16pp inc; nd np [LC]
  b) Several orch parts of principal numbers in Sousa's hand; nd np [LC]
  c) ("Here Goes") v/pi 1pp inc; nd np [LC]
  d) ("The Lily Bells") v/pi 2pp; nd np [LC]
  e) ("The Lily Bells") orch 4pp inc; nd np [UI]
  f) ("The Lily Bells") bd 5pp; 16Jan1895 Bordentown, N.J. [LC]
  g) ("The Lily Bells") cornet/bd; 8Aug1914 Sands Pt. [LC]
  h) (March) orch 2pp inc; nd np [LC]
  i) (Overture) orch 4pp; nd np [LC]
Pub: Stoddart (individual songs); Hitchcock ("Flirtation"); Chappell ("The Lily Bells"); Church ("The Lily Bells")
©: ("Flirtation," "Love's Beguiling," "Oh My! De Sight") v/pi: Stoddart 30Aug1880; not ren

_____

ager of both *Flirtation* and *Our Flirtations*. Sousa was apparently not associated with the earlier show.

("The Lily Bells") v/pi: Stoddart 30Aug1880 again Church 30Sep1914; not ren
(Waltzes) pi: Stoddart; 18Sep1880; not ren
("The Lily Bells") cornet with bd: Chappell 2Feb1920; not ren
Also see Marches: "Our Flirtation"

THE PHOENIX (1875)
(BOHEMIANS AND DETECTIVES)
(JIM BLUDSO)

Milton Nobles, the author and actor, wrote his own stage play and named it after the principal character, Jim Bludso. After a short period it was renamed *Bohemians and Detectives*. When the play came to Washington, D.C., in the summer of 1875, Sousa was engaged temporarily as orchestra leader. Several months later, Nobles called Sousa to Chicago to act in the same capacity. Music for the show consisted mostly of currently popular tunes, but Sousa added a few of his own compositions.

Because of an incident in the story bearing a resemblance to the story of the mythological phoenix bird, Sousa suggested to Nobles that *The Phoenix* would be an appropriate title for his play, and it was subsequently adopted.

MSS: (Medley Overture) 1st vi/conductor 9pp; 1878[?] Phila. [LC]
Not pub or ©

OVERTURES

THE LAMBS' GAMBOL (1914)

Sousa was an honorary member of the Lambs' Club of New York and participated in several of their annual gambols. For their 1914 gambol he wrote "The Lambs' March" and this overture. It is reminiscent of minstrel medleys and includes "Mammy's Lullaby," "El Capitan's Song," and "Seeing Nelly Home."

MSS: N/A
Pub: Church
©: Orch: Church 7May1915; ren JvMS 22Mar1943

THE RIVALS (1877)

Sousa probably wrote this medley overture in either 1877 or 1879 for Sheridan's play, *The Rivals*. He might have been playing violin in the orchestra at one of two Philadelphia theaters where the play was performed.[1] The more likely date is 1877, because when the play was run in 1879 Sousa was busily engaged in the orchestration and rehearsal of *H.M.S. Pinafore* for the Philadelphia Church Choir Company.

MSS: N/A
Not pub or ©

---

[1] The Chestnut Street Theatre in November, 1877, or Mrs. Drew's Arch Street Theatre in February, 1879.

SANS SOUCI
(See VAUTOUR)

TALLY-HO! (1886)

Sousa composed this overture for his friend Joaquin Miller's play of the same name. A song he composed the previous year was also entitled "Tally-Ho!"

MSS: Orch 8pp inc; nd np [LC]
Pub: Coleman
©: Orch: Coleman 27Dec1886; ren JPS 13Feb1914
Pi: Coleman 3Apr1894; ren JPS 6Feb1922
Bd: Coleman 26Jun1894; ren JPS 6Feb1922

VAUTOUR (1886)

Presumably written for a stage play, this overture was often programmed by the Sousa Band with the subtitles "The Vulture" or "The Vampire." Curiously, a foreign edition published by Lafleur & Son was entitled "Sans Souci."

MSS: a) Orch 13pp inc; nd np [LC]
b) Several bd parts in Sousa's hand; nd np [Morton]
Pub: Coleman
©: Orch: Coleman 27Dec1886; ren JPS 13Feb1914
Bd: Coleman 14Jul1894; ren JPS 6Feb1922
Also pub for pi but not ©

CONCERT PIECES

THE SUMMER GIRL (1901)

According to an inscription on the only known manuscript of this "idyl," it was intended for use as one movement of the makeshift suite *Maidens Three* (1901). The only published edition was a piano transcription by Charles Kunkel of St. Louis.

MSS: Pi 2pp; nd np [LC]
Pub: Church
©: Pi: Charles Kunkel (arranger) 30Jan1903; ren Charles Kunkel 13Jan1931

WILLOW BLOSSOMS (1916)

Although the publisher occasionally advertised this composition as a march, it is actually more a fox trot and was programmed mostly as a "legend" at Sousa Band concerts. It was dedicated to the management and patrons of Philadelphia's Willow Grove Park and was based on the legend that fairies waved their magic wands and caused the willows to cease weeping in the beauty of the music.

MSS: N/A
Pub: Harms (pi); Chappell (bd)
©: Pi: Harms 17Aug1916; ren JvMS 18Aug1943
Bd: Chappell 26Jan1920; ren JPrS & HSA 28Jan1947

INSTRUMENTAL SOLOS

(Also see Arrangements and Transcriptions)

AN ALBUM LEAF (circa 1863)
For violin

Possibly the first composition Sousa ever put on paper, this piece was written when he was about ten years old and studying in the private conservatory of John Esputa, Jr. Esputa callously listened to the piece and then belittled Sousa's effort by calling it "bread and cheese, and cheese and bread." Sousa was deeply hurt by this disparagement and spoke of it often. In his autobiography he tells of keeping the manuscript as one of his most treasured possessions. Unfortunately, it has never been found.

MSS: N/A
Not pub or ©

BELLE MAHONE (1885)
For saxophone

Harold B. Stephens, saxophone soloist with the Sousa Band for the 1925 and 1926 seasons, related the composer's own story of how this piece originated. The work takes the form of variations on a theme and was written for the celebrated saxophonist E. A. Lefebre.[1] Lefebre played it with the Sousa Band on several engagements and apparently took the only copy with him when he left the band. It turned up several years later in the hands of Jean H. B. Moere-

mans, another Sousa Band saxophone soloist, but has since been lost.[2]

MSS: N/A
Not pub or ©

NYMPHALIN (1880)
(REVERIE)
For violin

Helen Sousa Abert, the composer's daughter, considered "Nymphalin" her father's most beautiful composition.[3] It was sometimes programmed as "Reverie" and was played by practically every violin soloist who performed with the Sousa Band. Mary Gailey, who played the opening weeks for three seasons with the Sousa Band at Willow Grove Park in Philadelphia,[4] did not share Helen's enthusiasm for the piece. One night while dining with Sousa she remarked that the piece lacked brilliance. Judging from her choice of solos, Miss Gailey's forte was the fiery music of Sarasate and Wieniawski. She apparently did not grasp Sousa's meaning of "Nymphalin," and her candid observation cost her dearly. Sousa, a violinist himself, was astounded by her remark. He called for music paper, wrote an almost impossibly

---

[1] A Sousa Band program of September 28, 1903, in Pittsburgh states that the piece was written in 1885. At that time Sousa was leader of the U.S. Marine Band and Lefebre was saxophone soloist with Gilmore's Band.

[2] As told to the author in letters of March 10, 1964, and September 14, 1969. Stephens corresponded with Moeremans in his native Belgium until the time of his death in 1937 or 1938, and Moeremans stated that he had no knowledge of the solo's whereabouts.

[3] Interview with the author, November 5, 1963.

[4] 1916, 1917, and 1918.

difficult cadenza to be inserted in the piece, and instructed her to play it that evening.[5]

MSS: a) V/pi 2pp; nd np [LC]
         b) Bd 2pp inc; nd np [LC]
         c) Several bd parts in Sousa's hand; nd np [UI]
         d) Cadenza only 1pp; nd np [in possession of Harold P. Geerdes of Grand Rapids, Mich.]
Pub: Shaw (pi); Coleman (others)
©:   Pi: Shaw 24Apr1880; not ren
       Vi/orch: Coleman 28Dec1889; ren JPS 18Aug1917

---

[5] This story is based on the account of Mary Gailey (Mangrum) and was revealed to the author by Harold P. Geerdes of Grand Rapids, Michigan, in a letter of June 4, 1969.

Pi: Coleman 27Jun1894; ren JPS 6Feb1922
Also pub for vi/pi and vi/bd but not ©

LA REINE D'AMOUR (1879)
For cornet

This elementary piece was called a "polka de concert" and published only in a collection of cornet solos with piano accompaniment called *Evening Hours*. It is the only original Sousa composition in the book and should not be confused with the Sousa waltz of the same name.

MSS: N/A
Pub: Shaw
©:   Covered by © of the collection

TRUMPET AND DRUM PIECES

FOUR MARCHES FOR REGIMENTAL DRUMS AND TRUMPETS (1884)

These short pieces were written while Sousa was leader of the U.S. Marine Band. They are scored for trumpet I, trumpet II, and drums and were published together on one sheet.

MSS: N/A
Pub: Coleman
©: Trumpets & drums: Coleman 19Dec1884; not ren

FUNERAL MARCH
GALLANT AND GAY WE'LL MARCH AWAY
GOOD BYE, SWEET NANNIE MAGEE
LET'S HURRAH! WE ARE ALMOST THERE
HANNAH, MY OWN TRUE LOVE
HERE'S YOUR HEALTH, SIR!
WITH STEADY STEP
WALTZ
} (1886)

Among practice pieces in Sousa's instruction book *The Trumpet and Drum* are these eight original compositions. Excerpts from two of them were later incorporated into marches: "With Steady Step" in "Semper Fidelis" (1888) and "Here's Your Health, Sir!" in "The Thunderer" (1889).

MSS: N/A
Pub: ? (Later by Fischer)
©: Covered by © of *The Trumpet and Drum*

ARRANGEMENTS AND TRANSCRIPTIONS

The arrangements and transcriptions in this section are those which Sousa made of the works of other composers. Adaptations of his own works are not included. No attempt has been made to distinguish between arrangements and transcriptions because considerable musicological research would be involved, and this is beyond the scope of this book.

Even though the list may appear impressive, it is probably not complete. When Sousa became leader of the U.S. Marine Band, he had to make his own adaptations of classical works because of the unavailability of these works in band instrumentations. It is believed that he took most of these with him when he left the band, and that he later disposed of them. Many works also disappeared from the Sousa Band library over the years and are therefore unavailable for study. The only works appearing herein are those for which there is sufficient evidence to justify their listing. Dates are given only where they are inscribed on the manuscripts or where it has been possible to estimate them with reasonable accuracy.

Classical Works

ANGELES (1921)
by Bizet

MSS: Bd 10pp; 29Jun1921 Sands Pt. [LC]
Not pub or ©

THE BARTERED BRIDE: OVERTURE
(1920 or before)
by Smetana

MSS: N/A (for bd)
Not pub or ©

CANADIAN SUITE (no date)
by Percy Godfrer

MSS: Bd 45pp; nd np [UI]
Not pub or ©

CAVALLERIA RUSTICANA: EASTER HYMN (1918)
by Mascagni

MSS: Bd 6pp inc; 4May1918 Cedar Rapids, Iowa [UI]
Not pub or ©

CHARLOTTE CORDAY: ENTR' ACTE VALSE DE LA SCENE DE BAL (1894)
by Peter Benoit

MSS: Several bd parts in Sousa's hand; 2nd clarinet part dated 2Aug1894 7:00 a.m. np [USMC]
Not pub or ©

CHIMES OF NORMANDY: GRAND SELECTION (no date)
by Planquette

MSS: N/A (for bd)
Not pub or ©

CLOS TA PAUPIERE (before 1897)
by Gounod

MSS: Several bd parts in Sousa's hand; nd np
[USMC]
Not pub or ©

COMES AUTUMN TIME: OVERTURE (1925)
by Leo Sowerby

MSS: Bd 13pp; 30Jun1925 Sands Pt. [UI]
Not pub or ©

CONCERTO IN E FOR VIOLIN: FINALE (no date)
by Mendelssohn

MSS: Several bd parts in Sousa's hand; nd np
[UI]
Not pub or ©

THE CREATION: THE HEAVENS ARE TELLING (1883)
by Haydn

This arrangement was apparently needed on short notice. Instead of extracting the instrumental parts by copying from the conductor's score in the usual manner, each page of the conductor's score had been cut into horizontal strips, with one strip for each instrument or group. These strips had been pasted on separate pages to make up the instrumental parts. To obtain the date and location which Sousa always wrote vertically in the margin of the final page, the author clipped fragments from the end of each part and pieced them together. They then read:

"John _____ ___usa, April 15th, _____, Washington, D.C." The date of 1883 was found on the first line of the flute part.

MSS: a) Bd 12pp; 15Apr1883 Washington, D.C. [USMC]
b) Alto saxophone part in Sousa's hand; nd np [USMC]
Not pub or ©

THE CREATION: IN SPLENDOR BRIGHT (1883)
by Haydn

The band parts of this piece are pasted back to back with the parts to "The Heavens Are Telling," with markings indicating that the two pieces were played in sequence with no pause.

MSS: Several bd parts in Sousa's hand; nd np
[USMC]
Not pub or ©

DEATH AND TRANSFIGURATION (no date)
by R. Strauss

MSS: N/A (for bd)
Not pub or ©

DON JUAN (no date)
by R. Strauss

MSS: Bd 35pp inc; nd np [LC]
Not pub or ©

DON JUAN: ARIA (before 1897)
by Mozart

MSS: Several bd parts in Sousa's hand; nd np
[Morton]
Not pub or ©

ERNANI: COME FLY WITH ME (before 1897)
by Verdi

MSS: Several orch parts in Sousa's hand;
nd np [Morton]
Not pub or ©

FAUST FANTASIA (before 1918)
by Gounod

MSS: N/A (for bd)
Not pub or ©

FERAMORS: BALLET MUSIC AND WEDDING MARCH (1893)
by Rubenstein

MSS: Bd 38pp; 9Feb1893 Washington, D.C.
[LC]
Not pub or ©

THE FLYING DUTCHMAN: OVERTURE (1893)
by Wagner

MSS: Bd 37pp; 7Feb1893 Washington, D.C.
[LC]
Not pub or ©

GOTTERDAMMERUNG: SIEGFRIED'S DEATH (no date)
by Wagner

MSS: Bd 6pp inc; nd np [LC]
Not pub or ©

HABANERA (1892)
by Sarasate

MSS: Bd 20pp; 4Jun1892 Sands Pt. [LC]
Not pub or ©

HUMORESQUE (1907)
by Dvorak

MSS: Bd 8pp; 5Oct1907 Great Falls, Mont.
[UI]
Not pub or ©

HUNGARIAN DANCE NO. 5 (no date)
by Brahms

MSS: Several bd parts in Sousa's hand; nd np
[UI]
Not pub or ©

HUNGARIAN RHAPSODY NO. 2 (1893)
by Liszt

MSS: Bd 37pp; 22Mar1893 Washington, D.C.
[LC]
Not pub or ©

INDIGO AND THE FORTY ROBBERS: SELECTIONS (1878)
by J. Strauss

MSS: Bd 2pp inc; 7Nov1878 Phila. [LC]
Not pub or ©

INTRODUCTION AND RONDO CAPRICCIOSO (no date)
by Saint-Saëns

MSS: Bd sketch and most bd parts in Sousa's
hand; nd np [UI]
Not pub or ©

KAISER FRANZ JOSEPH MARCH (1885)
by E. Strauss

MSS: N/A (for bd)
Pub: Coleman
©: Bd: Coleman 12Dec1885; not ren

KERMESSE DE ST. CLOUD (1892)
by Joseph Leopold Rockel

MSS: Bd 5pp; 10Sep1892 New York City
[USMC]
Not pub or ©

LAKME: INDIAN BELL SONG (1902)
by Delibes

MSS: Several bd parts in Sousa's hand; nd np
[USMC]
Not pub or ©

LOHENGRIN: ELSA'S DREAM (1893)
by Wagner

MSS: Several bd parts in Sousa's hand; nd np
[Morton]
Not pub or ©

LOHENGRIN: INTRODUCTION TO ACT III (before 1921)
by Wagner

MSS: N/A (for bd)
Not pub or ©

LOHENGRIN: INTRODUCTION TO ACT III (no date)
by Wagner

MSS: (Ending only) orch 3pp; nd np [LC]
Not pub or ©

LOHENGRIN: LOHENGRIN'S NARRATIVE (before 1897)
by Wagner

MSS: Bd parts in Sousa's hand; nd np
[Morton]
Not pub or ©

LOUISE: ROMAN MUSICAL (1908)
by Gustave Charpentier

MSS: Several bd parts in Sousa's hand; harp
part dated 22Aug1908 np [UI]
Not pub or ©

LOURE (1903)
by Bach

MSS: a) Bd 6pp; 2Apr1903 Bristol, England
        [UI]
     b) Several bd parts in Sousa's hand;
        nd np [UI]
Not pub or ©

LUCIA: SCENA AND TRIA (before 1897)
by Donizetti

MSS: Coda on bd parts in Sousa's hand; nd np
     [USMC]
Not pub or ©

LUCIA: SEXTETTE (before 1897)
by Donizetti

MSS: N/A (for bd)
Not pub or ©

LULLABY (1903)
by Brahms

MSS: Bd 2pp; 1Apr1903 Bath, England [UI]
Not pub or ©

THE MAIDS OF CADIZ (1924)
by Delibes

MSS: Bd 7pp; 29Sep1924 Providence, R.I.
     [LC]
Not pub or ©

MANON: GAVOTTE (1895)
by Massenet

MSS: Several bd parts in Sousa's hand; 1st
     clarinet part dated 17Jan1895 np
     [USMC]
Not pub or ©

MARCH DE NUIT (probably 1893)
by Louis Gottschalk

MSS: Several bd parts in Sousa's hand; one
     part in copyist's hand dated 6Oct1893
     St. Louis [USMC]
Not pub or ©

MARCHE MILITAIRE FRANCAISE
(no date)
by Saint-Saëns

MSS: Several bd parts in Sousa's hand; also
     additions to French bd transcription
     by V. Bonnelle in Sousa's hand nd np
     [UI]
Not pub or ©

MARTHA: AIR (before 1897)
by Flotow

MSS: Bd parts in Sousa's hand; nd np
     [Morton]
Not pub or ©

**DIE MEISTERSINGER: WALTHER'S
PRIZE SONG** (before 1897)
by Wagner

MSS: Several bd parts in Sousa's hand; nd np
     [Morton]
Not pub or ©

**MERRY WIVES OF WINDSOR:
OVERTURE** (1905)
by Nicolai

MSS: Several bd parts in Sousa's hand; harp
     part dated 2Jan1905 "In the Atlantic"
     [UI]
Not pub or ©

NOCTURNE IN E-FLAT (no date)
by Chopin

MSS: Bd 6pp inc; nd np [LC]
Not pub or ©

OTHELLO: SELECTIONS (no date)
by Verdi

MSS: N/A (for bd)
Not pub or ©

THE PEARL FISHERS: SELECTIONS
(no date)
by Bizet

MSS: Bd 2pp inc; nd np [LC]
Not pub or ©

PEER GYNT SUITE (1892)
by Grieg

MSS: Bd 31pp, in bound volume; 9Jan1892
     Washington, D.C. [LC]
Not pub or ©

PIRATES OF PENZANCE: OVERTURE
(no date)
by Arthur Sullivan

MSS: a) Orch 1pp inc; nd np [LC]
     b) Several orch parts in Sousa's hand;
        nd np [UI]
Not pub or ©

PIRATES OF PENZANCE: SELECTIONS
(1880)
by Arthur Sullivan

MSS: a) Bd 57pp; 3Dec1880 Washington,
D.C. [USMC]
b) Several bd parts, in copyist's hand,
amended in Sousa's hand; nd np
[USMC]
Not pub or ©

PRELUDE L'APRES-MIDI D'UN FAUNE
(1921)
by Debussy

MSS: Bd 18pp; 29Mar1921 Sands Pt. [UI]
Not pub or ©

IL PROFETA: AH! MON FILS (1893)
by Meyerbeer

MSS: Several bd parts in Sousa's hand;
bassoon part dated 21Oct1893
St. Louis [USMC]
Not pub or ©

RONDO CAPRICCIOSO (no date)
by Mendelssohn

MSS: Bd 2pp inc; nd np [LC]
Not pub or ©

SALUT D'AMOUR (1903)
by Elgar

MSS: Several bd parts in Sousa's hand; tuba
part dated 12Apr1903 Bath, England
[UI]
Not pub or ©

SEE THE CONQUERING HERO COMES
(1893)
by Handel

MSS: Bd 5pp; 27Apr1893 New York City [LC]
Not pub or ©

SERENADE (1892)
by Joachim Raff

MSS: Several bd parts in Sousa's hand; nd np
[USMC]
Not pub or ©

LE SOIR (1893)
by Thomas

MSS: Several bd parts in Sousa's hand; nd np
[USMC]
Not pub or ©

**SONATA (PIANO) OPUS 14, NO. 2:
ANDANTE** (1893)
by Beethoven

MSS: Bd 11pp; 13Feb1893 Washington, D.C.
[LC]
Not pub or ©

THE SORCERER'S APPRENTICE
(before 1921)
by Dukas

MSS: N/A (for bd)
Not pub or ©

**SYMPHONY IN E ("THE NEW
WORLD"): LARGO** (before 1920)
by Dvořák

MSS: N/A (for bd)
Not pub or ©

TANNHAUSER: EVENING STAR
(before 1897)
by Wagner

MSS: Several bd parts in Sousa's hand; nd np
[Morton]
Not pub or ©

TANNHAUSER: OVERTURE (1897)
by Wagner

MSS: Bd 82pp; 12May1897 Keene, N.H. [UI]
Not pub or ©

TOCCATA AND FUGUE IN D MINOR
(no date)
by Bach

MSS: Bd 1pp inc; nd np [LC]
Not pub or ©

LE TORTORELLE (no date)
by Luigi Ardita

MSS: Orch 1pp inc; nd np [LC]
Not pub or ©

LA TOSCA: PRAYER (1911)
by Puccini

MSS: Bd 4pp; 13Jun1911 Melbourne, Australia
[UI]
Not pub or ©

TRIAL BY JURY: SELECTIONS (1877)
by Arthur Sullivan

MSS: N/A (for bd)
Not pub or ©

**TRISTAN AND ISOLDE: PRELUDE
AND LOVE DEATH** (before 1921)
by Wagner

MSS: N/A (for bd)
Not pub or ©

THE VICTORY BALL (1923)
by Ernest Schelling

MSS: N/A (for bd)
Not pub or ©

WIEGENLIED (before 1897)
by Hans Sitt

MSS: Several bd parts in Sousa's hand; nd np
[USMC]
Not pub or ©

Operetta Orchestrations

THE CONTRABANDISTA (1879)
Original libretto by F. C. Burnand
Revised libretto by Charles Gaylord
Music by Arthur Sullivan

According to Sousa's autobiography, he was touring the New England states in late 1879 as conductor of a company which was producing Gilbert and Sullivan's *H.M.S. Pinafore*. Concurrently, the company was working on *The Contrabandista* for their next production. The playwright Charles Gaylord revised the libretto of *The Contrabandista,* and Sousa made this orchestration.

MSS: N/A
Not pub or ©
(See also Operettas: *The Smugglers*)

H.M.S. PINAFORE (1879)
Libretto by William Gilbert
Music by Arthur Sullivan

The Gilbert and Sullivan operetta closest to Sousa's heart was *H.M.S. Pinafore*. He arranged several of the songs for various instruments, but the most significant effort was this orchestration of the entire operetta.

In his autobiography, Sousa related that Arthur Sullivan thought this orchestration excellent. It was used by the Philadelphia Church Choir operetta company in their seasons in New York and Philadelphia, as well as on tour, all under his direction. It was also used by an Australian company which preferred it to the original edition.

In a newspaper interview, Sousa re-

vealed that he had made the complete orchestration in the incredibly short time of forty-two hours, adding some unusual orchestral effects.[1] At the time, he had seen nothing but a piano score.[2]

MSS: Opa 21pp inc; nd np [LC]
Not pub or ©

THE LION TAMER (1891)
Libretto by J. Cheever Goodwin
Music by Richard Stahl

Sousa revised and orchestrated the score of this production at the request of producer Francis Wilson. As a bonus, Sousa inserted an original march. He too received a bonus for completing the work on short order: a handsome gold watch. Wilson and Sousa later parted ways, however, over money matters concerning the unfinished operetta *The Devil's Deputy*. Sousa then revived the bonus march and published it under two different titles: "On Parade" and "The Lion Tamer."

MSS: a) (Complete opa) 236pp in two bound
volumes, inc; 19Dec1891 Washington,
D.C. [LC]
b) (Overture) opa 4pp inc; nd np [LC]
Not pub or ©

THE MERRY MONARCH (1890)
Libretto by J. Cheever Goodwin
Music by Emmanuel Chabrier
and Woolson Morse

The *Merry Monarch* and *The Lion Tamer*

---

[1] *New York Advertiser,* August 27, 1893.
[2] Undated Boston newspaper, circa 1929, in the Boston Public Library Sousa scrapbook.

were the two complete works known to have been instrumented for the New York producer-comedian Francis Wilson. There may have been others, but their existence has not been established. The music of *The Merry Monarch* is mostly from Chabrier's *The Merry Monarch,* with additional numbers by Woolson Morse.

MSS: (Complete opa) 211pp in two bound volumes; 11Aug1890 Washington, D.C. [LC]
Pub: Coleman
©: (Overture) orch: Coleman 10Jan1891; not ren
Overture also pub for pi but not ©

THE OOLAH (1889)
Adaptation of Charles Lecocq's operetta *La Jolie Persane* by Sidney Rosenfeld

On September 26, 1892, the Sousa Band made its debut in Plainfield, New Jersey. The next day newspapers carried accounts of the concert, and one reviewer referred to this orchestration by Sousa but gave no details.[3] Other than this casual mention, Sousa's contribution was in question until 1971, when a few pages of his preliminary score were found among unidentified manuscripts at the Library of Congress.

MSS: V/pi 4pp inc; nd np [LC]
Not pub or ©

THE SORCERER (1878)
Libretto by William Gilbert
Music by Arthur Sullivan

This orchestration was prepared with the assistance of J. Fred Zimmerman, the conductor of the orchestra at Mrs. John Drew's Arch Street Theatre in Philadelphia. Sousa was playing violin in the theater orchestra at the time.

MSS: N/A
Not pub or ©

---

[3] Unidentified article, presumably from a Plainfield newspaper of September 27, 1892, in the Sousa Band press book of that year.

Opera and Operetta Arrangements for Piano

BOCCACCIO: POTPOURRI NO. 1 (1880)
by Suppe

MSS: N/A
Pub: Stoddart; Hitchcock
©: Stoddart 30Mar1880; not ren

BOCCACCIO: POTPOURRI NO. 2 (1880)
by Suppe

MSS: N/A
Pub: Stoddart; Hitchcock
©: Stoddart 8May1880; not ren

LA CAMARGO: POTPOURRI (1880)
by Charles Lecocq

MSS: N/A
Pub: Stoddart; Hitchcock
©: Stoddart 19Apr1880; not ren

CARMEN: GRAND POTPOURRI (1879)
by Bizet

MSS: N/A
Pub: Stoddart; Hitchcock
©: Stoddart 13Feb1879; not ren

FORTY ROBBERS
(See INDIGO AND THE FORTY ROBBERS)

H.M.S. PINAFORE: POTPOURRI NO. 1 (1879)
by Arthur Sullivan

MSS: N/A
Pub: Stoddart
©: Stoddart 10Feb1879; not ren

H.M.S. PINAFORE: POTPOURRI NO. 2 (1880)
by Arthur Sullivan

MSS: N/A
Pub: Stoddart
©: Stoddart 30Mar1880; not ren

INDIGO AND THE FORTY ROBBERS: POTPOURRI (1878)
by J. Strauss

MSS: N/A
Pub: Stoddart; Hitchcock
©: Stoddart 4Oct1878; not ren

THE LITTLE DUKE: POTPOURRI
(1879)
by Charles Lecocq

MSS: N/A
Pub: Stoddart; Hitchcock
©:   Stoddart 13Apr1879; not ren

PAUL AND VIRGINIA: POTPOURRI
(1880)
by Felix Marie Masse

MSS: N/A
Pub: Stoddart; Hitchcock
©:   Stoddart 7Apr1880; not ren

THE SEA CADET: SELECTIONS (1880)
by Richard Genee

MSS: N/A
Pub: Stoddart
©:   Stoddart 3Mar1880; not ren

THE SORCERER: POTPOURRI (1879)
by Arthur Sullivan

MSS: N/A
Pub: Stoddart; Hitchcock
©:   Stoddart 1Mar1879; not ren

THE THREE DRAGOONS: SELECTIONS
(1899)
by Reginald DeKoven

MSS: N/A
Pub: Church
©:   Church 3Apr1899; not ren

TRAVIATA: SELECTIONS (1880)
by Verdi

MSS: N/A
Pub: Stoddart; Hitchcock
©:   Stoddart 7Aug1880; not ren

TRIAL BY JURY: POTPOURRI (1879)
by Arthur Sullivan

MSS: N/A
Pub: Stoddart; Hitchcock
©:   Stoddart 21Feb1879; not ren

WE SAIL THE OCEAN BLUE
from *H.M.S. Pinafore*
by Arthur Sullivan

MSS: N/A
Pub: Stoddart
©:   Stoddart 10Feb1879; not ren

Various Dance Forms

AH! AT LENGTH 'TIS HERE (1877)
Polka
by Ferdy Gumbert

MSS: Orch 5pp; 5Apr1877 Phila. [LC]
Not pub or ©

ALABAMA DANCE (1894)
by J. F. Gilder

MSS: N/A (for bd)
Pub: Church
©:   Bd: Church 6Dec1894; not ren

AMERICAN DANCES (no date)
by Harry Rowe Shelley

MSS: Bd 27pp; nd np [LC]
Not pub or ©

LE BEAUX SABREUR (no date)
Gavotte Militaire
by J. A. Darling

MSS: Bd 1pp inc; nd np [LC]
Not pub or ©

BOA NOITE (1887)
Brazilian Polka
by Cezario A. G. Vellela

MSS: Several bd parts in Sousa's hand; E-flat
        cornet/conductor part dated
        15Apr1887 Washington, D.C.; 1st
        B-flat cornet part dated 14Apr1887
        np [USMC]
Not pub or ©

COUNTRY GARDENS (1923)
English Folk Dance
by Percy Grainger

MSS: Bd 12pp; 27Mar1923 New York City
        [LC]
Not pub or ©

DANCE OF THE GNOMES (before 1897)
by Homer N. Bartlett

MSS: Several bd parts in Sousa's hand; nd np
        [USMC]
Not pub or ©

GAVOTTE (before 1897)
by Hans Sitt

MSS: Several bd parts in Sousa's hand; nd np
 [USMC]
Not pub or ©

JUBA (1926)
Dance
by Robert Nathaniel Dett

MSS: Bd 12pp; 4May1926 Sands Pt. [USMC]
Not pub or ©

KUTSCHKE POLKA (1880)
by Ludwig Stasny

MSS: Bd 2pp; 5Oct1880 Phila. [UI]
Not pub or ©

MA-MA-MA MINE GA-GA (1890)
Apache Indian Scalp Dance
Traditional

MSS: N/A (for bd)
Pub: Coleman (only in bd edition of *National,
 Patriotic and Typical Airs of All
 Lands*)
Not © for bd

MENTOR MAZURKA (no date)
by J. H. Rathrone

MSS: Orch 4pp inc; nd np [UI]
Not pub or ©

THE OWL AND THE PUSSY CAT
(no date)
Polka
by George Ingraham

MSS: Several orch parts in Sousa's hand; nd
 np [LC]
Not pub or ©

PSYCHE GAVOTTE (before 1897)
by J. W. Bischoff

MSS: Several bd parts in Sousa's hand; nd np
 [USMC]
Not pub or ©

SECRET LOVE (1876)
Gavotte
by Johann Rasch

MSS: Orch 3pp; 24Nov1876 Phila. [LC]
Not pub or ©

THE WEDDING OF THE LILY AND
THE ROSE (before 1897)
Schottische Caprice
by Thomas Le Mack and W. Andrew Mack

MSS: Several bd parts in Sousa's hand; nd np
 [USMC]
Not pub or ©

Songs

AN AIR OF THE DECCAN (1889)
Traditional Song of Berar

MSS: Bd 3pp; Aug1889 Washington, D.C.
 [LC]
Pub: Coleman (only in bd edition of *National,
 Patriotic and Typical Airs of All
 Lands*)
Not © for bd

AN AIR OF ZAMBOANGA (1893)
Traditional

This was arranged for band from a typical
tune of Zamboanga which Sousa included
in his *National, Patriotic and Typical Airs
of All Lands* (1890).

MSS: N/A (for bd)
Pub: Coleman (only in bd edition of *National,
Patriotic and Typical Airs of All
Lands*)
Not © for bd

ANNIE LAURIE (no date)
Traditional

MSS: Several bd parts in Sousa's hand; nd np
 [UI]
Not pub or ©

AWAKE, AWAKE (1873)
from *Fountains Abbey*
by ?

MSS: V (for male quartet) 1pp; nd np [LC]
Not pub or ©

BABY DEAR (1889)
Lullaby
by Harry C. Leighter

MSS: Bd 2pp; 20May1899 Washington, D.C.
[LC]
Not pub or ©

LA BAYAMESA (1898)
Traditional

MSS: N/A (for v/pi)
Pub: Coleman
©: V/pi: Coleman 23May1898; not ren

CARRY ME BACK TO OLD VIRGINNY
(before 1926)
by E. P. Christy

MSS: N/A (for four French horns — accompaniment for soprano solo)
Not pub or ©

COMIN' THRO' THE RYE (before 1897)
Traditional

MSS: Bd parts in Sousa's hand; nd np [Morton]
Not pub or ©

COMING HOME (1929)
by Charles Willeby

MSS: Bd 4pp; 30Apr1929 New York City [LC]
Not pub or ©

DEATH'S AT THE DOOR
(See THE VOICE OF A
DEPARTING SOUL)

DIXIE (no date)
by Dan Emmet

MSS: N/A (for bd)
Not pub or ©

ECHO SONG (before 1897)
by ?

MSS: Several bd parts in Sousa's hand; nd np
[USMC]
Not pub or ©

FINLAND LOVE SONG (no date)
by E. S. Engeloberg

MSS: Bd 1pp inc; nd np [LC]
Not pub or ©

FLOWER SONG OF CHINA (1889)
Traditional

This was an arrangement of the song "Moo-lee-wha," or "Flower Song," which Sousa included in his *National, Patriotic and Typical Airs of All Lands* (1890).

MSS: N/A (for bd)
Pub: Coleman (only in bd edition of *National, Patriotic and Typical Airs of All Lands*)
Not © for bd

FOREVER AND FOREVER (1882)
by Francesco Paolo Tosti

MSS: N/A (for bd)
Not pub or ©

GOOD NIGHT! BELOVED (1885)
by M. W. Balfe

MSS: Bd 6pp; 17Sep1885 Washington, D.C.
[LC]
Not pub or ©

HAPPY DAYS (1895)
by Henly Thomson and Anton Strelezky

MSS: Bd 5pp; 6Feb1895 New York City
[USMC]
Not pub or ©

I DREAMT (1877)
by F. Schira

MSS: Orch 4pp; 20Aug1877 Phila. [LC]
Not pub or ©

JUNE BROUGHT THE ROSES (no date)
Words by Ralph Stanley
Music by John Openshaw

MSS: Several bd parts in Sousa's hand; nd np
[UI]
Not pub or ©

KYRIE (no date)
by Paolo Georza

MSS: Orch 1pp inc; nd np [LC]
Not pub or ©

**THE LARK NOW LEAVES ITS WAT'RY
NEST** (1922)
by Horatio Parker

MSS: N/A (for bd)
Not pub or ©

LISTEN TO MY TALE OF WOE (1888)
by Hubbard T. Smith

MSS: N/A (for orch)
Pub: Ellis
©:   Orch: Ellis 6Apr1888; not ren

THE LITTLE CHATTERBOX (no date)
by R. Eilenberg

MSS: Bd 2pp; nd np [LC]
Not pub or ©

THE LOST CHORD (no date)
by Arthur Sullivan

MSS: N/A (for bd)
Not pub or ©

MARGERY: AN ECHO SONG (1885)
by J. W. Bischoff

MSS: Orch 3pp inc; 26Apr1885 Washington,
       D.C. [LC]
Not pub or ©

MARGUERITE (1893)
Words by R. Willrose
Music by V. Fassone

MSS: Bd parts in Sousa's hand; 1st clarinet
       part dated 3Jul1893 Manhattan Beach,
       N.Y. [USMC]
Not pub or ©

MI CHILENA (no date)
by F. Soler

MSS: Bd 1pp inc; nd np [LC]
Not pub or ©

MIGHTY LAK A ROSE (no date)
by Ethelbert Nevin

MSS: Several bd parts in Sousa's hand; nd np
       [UI]
Not pub or ©

NEVER SEEMED THE WORLD MORE
FAIR (no date)
by ?

MSS: Orch 1pp inc; nd np [LC]
Not pub or ©

NIGHTS IN THE WOODS (no date)
by Harold de Bozi

MSS: N/A (for bd)
Not pub or ©

NUKAHIVAH (1889)
Traditional song of Nukahivah Island

MSS: Bd 3pp; 11Sep1889 Washington, D.C.
       [LC]
Pub: Coleman (only in bd edition of *National,
       Patriotic and Typical Airs of All
       Lands*)
Not © for bd

OH PROMISE ME (before 1897)
Words by Clement Scott
Music by Reginald de Koven

MSS: Several bd parts in Sousa's hand; nd np
       [USMC]
Not pub or ©

OLD FOLKS AT HOME (before 1897)
by Stephen Foster

MSS: Several bd parts in Sousa's hand; nd np
       [USMC]
Not pub or ©

PETER PAN (after 1916)
by William Stickles

MSS: N/A (for bd)
Not pub or ©

PLAIN TUNES FROM THE HILLS (1889)
A) KUTCH KEWHANA (Bengal)
B) KAYAH THAN (Burma)
Traditional

These traditional melodies of East Indian
tribes were arranged for band from songs
included in Sousa's *National, Patriotic and
Typical Airs of All Lands* (1890).

MSS: N/A (for bd)
Pub: Coleman (only in bd edition of *National,
       Patriotic and Typical Airs of All
       Lands*)
Not © for bd

QUEEN OF THE EARTH (no date)
by H. L. D'Arcy Laxone

MSS: Orch 2pp inc; nd np [UI]
Not pub or ©

THE QUILTING PARTY (no date)
Traditional

MSS: Several bd parts in Sousa's hand; nd np
      [UI]
Not pub or ©

ROBIN ADAIR (before 1897)
by Keppel

MSS: Several bd parts in Sousa's hand; nd np
      [USMC]
Not pub or ©

SERENATA (before 1897)
by Louis Conrath

MSS: N/A (for bd)
Not pub or ©

**SOFT, ZEPHYRS SPREAD THY DAINTY
WING** (no date)
by ?

MSS: V/orch 7pp; nd np [LC]
Not pub or ©

THE SOVEREIGN OF THE SKIES (1923)
by George Harold Morgan

Sousa arranged George (Red) Morgan's
song as an accompaniment for his soprano
Nora Fauchald, who later became Mrs.
Morgan.

MSS: N/A (for bd)
Not pub or ©

TA-RA-RA-BOOMDERE (no date)
by Henry J. Sayers

MSS: Bd 1pp inc; nd np [LC]
Not pub or ©

TOO UTTALY UTTA (1888)
by Hubbard T. Smith

MSS: N/A (for orch)
Pub: Ellis
©:   Orch: Ellis 8May1888; not ren

'TWAS APRIL (1888)
by Ethelbert Nevin

MSS: Several bd parts in Sousa's hand; nd np
      [USMC]
Not pub or ©

US FOUR TRAMPS (1894)
by Hubbard T. Smith

MSS: N/A (for orch)
Pub: Ellis
©:   Orch: Ellis 19Dec1894; not ren

VILLANELLE (1922)
by Eva Dell' Acqua

MSS: N/A (for bd)
Not pub or ©

THE VOICE OF A DEPARTING SOUL
(1892)
(DEATH'S AT THE DOOR)
by Patrick S. Gilmore

MSS: Several bd parts in Sousa's hand; nd np
      [Morton]
Not pub or ©

VOLKSLIEDCHEN MARCHEN (1910)
by Karl Komzak

MSS: Several bd parts in Sousa's hand;
      23Sep1910 Pittsburgh [UI]
Not pub or ©

WAKE UP (before 1910)
Words by Harold Simpson
Music by Montague A. Philips

MSS: Bd 4pp; nd np [LC]
Not pub or ©

WEARY AND FOOTSORE (1873)
from *Fountains Abbey*
by ?

MSS: V/pi 1pp; Apr1873 np [LC]
Not pub or ©

WHEN MYRA SINGS (1923)
Words by George Granville,
Lord Landsdowne
Music by "A. L."

MSS: Several bd parts in Sousa's hand; 1st
      clarinet part dated 24Oct1923 np [UI]
Not pub or ©

YOU AND I (no date)
by Liza Lehman

MSS: N/A (for bd)
Not pub or ©

YOU'RE THE FLOWER OF MY HEART, SWEET ADELINE (1930)
Words by Richard H. Gerard
Music by Harry Armstrong

MSS: Bd 18pp; 19Aug1930 Sands Pt. [LC]
Not pub or ©

(UNTITLED SONG) 1930
by ?

MSS: Bd 4pp; 3Oct1930 Sands Pt. [LC]
Not pub or ©

Instrumental Solos or Ensembles

(Reference) CARMEN MARCH (1879)
from *Carmen*
by Bizet

MSS: N/A (for vi or flute, with pi)
Pub: Shaw (also included in collection, *Evening Pastime*)
©: Vi or flute, with pi: Shaw 21Apr1879; not ren

CAVITANA FOR TROMBONE (no date)
by E. Hasselmann

MSS: N/A (for trombone with bd)
Not pub or ©

EVENING HOURS (1879)
A collection of solos for cornet, with piano

A notable step in the musical development of the young Sousa came when he was engaged by the Philadelphia music publisher, W. F. Shaw, to arrange two sets of instrumental solos with piano accompaniment. The first book was for violin or flute and was called *Evening Pastime*. The second, *Evening Hours*, was for cornet.

The twenty-eight selections in *Evening Hours* were more elementary than those in *Evening Pastime*, and several hymns were included. It contained only one original Sousa composition, a polka entitled "La Reine d'Amour."

CONTENTS:
Bell Trio (from *H.M.S. Pinafore*) (Sullivan)
Beulah Land (Sweney)
Blue Alsatian Mountains (Adams)
First Kiss — Waltz (Lamothe)
Going from de Cotton Fields (Westendorf)
Grant's Presentation Grand March (Latour)
H.M.S. Pinafore — Potpourri (Sullivan)
Hunter's March (Faust)
I Kissed You in a Dream — Fantasy (Rutledge)
I'm Called Little Buttercup (from *H.M.S. Pinafore*) (Sullivan)
I Left It All with Jesus (English)
I Love My Love (Pinsuti)
I Love to Tell the Story (Fischer)
Jesus, Savior of My Soul (German)
La Reine d'Amour — Polka de concert (Sousa)
Let Me Dream Again (Sullivan)
The Little Duke — Potpourri (Lecocq)
Nancy Lee (Adams)
Onward, Christian Soldiers (Sullivan)
Perplexity (Abt)
Poor Little Wedded Man (from *The Little Duke*) (Lecocq)
Rock of Ages (Hastings)
Remembrance (Lange)
Singing Lesson (from *The Little Duke*) (Lecocq)
Sun of My Soul (German)
Ten-Pin Galop (Zikoff)
There Is a Fountain Filled with Blood (Western melody)
You and I (Claribel)

MSS: N/A (for cornet with pi)
Pub: Shaw
©: Cornet with pi: Shaw 25Oct1879; not ren

EVENING PASTIME (1879)
A collection of solos for violin or flute, with piano

This volume of Sousa arrangements contained eighty-seven solos for violin or flute, with piano accompaniment. Several of the selections were published and copyrighted separately. Among these, the "Carmen March" is sometimes mistakenly considered an original Sousa composition, but it is actually a medley of five of the melodies

from Bizet's opera in a setting for solo instruments. Another selection, "Triton," was
later expanded into a march and is catalogued as such.

Not all the selections were strictly
arrangements. "Adamsonia" and "Home
Sweet Home with Variations" received
original treatment by Sousa and are catalogued with the Fantasies for Individual
Instruments. These were also published
and copyrighted separately.

One other exception is the "Resumption
March," which was an original composition of Sousa's. It predated the publication
of *Evening Pastime* and is catalogued with
the marches.

CONTENTS:

Song of the Hunchback (from *The Little Duke*) (Lecocq)
The Sorcerer — Potpourri (Sullivan)
Spring (Lichner)
Spring Song (Mendelssohn)
Summer (Lichner)
Sunshine Polka (Kinkel)
Swedish Wedding March (Soderman)
Tarantella (Mendelssohn)
Ten-Pin Galop (Zikoff)
The Adieu (from *The Little Duke*) (Lecocq)
Trial by Jury — Potpourri (Sullivan)
Triton — March (Molloy)
Time Was When Love and I (from *The Sorcerer*) (Sullivan)
We Sail the Ocean Blue (from *H.M.S. Pinafore*) (Sullivan)
What Will Jack Say [?] (Pinsuti)
When First My Old Love (from *Trial by Jury*) (Sullivan)
Where Was Moses When the Light Went Out [?] (Traditional)
Whoa, Emma! (Read)
Woodland Vows — Schottische (Mack)

MSS: N/A (for vi or flute, with pi)
Pub: Shaw
©:   Vi & pi: Shaw 16Apr1879; not ren
     Vi; flute; flute & pi; Shaw
     10May1879; not ren

FANTASIE BRILLANTE (1885)
by Jean Baptiste Arban

MSS: Cornet with bd 15pp; 29Dec1885 np
     [in possession of Leonard V. Meretta,
     Western Michigan Univ.]
Not pub or ©

INDIAN LOVE CALL (1925)
from *Rose Marie*
by Rudolf Friml

MSS: (For alto saxophone with bd) alto sax-
     ophone part 1pp; 4Jul1925 Hershey,
     Pa. [in possession of Harold B.
     Stephens, Long Beach, Calif.]
Not pub or ©

KA-LU-A (1922)
from *Good Morning, Dearie*
by Jerome Kern

MSS: Xylophone with bd 7pp; 1Aug1922
     Willow Grove, Pa. [LC]
Not pub or ©

(Reference) MEDLEY QUADRILLE (1879)
by various composers

This piece was first published in the *Evening Pastime* collection (1879). The individual songs making up the medley were also published as separate songs in the same collection. Included were: "It's Funny When You Feel That Way" (Hunt); "Johnny Morgan" (Read); "If I Only Knew How It Was Done" (Skelly); "The Haunted Kickaboo" (Offenbach); "Where Was Moses When the Light Went Out?" (Traditional); and "Whoa, Emma!" (Read).

MSS: N/A (for vi or flute, with pi)
Pub: Shaw
©:   Vi or flute, with pi: Shaw
     29May1879; not ren

MELODY (after 1920)
by Charles G. Dawes

MSS: (For six flutes with bd) several bd parts
     in Sousa's hand; nd np [UI]
Not pub or ©

(Reference) RING FORTH, YE BELLS (1879)
from *The Sorcerer*
by Arthur Sullivan

MSS: N/A (for vi or flute, with pi)
Pub: Shaw (also included in collection,
     Evening Pastime)
©:   Vi or flute, with pi: Shaw
     21Apr1879; not ren

SILKEN BANDS (1888)
Waltz
by J. W. Bischoff

MSS: N/A (for cornet with bd)
Pub: Ellis
©:   Cornet & bd: Ellis 1Sep1888; not ren

STANCES (1893)
Song
by Flegier

MSS: E-flat cornet with bd 7pp; 29Apr1893
     New York City [LC]
Not pub or ©

TAPS (no date)
Traditional

MSS: (For brass instruments and drums) parts
     in Sousa's hand; nd np [UI]
Not pub or ©

Marches

BOULANGER'S MARCH
(See EN REVENANT DE LA REVUE)

CHEERFULNESS MARCH (1885)
by Neuman

MSS: N/A (for bd)
Pub: Coleman
©: Bd: Coleman 30Dec1885; not ren

DUDE'S MARCH
(See GIGERL MARCH)

EN REVENANT DE LA REVUE (1887)
(BOULANGER'S MARCH)
by ?

MSS: Bd 3pp inc; nd np, but notation on first
page refers to first performance at the
White House on 16Jul1887 [LC]
Pub: Coleman
©: Bd; pi: Coleman 30Jul1887; not ren

GIGERL MARCH (1890)
(DUDE'S MARCH)
by J. F. Wagner

MSS: Bd 5pp; 1Jul1890 Washington, D.C.
[LC]
Pub: Coleman
©: Orch: Coleman 22Dec1890; not ren
Also pub for bd but not ©

GREETING TO CAPE MAY
(probably 1879)
by Simon Hassler

MSS: N/A (for orch)
Not pub or ©

HAMLET (1877)
by Simon Hassler

MSS: a) Bd 4pp; 29Jun1877 Phila. [UI]
b) Pi 2pp; 2Jul1877 Phila. [UI]
Not pub or ©

THE JOLLY STUDENTS MARCH (1892)
by P. Fahrbach, Jr.

MSS: N/A (for bd)
Pub: Coleman
Not ©

THE LEAGUE OF NATIONS (1925)
by George Thurman Bye

MSS: Bd 9pp; 13Jul1925 Sands Pt. [UI]
Not pub or ©

MARCH OF THE BLUES (1927)
by Irving Bibo

MSS: N/A (for bd)
Pub: Bibo
©: Bd: Bibo 9Aug1927; ren Stasny Music
Corp. 9Aug1954

MARCHING THROUGH GEORGIA
(PATROL) (1891)
(THE SOUTHERN PATROL)
by Henry Clay Work

MSS: Bd 10pp; 1891 np [USMC]
Not pub or ©

ORPHEUM MARCH (1877)
by Johann Slack

MSS: Orch 3pp; 29Oct1877 Phila. [LC]
Not pub or ©

ROYAL MARCH (of Spain)
(1889 or before)
Traditional

MSS: Several bd parts in Sousa's hand; nd np
[USMC]
Pub: Coleman (only in bd edition of *National,
Patriotic and Typical Airs of All
Lands*)
Not © for bd

THE SOUTHERN PATROL
(See MARCHING THROUGH GEORGIA)

Miscellaneous

LA BIEN AMADA (1926)
by Jose Padilla

MSS: Bd 7pp; 28Apr1926 Sands Pt. [LC]
Not pub or ©

BOLIVIA NOS EL HA (1889)
National Air of Bolivia
by De Benedicto Vincentti

MSS: Bd 5pp; Aug1889 Washington, D.C.
[LC]
Pub: Coleman (only in bd edition of *National, Patriotic and Typical Airs of All Lands*)
Not © for bd

CENTENNIAL HYMN (no date)
by J. E. Schnoelzer

MSS: N/A (for orch)
Not pub or ©

CENTENNIAL ODE (no date)
by J. Mosenthal

MSS: N/A (for orch)
Not pub or ©

COLUMBIA THE GEM OF THE OCEAN
(See RED, WHITE AND BLUE)

CONSTANCY (no date)
by G. Rizzo

MSS: Bd 6pp; nd np [LC]
Not pub or ©

DANCE (1888)
by ?

At the end of the manuscript of this short piece are the markings "End of Play" and "Finale" but no clue as to the nature of the stage work for which it was written.

MSS: Orch 1pp; 27Aug1888 Phila. [LC]
Not pub or ©

THE FAIRY PIPERS (no date)
by A. Herbert Bremer

MSS: Bd 7pp inc; nd np [LC]
Not pub or ©

GOD SAVE THE QUEEN
(See MY COUNTRY 'TIS OF THEE)

HAIL COLUMBIA (1889)
by Philip Phile (Fyles) and Joseph Hopkinson

MSS: N/A
Pub: Coleman (also included in bd edition of *National, Patriotic and Typical Airs of All Lands*)
Not © for bd

HAIL TO THE CHIEF (1889)
by James Sanderson and Sir Walter Scott

MSS: N/A (for bd)
Pub: Coleman (also included in bd edition of *National, Patriotic and Typical Airs of All Lands*)
Not © for bd

HYMN OF THE PROCLAMATION OF THE REPUBLIC (of Brazil)
Music by Leopoldo Miguez
Words by Medeiros and Albuquerque

MSS: Bd 4pp; 24May1890 Washington, D.C.
[in possession of Leonard V. Meretta, Western Michigan Univ.]
Pub: Coleman (only in bd edition of *National, Patriotic and Typical Airs of All Lands*)
Not © for bd

IMOGENE WALTZES (1877)
by Simon Hassler

MSS: Orch 3pp; 28Feb1877 Phila. [LC]
Not pub or ©

THE IRISH WEDDING (1890)
by Charles Puerner

MSS: Bd 10pp; Aug1890 Washington, D.C.
[LC]
Not pub or ©

LEAD, KINDLY LIGHT (1901)
by John B. Dykes

MSS: N/A (for bd)
Not pub or ©

MARIA VALSE (1881)
by Mary Reardon

MSS: Bd 4pp inc; 7Nov1881 Washington, D.C.
[LC]
Not pub or ©

THE MARSEILLAISE (1881)
by Claude Joseph Rouget

MSS: Bd 3pp; 12Sep1881 np [LC]
Not pub or ©

MASS (no date)
by John Esputa, Jr.

MSS: N/A (for v/orch)
Not pub or ©

THE MONONGAHELA WALTZ (1904)
by ?

MSS: N/A (for bd)
Not pub or ©

MY COUNTRY 'TIS OF THEE (1889)
(GOD SAVE THE QUEEN)
by Henry Carey

MSS: N/A (for bd)
Pub: Coleman (also included in bd edition of
*National, Patriotic and Typical Airs
of All Lands*)
Not © for bd

NEARER, MY GOD TO THEE (1889)
by Lowell Mason

MSS: N/A (for bd)
Pub: Coleman
Not ©

OH GOD, OUR HELP IN AGES PAST
(no date)
by William Croft

MSS: Bd 2pp; nd np [LC]
Not pub or ©

AN OLD PORTRAIT (1924)
by James Francis Cooke

MSS: Bd 10pp; 2Sep1924 Willow Grove, Pa.
[UI]
Not pub or ©

QUANT' IO T'AMO (no date)
by G. Satta

MSS: Several bd parts in Sousa's hand; nd np
[UI]
Not pub or ©

RED, WHITE AND BLUE (1889)
(COLUMBIA THE GEM OF THE
OCEAN)
by David T. Shaw

MSS: N/A (for bd)
Pub: Coleman (also included in bd edition of
*National, Patriotic and Typical Airs
of All Lands*)
Not © for bd

**ROCKED IN THE CRADLE OF THE
DEEP** (before 1890)
by Joseph Philip Knight

MSS: N/A (for male quartet and orch)
Not pub or ©

**SHEEP AND GOAT WALKIN' TO THE
PASTURE** (1925)
by David W. Guion

MSS: Bd 12pp; 4Apr1925 Sands Pt. [LC]
Not pub or ©

THE STAR SPANGLED BANNER
(first version) (1890)
by Francis Scott Key

On the second of two stanzas, this version
has variations by the woodwind instruments "à la Wagner," or in the style of
Wagner's *Tannhauser* Overture. It was
first published for band in a special edition
of Sousa's book, *National, Patriotic and
Typical Airs of All Lands* (1890), and
later published separately (1892). A recording by Sousa's Band was made by Ber-
liner (circa 1899) and labeled as "Sousa's
arrangement," but it was probably this
same arrangement minus the Wagner variations, not another version. Sousa had
adapted "The Star Spangled Banner" in a
similar manner in his earlier orchestral fantasy, "The International Congress" (1876).

MSS: N/A
Pub: Coleman
Not © for bd

THE STAR SPANGLED BANNER
(second version) (1918)
by Francis Scott Key
Harmonized by Walter Damrosch and
arranged for band for Sousa

Sousa, along with Walter Damrosch and
three others, was appointed to a committee
established by the U.S. Bureau of Education to standardize "The Star Spangled
Banner." This version is the result.

MSS: N/A
Pub: Schirmer
©: Bd: Schirmer 27Feb1918; ren Schirmer
28May1945

THE SUICIDE (1899)
by ?

MSS: Orch 2pp inc; 14Oct1899 New York
City [LC]
Not pub or ©

TURKEY IN THE STRAW (1921)
Traditional
Arranged by David W. Guion and
transcribed by Sousa

MSS: Bd 14pp; 4May1921 Sands Pt. [LC]

Pub: Schirmer
©: Bd: Schirmer 8Dec1931; ren David W.
Guion & HSA 16Feb1959

DIE WACHT AM RHEIN (1889)
(THE WATCH ON THE RHEIN)
by Karl Wilhelm

MSS: N/A (for bd)
Pub: Coleman (also included in bd edition of
*National, Patriotic and Typical Airs
of All Lands*)
Not © for bd

WE'RE DRIFTING ON (1892)
by Luther B. Noyes

MSS: N/A (for mixed voices and pi)
Pub: National
©: V/pi: National 29Jun1892; not ren

YANKEE DOODLE (1889)
Traditional

MSS: N/A
Pub: Coleman (also included in bd edition of
*National, Patriotic and Typical Airs
of All Lands*)
Not © for bd

LITERARY WORKS

Sousa's reputation as a composer overshadows his reputation as an author to such an extent that most people know nothing of his writings. He wrote seven books, including an autobiography and three novels. He also penned over a hundred articles and letters to the editor. Abstracts of these writings are presented in this section, and they are listed alphabetically within each classification.

Manuscript data is not given for the articles and letters to the editor because very few of the handwritten manuscripts or typescripts have ever been found. Copyright data, on the other hand, has been omitted in the interest of brevity. None of the articles or letters were copyrighted as individual pieces but were instead covered by the copyrights of the publications in which they appeared.

Books

THE FIFTH STRING (1902)
Novel

The Fifth String was the first of Sousa's three novels and could more correctly be called a novelette because of its length; it has 125 pages with generous margins, not counting six color illustrations by the notable American artist Howard Chandler Christy. The book sold over 50,000 copies, probably owing to Sousa's magic name, in spite of generally unfavorable reviews. While critics thought his writing somewhat awkward, they did acknowledge cleverness in the plot, which was a new twist on the old story of selling one's soul to the Devil to gain supernatural powers. It is written in a very direct style and is free of padding, but it lacks polish. It was first offered to the *Ladies' Home Journal* for $5,000, but before the manuscript was submitted for their consideration a more attractive contract was signed with Bowen-Merrill.

Sousa did less philosophizing in this novel than in the two which followed. However, certain of his real-life experiences may be found disguised in the story (such as his mild contempt for concert managers; the book was written shortly after his distasteful lawsuit with the heirs of his former manager, David Blakely). His love for the violin is also visible. Then too, there is a variation of his own experience with the father of an early sweetheart who disallowed her marriage to a musician.

CHARACTERS:

Angelo Diotti, virtuoso violinist from
  Tuscany
Mildred Wallace, beautiful daughter of a
  prominent New York banker
Mr. Wallace, Mildred's father
Uncle Sanders, executive of Wallace's bank
  and friend of the family
Mr. Perkins, impresario and Diotti's
  manager
Mrs. Llewellyn, wealthy patron of musicians
The Devil

SYNOPSIS:

On the evening preceding Diotti's New York debut, he is the honored guest at a reception held by Mrs. Llewellyn. There he meets the captivatingly beautiful Mildred Wallace. To his astonishment he learns that Mildred seems incapable of being moved by the greatest efforts of even the finest artists, though she admires their skill.

At his debut concert, Diotti spies Mildred in the audience and attempts to stir her soul with his artistry. He wins the audience completely, but Mildred's heart is untouched. Feeling that she is superior to his best efforts, he humbles himself and seeks solitude on the island of Bahama. There he studies and practices diligently in an effort to become perfect. Frustrated by the slow pace of his progress, he dashes his violin to the ground and carelessly calls upon the prince of darkness.

The Devil appears and beckons an ancient craftsman, who brings an enchanted violin. It has the usual four strings — which the Devil refers to as the strings of pity, hope, love, and joy — plus a mysterious black string, the string of death. This string is wrapped with the hair of the first mother of man, dating from the Garden of Eden, and he who plays on it must forfeit his life. Diotti tries the violin, avoiding the black string, and realizes that with it he can capture the heart of Mildred and conquer the musical world.

Diotti returns to New York and again spots Mildred in the audience at his next concert. His playing enraptures not only the audience, but Mildred as well. They fall in love. Mildred's father is opposed to her marrying a musician, however. He enlists the aid of his aging associate Sanders, whom Mildred respects, to attempt to separate the young lovers. When Diotti plays for them at a party, Sanders notices the fifth string and how Diotti carefully avoids it. He privately suggests to Mildred that the string is made from the hair of another woman in Diotti's life.

Diotti and Sanders leave the party together and escape the cold with hot toddy at Sanders's home. A snowstorm comes up,

and Diotti is obliged to stay overnight. After he retires, Sanders is overcome by curiosity and makes his way quietly downstairs to examine Diotti's violin. A violinist himself in his youth, he cannot resist trying the mysterious fifth string. He is heard by Diotti, who comes downstairs and finds him dead, victim of the violin's fatal power.

Mildred is grieved at Sanders's death and, remembering his remarks about the violin, questions Diotti. He explains its unusual construction, but she refuses to believe that playing on the black string would bring harm. Instead, she jealously believes that it in some way represents another woman's love. At the next concert she threatens to leave him forever unless he plays on the fifth string, thus proving that he loves only her. In desperation he strides to the stage and plays a weird melody on the forbidden string. As the melody becomes higher and softer the string snaps and Diotti falls limp to the floor, dying with a faint smile on his face.

MSS: N/A
Pub: Bowen-Merrill (later Bobbs-Merrill), Indianapolis; later by Grossett and Dunlap, New York City
©: Bowen-Merrill 6Jan1902 again Bobbs-Merrill 13Sep1907; ren JPS 5Mar1929

A HANDBOOK OF INSTRUCTION FOR THE FIELD-TRUMPET AND DRUM
See THE TRUMPET AND DRUM

MARCHING ALONG (1928)
Autobiography

The subtitle of this book, *Recollections of Men, Women and Music,* is a good indication of the reading matter to be found within its covers. It is filled with personal glimpses of Sousa's associations with people of all walks of life. His associations with five presidents of the United States are particularly interesting. The accounts of his travels, triumphs, and failures are engagingly presented. The volume was long awaited, and it reveals a Sousa seldom seen by the public. It is readable and entertaining.

Marching Along is by no means the complete story of John Philip Sousa. It was written four years before his death, and several milestones of his career were omitted. From a biographer's point of view, considerable reading between the lines is necessary because the chronology is sometimes incorrect and important details are often lacking.

Sousa has drawn heavily on previously written articles, and it is likely that he had this autobiography in mind when writing some of them. Nearly all of the book appeared three years earlier in serial form in the *Saturday Evening Post.* The series was entitled "Keeping Time." Also, he borrowed some material from his *Through the Year with Sousa* (1910).

Unfortunately, the list of compositions at the end of the book is very inaccurate. It is incomplete, of course, partly because Sousa was active in composition after the book was published, but mainly because of many omissions. Indeed, well over a hundred compositions are missing from this index. There are also a few double listings. And none of his 309 arrangements and transcriptions is mentioned. One might surmise that Sousa had little to do with the preparation of the index.

MSS: N/A
Pub: Hale, Cushman and Flint, Boston
©:   Hale, Cushman and Flint 26Apr1928;
      ren JPrS & HSA 12Mar1956

NATIONAL, PATRIOTIC AND TYPICAL AIRS OF ALL LANDS (1890)

In his years as leader of the U.S. Marine Band, Sousa had collected a wide range of music characteristic of various countries. Even though it was not required of him, the U.S. Marine Band was thus prepared for Washington visits by foreign dignitaries. This caught the attention of Benjamin F. Tracy, secretary of the navy. One day when he complimented Sousa on his industry, Sousa asked permission to expand the collection and publish it by his authority. Tracy issued an order to that effect on October 18, 1889, and Sousa went to work

on the book. Most of his research was done at the Library of Congress.

The work is scholarly, and it was well received at home and abroad. Among the 239 compositions were many grass roots songs, like those of American Indians. Sousa added harmony to some of the tunes. His explanatory notes are very informative.

The work was immediately put to official use by the navy. "The Star Spangled Banner" was played at morning colors and "Hail Columbia" at evening colors aboard ships, again by direction of Secretary Tracy. This, incidentally, was the first official recognition of "The Star Spangled Banner." Some of the airs were later extracted and published in a separate set of books.

MSS: (Eskimo Indian Songs [3]) 1pp; nd np
      [LC]
Pub: Coleman; later by Fischer
©:   E-flat cornet book: Coleman
      11Nov1889; ren JPS 18Aug1917
      V/pi: Coleman 22Nov1890; ren JPS
      31Aug1918
Also pub for other bd instruments but not ©

PIPETOWN SANDY (1905)
Novel

The importance of this novel lies not in its literary value but in the glimpses of Sousa's boyhood as seen through the eyes of one of the principal characters, Gilbert Franklin. The story, spread out by incidents which add color but contribute little to the plot, takes place in the southeastern section of Washington, D.C., the scene of Sousa's boyhood. He calls this section Pipetown in the novel. Some of his own poetry is included, and some of this might have been written much earlier, perhaps while he was a member of the Vis-à-Vis, a Washington literary club.

Reviewers pointed out the similarity between this novel and Mark Twain's *Huckleberry Finn.* It sold over 15,000 copies. At 383 pages, it is longer than both of his other novels combined.

CHARACTERS:

Sandy Coggles, adventuresome and not too
   studious schoolboy
Mrs. Coggles, Sandy's mother

Gilbert Franklin, Sandy's friend, a quiet, scholarly schoolboy
Mr. Franklin, Gilbert's father, a lawyer
Mrs. Franklin, Gilbert's mother
Lillian Franklin, Gilbert's younger sister
Gilbert's grandmother
Tom Foley, incorrigible student
Dennis Foley, Tom's vagabond father
Mrs. Foley, Tom's mother
John Hildey, accomplice of Dennis Foley
Zorah Dabney ⎫
Dink Dabney ⎪
Leander Daindridge ⎬ neighborhood boys
Curley Harris ⎪ and girls
Wheareat Curley ⎪
Fatty Beeks ⎪
Matt Johnson ⎭
Titcomb Jebb, proprietor of neighborhood general store
Jedge, neighborhood philosopher
Delia, the Franklin's Negro cook
Miss Latham, teacher at Pipetown's boys' school
Bill Dabney, neighbor, father of Zorah and Dink Dabney
Buck Wesley, neighbor
Police sergeant

SYNOPSIS:

Sandy and the frail, sickly Gilbert become pals. Gilbert helps Sandy with his lessons, and in turn Sandy helps Gilbert grow stronger through athletics. By learning boxing, Gilbert is able to beat the local bully, Tom Foley.

Tom's father, Dennis Foley, has never returned from the Civil War and is presumed dead, but Mrs. Foley has not remarried because of the chance that he might still be alive. She is being courted by Titcomb Jebb, who tries to win her with his poetry.

Mrs. Foley finally agrees to marry Jebb if it can be proved that her first husband is dead. An advertisement is placed in the newspapers of several cities offering a reward for information. Dennis Foley is not dead; he and an accomplice, John Hildey, have become thieves operating in other parts of the country. The advertisement reaches them in Chicago, and Foley sends Hildey to declare that he is indeed dead. They plan to split the reward money. Hildey convinces everyone that Foley is dead and does collect the money. He does

not return to Foley, however, but spends most of the money on drinking and gambling.

Foley, getting impatient, returns to Pipetown and confronts Hildey. They argue bitterly but agree to resume their thievery and make plans to kidnap Lillian Franklin for ransom. Foley makes one unsuccessful attempt alone but is seen by Sandy, whom he knocks unconscious.

In the meantime, Mrs. Foley and Titcomb Jebb set the marriage date. The frustrated Foley appears at the wedding, which is halted. But Sandy recognizes him as the one who tried to kidnap Lillian, and he is jailed.

Foley is not long in jail, however, because Hildey breaks him out. Together they succeed in kidnapping Lillian, and they hold her hostage in a cave by the river. It happens that Sandy knows that area well; following a hunch, he leads Gilbert and some other boys to the hideout. While Foley and Hildey are away, they rescue Lillian and start down the river in their boat. The kidnappers return in time to spot them and give pursuit. The kidnappers' boat fails to negotiate a rapids, capsizes, and they both drown.

In proper storybook fashion, the novel ends happily, with the heroes called upon time and time again to tell the story of Lillian's rescue and their wild chase. Jebb and Mrs. Foley are finally married.

MSS: a) Handwritten and typed draft [LC]
     b) Typescript with corrections in Sousa's hand [LC]
Pub: Bobbs-Merrill, Indianapolis
©: Bobbs-Merrill 10Aug1905; ren JvMS 20Jul1933

THROUGH THE YEAR WITH SOUSA
(1910)
Musical Almanac

For each day of the year, Sousa provides a musical sketch, an excerpt from one of his literary works, some of his miscellaneous verse, a lyric from one of his operettas, or one of his views on many subjects. For interest he also lists the names of one or more musicians whose birthdays fall on each day.

The musical sketches are of Sousa's own music and are in his own hand. Some are appropriately chosen for the date, such as "Sound Off" for New Year's Day, "The Liberty Bell" for Independence Day, and "Hail to the Spirit of Liberty" for Bastille Day. Of historical interest are his sketches of "The Phoenix March" (1875) and "Recognition March" (date unknown). The almanac provides the only glimpse of these two compositions; neither was ever published, and the whereabouts of their manuscripts is not known.

MSS: N/A
Pub: Thomas Y. Crowell & Co., New York City
©:   Thomas Y. Crowell & Co. 15Sep1910; ren JvMS 20Apr1938

THE TRANSIT OF VENUS (1919)
Novel

Sousa's third and last novel did not enjoy the popularity of either *The Fifth String* or *Pipetown Sandy,* even though it is better written. It is free of padding but not free of sermonizing, and much of Sousa's philosophy of life comes through. It is 250 pages long — well over twice the length of *The Fifth String*. The publishers wanted to reissue the book as *The Alimony Club,* but their plans did not materialize.

CHARACTERS:

Edward Stoneman, handsome young playboy
John Stoneman, Edward's millionaire father
Nancy Burroughs, attractive opera singer
Mrs. Burroughs, Nancy's dominating mother
Miranda Bradley, vivacious scientist
Captain Bradley, yacht skipper and Miranda's uncle
Mr. Curlip, president of the Alimony Club
Mr. Skaggs ⎫
Mr. Anderson ⎪ members of the Alimony
Mr. Scroggins ⎬ Club
Mr. Barstars ⎭
Von Stuefen, German newspaperman

SYNOPSIS:

Edward Stoneman throws a lavish party in New York for Nancy Burroughs, whom he considers marrying. Mrs. Burroughs, cognizant of Edward's wealth, persuades Nancy to drop another suitor and prepare herself for Edward's expected proposal. But Edward's plans are wrecked by his father, who lectures him about irresponsibility and vows to disinherit him if he marries. Edward settles down to work at a brokerage firm which his father had established for him. He works so hard that after a few months his health is endangered and he is forced to take a long vacation.

He elects to take a cruise in a yacht which has been hired for an astronomical expedition to witness the transit of Venus. The only other passengers are a scientist and five wealthy divorced men — the charter members of the unique Alimony Club. They are taking a two-month cruise to avoid women, as stipulated in their club rules. But once at sea they discover that the scientist is a girl. The scientist originally scheduled for the trip had died at the last moment, and the only substitute the captain could find on such short notice was his own niece, Miranda. The men argue over whether to put her ashore at the first port. But her beauty and charm wins them over, and she stays.

Soon Curlip, president of the Alimony Club, and the other members are courting Miranda, as is Edward. One by one they leave the expedition for various reasons, and only Miranda, Edward, and Curlip are left. When Miranda saves Edward's life by shooting a sea elephant which attacks and wounds him, the attraction between them grows. Curlip, however, is still competing for her affections.

The party stops at Cairo, where they attend a performance of *Aida*. The star of the opera happens to be none other than Nancy Burroughs, Edward's former sweetheart. And it turns out that Curlip was Nancy's other suitor whom she had rejected months earlier in favor of Edward. But Edward is now much in love with Miranda, so Nancy and Curlip rekindle their romance and are married.

Back in New York, Edward finds that his business has prospered. He is able to free himself of his father's financial influence, and he and Miranda announce their marriage.

MSS: Handwritten and typed draft [LC]
Pub: Small, Maynard & Co., Boston
©:   Small, Maynard & Co. 14Feb1920;
      ren JPrS & HSA 26Dec1947

THE TRUMPET AND DRUM (1886)

While leader of the U.S. Marine Band, Sousa was well aware of trumpet and drum corps activities in Washington, both civil and military. Perfectionist that he was, he saw a need for greater precision in their playing. His contribution to their betterment was this handbook of instruction. It was his first book. It includes basic music theory, exercises for trumpet, exercises for drums, standard bugle calls, and eight original compositions for trumpet and drum in its 123 pages.

MSS: N/A
Pub: Fischer
©:   JPS 27Dec1886; ren JPS 12Dec1914

Articles

"According to Sousa"
Daily Express (London), January 11, 1905

Asked by the editors to comment on his podium manner, Sousa discusses this and his philosophy of conducting. He compares the inspirations of a conductor to the inspirations of a composer and tells how "The Stars and Stripes Forever" was born.

"All But One Had to Bark"
(See "Facetiae in Music")

"All's Well with the Musical World"
Wurlitzer Magazine (Cincinnati),
December 10, 1920
Reprinted in the 1921 Sousa Band
tour program

Sousa surveys the state of the art of music and concludes that it is stable and now receives greater recognition than ever before. He observes that interest is uniform throughout America on all levels of participation. Begrudgingly, he acknowledges the progress of jazz but notes that Beethoven and others still march onward, unaffected.

"American Music in Paris"
Wire service article, May 12, 1900

During the Sousa Band's first overseas tour, Sousa cabled this article from the Paris Exposition. He gives his impressions of the exposition and reports that the band has been well received.

"American Musical Taste"
Modern Music and Musicians, Part 2,
Volume 3, edited by Louis C. Elson.
New York: The University Society, 1912

America's taste in music is improving, Sousa asserts, and her demand for music is the most cosmopolitan demand in the world. He presents an essay on composing, emphasizing the necessity for inspiration, and explains why he has catered to the American musical taste.

"Appreciations of Rachmaninoff from
Famous Musicians in America"
Etude, October, 1919

Several notable American musicians, including Leopold Stokowski, Charles Wakefield Cadman, and Sousa, contributed to this symposium. Rachmaninoff had been in the United States for two years when the article was written. The contributors testify to his genius, influence, and character.

In Sousa's contribution he states that Rachmaninoff must be considered one of the greats because he has given the world music of lasting value. For instance, he tells how the "C-Sharp Minor Prelude" has won the hearts of the public.

"As to Military Bands"
Independent, September 2, 1897

The history of the military band is traced back to biblical days, and Sousa declares that David was the first important bandmaster. He discusses the role of the military band in various countries. He also discusses the evolution of instruments and gives the current instrumentation of his own band.

"The Band"
American Bandsman, November 15, 1908

This article was intended to be the first of a series Sousa was to write for the *American Bandsman,* but there is no evidence of others having been written. In this one he discusses band development of the past two centuries and tells why he believes a good band is superior to a good symphony orchestra. He foresees a great future for bands in America.

"Being a Musician"
Circle, September, 1909

Several American celebrities were asked to contribute articles for a series called "In the Days of Their Youth," and Sousa submitted this entertaining article. He relates several humorous incidents of his youth and tells of the factors which molded his future.

"The Business of the Bandmaster"
Criterion, August, 1905

The operation of a professional band, according to Sousa, is little different from any other business operation. In auditioning thousands of musicians in his career as a conductor, he has learned that the principle of "survival of the fittest" is predominant. His own concept of the leader-musician relationship is presented, and prerequisites for the musicians of his own band are enumerated. Deviating from the theme of the article, he discusses such subjects as originality, national flavors of music, the social position of musicians, and the future of music in America.

"A Century of Music"
New York World, December 31, 1899

At the close of the nineteenth century, the *New York World* invited a number of prominent Americans to summarize affairs of the century in their respective fields of endeavor. Sousa was asked to report on important musicians. After expounding the virtues of music, he names twenty-three composers whom he believes contributed most to nineteenth-century music, modestly excluding himself. Not to be discounted are several unnamed instrumental performers. Curiously, singers are not mentioned.

"Commander John Philip Sousa Tells of His Tour with the Offenbach Orchestra"
Etude, July, 1930

Sousa tells of touring with the *Matt Morgan's Living Pictures* show as orchestra leader [in the spring of 1876] and of his experiences while playing under Offenbach's direction at the Centennial Exposition in Philadelphia [later that spring]. His article was printed as an insert in a lengthy article about Offenbach.

"The Days of My Youth"
(See "Being a Musician")

"Development of Military Band"
Focus (New York), February 7, 1903

Sousa traces the history of the military band to its origin in antiquity and tells of the invention and development of various band instruments. He gives the Sousa Band's instrumentation for the 1902-3 season and explains the character and function of each instrument. He encourages the amateur musician and predicts that American military bands will soon be manned almost exclusively by American, not European, musicians. Much of this article was quoted from an earlier article, "Queer Instruments in the Modern Military Band."

"Differences of Opinion as to Correct Metronomic Tempo Indications"
Metronome, April, 1917

The editors of *Metronome* solicited the opinions of several prominent band conductors on what should be the correct tempo markings for Suppe's *Pique Dame* Overture. In Sousa's response he cites his own preferences and adds some generalized remarks about why conductors often deviate from the tempi specified by composers.

"The Experiences of a Bandmaster"
Youth's Companion, September 27, 1900

Sousa presents anecdotes of his conducting career, first with the U.S. Marine Band and then with the Sousa Band. He revised most of the stories and used them later in *Through the Year with Sousa* and/or *Marching Along.*

"A Fable with a Moral"
M.A.P. (London), January or February, 1911

For the performance of a symphony, Sousa points out that it is necessary to have a composer, an orchestra, a conductor, and an audience. This fable tells what can happen if one element is overlooked.

"Facetiae in Music"
Town Topics (New York), December 12, 1907

Several of Sousa's favorite anecdotes are related in this article. One story might well be considered a confession — he tells of drinking excessively in celebrating the enthusiastic reception given his band at its first concert in Berlin. Another anecdote, concerning his experience as a bass drummer in an amateur "mountaineer" band, was reprinted in several American newspapers under the title "All but One Had to Bark."

"Following the Band"
Country Gentleman, September, 1928

Sousa touches on many musical subjects, but the main purpose of this lengthy article is to give encouragement to young musicians. He advises them to make efficient use of their time and cites success stories of several outstanding Sousa Band

members. He expresses optimism over the future of the professional musician in America, stating that America can be the greatest musical nation "if everybody follows the band."

"The Force of Music"
American Legion Weekly, September 1, 1922

The theme of this article is that music fulfills one of mankind's crying needs and plays a vital role in all periods of one's life. Sousa traces the history of music back to biblical times and discusses the uses of various types of music. He also discusses patriotic music of the United States.

"From the Gardens of Paradise to the Great Industrial Plants"
Etude, June, 1923

Of the eight contributors to a symposium entitled "Music and Labor," Sousa alone does not stick to the script. The theme of this collection of articles and letters is the need for music in business and industry. Such notables as U.S. Secretary of Labor James J. Davis and Senator James Couzens of Michigan expound on the benefits which businesses and industries derive from the sponsorship of bands.

Sousa's article, however, is a short history of music. It starts with a discussion of how man's first music came by way of imitating animal sounds. Then it progresses to music of biblical times and on to modern times where industrial bands are promoted for two-thirds of a paragraph. The pun in the title is typical Sousa wit.

"The Future of Grand Opera in New York"
Sun (New York), August 10, 1913

Sousa was one of thirteen prominent New York music personalities contributing to this article speculating on the future of opera in the United States. He foresees specialization in the major opera houses; some will perform only German opera, some

French, some Italian, and so forth. As soon as this is established, New York will be the mecca for composers, librettists, and performers.

"The Future of Music in America"
Pacific Monthly, May, 1899

At the turn of the century Sousa is surveying the status of music in the United States. He states that the love of music is more universal there than in any other country and presents his argument. There is a considerable amount of inspired American music at the grass roots level, he observes, suggesting that an American school of music may grow from this. It is in this article that he first writes that he would rather be the composer of an inspired march than of a manufactured symphony.

"The Greatest Game in the World"
Baseball Magazine, February, 1909

Sousa believes that baseball is distinctively American and that it is superior to any other game played with ball and bat. He tells of his own passion for the game, citing experiences from his childhood. He also tells of the Sousa Band's baseball team and quotes from newspaper accounts of their games.

"Here's Sousa's First Self-Written Interview"
Los Angeles Times, October 16, 1911

Responding to a request from the editor, Sousa wrote this article to tell of the business aspects of touring with a large musical organization. Many interesting statistics and some rare anecdotes are given. The article was dictated to his secretary en route from San Bernardino to Los Angeles.

"His Experiences as a Bandmaster"
Pearson's Weekly (London), April, 1903

Presented here are several of Sousa's favorite anecdotes, derived, as the title implies, from his own experiences as a bandmaster.

"A Horse, a Dog, a Gun and a Girl"
American Shooter, August 15, 1916

Sousa gives suggestions for the proper care of horses. One of his favorite sayings apparently was coined in this article — that a horse, a dog, a gun, and a girl was his idea of heaven. A man should give his horse loving care, he says, because the horse is one of man's two most loyal companions. The other is the dog.

"How I Built the Sousa Band"
Life (Australia), January 9, 1911

While passing through Australia on the world tour of 1910-11, Sousa wrote this article to explain the instrumentation of his band and to tell of the band's formation and development.

"How I Earned My Musical Education"
Etude, November, 1908

Sousa is one of several notable American musicians contributing short articles in answer to the editor's inquiries regarding their musical educations. He replies that his father paid the bill for his early training, so it cannot be said that he earned it. However, it was a struggle after leaving the parental roof. He adds that he'd like to go back and do it all over again.

"How to Make Programs"
Musical Record, December, 1893

The public generally prefers entertainment to education when attending concerts, according to the theory advanced in this article. In effect, Sousa is defending his philosophy of programming. The article is part of a column entitled "Helpful Hints."

"The Ideal Band"
Independent, January 25, 1900

It is Sousa's opinion that an ideal band, which has never existed and never will exist, would require perfect instruments, players, and leadership, and that it would most likely be found in America. He expresses optimism concerning the future of the arts in America and says that competition is a major factor in its growth. He also tells of his opposition to governmental subsidization of art.

"If I Had to Begin All Over Again"
Etude, December, 1916

Sousa is one of several distinguished musicians contributing to this symposium, in which the contributors answer the editor's question of how they would relive their lives if given the opportunity to "start all over again." In Sousa's cleverly worded response, he reflects on milestones of his career and states that he would follow the same path he has followed since childhood.

"I'm Not Saying Good-bye"
Pearson's Weekly (London), September 1, 1911

At the time of this article the Sousa Band was on its world tour and was visiting Britain for the fifth and final time. Future bookings in the United States were so numerous that the band management had proclaimed this a "farewell tour" for Britain. In response to public sentiment Sousa wrote this article to clarify his position in the matter. He tells of several incidents which had made his foreign tours difficult but says that he too will be disappointed if he is unable to return.

"In the Days of My Youth"
M.A.P. (London), October 19, 1901

M.A.P. was running a series of autobiographical articles by celebrities, and this was Sousa's contribution. He tells of his early musical training and career, suggesting that it was his destiny to become a musician. At the conclusion of the article he outlines current activities of the Sousa family.

"In the Days of Their Youth"
(See "Being a Musician")

"Jazz Will Never Replace Great American Marches"
Wire service article, April 27-28, 1928

Weighing the merits of marches and jazz, Sousa declares that martial music appeals both to the emotions and the intellect, whereas jazz appeals only to those who crave strongly rhythmical music. He observes that American jazz is popular only in America, while American marches are popular the world over.

"John Philip Sousa on Trap Shooting in America"
Sketch (London), January 18, 1911

Sousa gives a brief history of clay pigeon shooting in the United States, discusses the major American tournaments, gives tips on shooting, and tells why the sport is appealing.

"John Philip Sousa Writes on 'Tunes' for Our Family Music Page Readers"
(See "Start with a Tune")

"Keeping Time"
Saturday Evening Post, November 7, 14, 21, 28; December 5, 12, 1925

This series of six lengthy articles later was used as the basis for Sousa's autobiography, *Marching Along* (1928).

"King David First Bandmaster"
Spokane (Wash.) *Chronicle,* August 6, 1915

The evolution of musical instruments always held a fascination for Sousa. In this article he discusses the instruments of current orchestras and bands and traces their development back to biblical times. He states that the first organizer of an instrumental ensemble mentioned in history was David and reasons that he had a basic understanding of tone-color effects.

"The King of Instruments?"
Etude, April, 1932

Printed posthumously, this was Sousa's last

article. It is a discourse on the drum family which would do credit to the most knowledgeable percussionist. An informative description of the most important percussion instruments is given, with explanations of their functions. A list of compositions in which they are featured is also given. The drum is the king of instruments, Sousa proclaims, because drums of one kind or another play important parts in 95 percent of all orchestral and band works.

"Leave German Music to Germans" *Musical Leader,* October 10, 1918

In this strongly worded World War I article, Sousa caustically comments on his interpretation of the German's attitude toward music. The German people believe they have a monopoly on good music, he asserts. The only answer to their vanity, as he sees it, is to leave German music to the native German and to "bludgeon him physically, mentally, morally, financially, and perpetually."

"Let's Go Down the Highroad of Music — Together" *Music Magazine,* September, 1929

As one who has traveled far down the highway of music, Sousa recommends that children study music and advises parents to encourage them. He sees America becoming the dominant nation in music. He commends students in general for laying the foundation for a nation of better minds and recognizes a spiritual awakening in the arts. Since there is a need for players of all instruments, the student is advised to select the one he likes best and to strive for perfection. Progress in popular music is acknowledged, and the student of jazz is advised to take that idiom seriously.

"Making America More Musical" *Woman's Home Companion,* July, 1925

Sousa notes a steady growth of America's musical life but assures the reader that there is no danger of overindulgence. He discusses music on the nonprofessional level, praising town and industrial bands and offering suggestions for the advancement of music. One of these suggestions is that intercity band leagues be formed. Town bands would compete against one another in major and minor leagues, as in baseball. Another suggestion is that schools investigate the advantages of classroom music instruction. He is critical of most jazz and states that children should be exposed to music of higher caliber.

"The March King Answers Questions from Beginners" (26 articles) *Chicago Daily News,* April 30-May 7, 1927, and December 6-14, 1928 (15 articles) *Cleveland News,* August 16-20, 1927 (5 articles) *Detroit News,* April 25-30, 1927 (6 articles)

Named temporary music editor of several large city newspapers, Sousa answers the inquiries of readers. The articles were timed to coincide with appearances of the Sousa Band in those cities. Another series was scheduled for the *Atlantic City Press* in July, 1927, but was run as a series of interviews instead.

"The Menace of Mechanical Music" *Appleton's Magazine,* September, 1906

Aside from the 1925 series of autobiographical articles in the *Saturday Evening Post,* this was the most significant of Sousa's magazine articles. It was written shortly after his participation in congressional hearings on copyright legislation held in 1906. It is a bitter assault on the recording and piano-roll industries, especially the former. The article created interest in the controversy and brought a volley of protests and endorsements. It was accompanied by a series of cartoons which left no doubt about his firm stand. The fact that the mild-mannered Sousa would be so severe and outspoken on any subject came as a surprise to the general public.

He notes that advances in technology have permitted a rapid growth in the number of mechanical reproducers of music.

He sees music, a sincere expression of the soul, being reduced to a mechanical, mathematical system. He states that phonographs and piano players, by eliminating the necessity of studying music, will cause the disappearance of amateur musicians and music teachers, leaving only professionals and mechanical devices.

He declares his willingness to be classified as an alarmist, risking this to bring his argument to the readers, and admits that he is swayed by a personal interest. Referring to an amendment to the copyright law which is currently being considered, he criticizes one particular phonograph company representative for brazenly exploiting the creative efforts of composers while expecting full government protection on his own phonograph patents. For this reason Sousa charges the manufacturers of mechanical reproducers of music with being blind to the moral and ethical questions involved.

Sousa feels that he, as a composer, should have the power of controlling his own compositions, interpreting one section in the U.S. Constitution as being protective of his own creations. He adds that composers will lose incentive without this protection and that all the parties will suffer.

"Misplaced Men Drag Way through Life" Wire service article, October, 1922

A person should work at what he likes best, says Sousa. Otherwise he might drag his way through life in a state of morbid apathy. Parents are advised to guide their children into occupations suited to their capacities and desires. A brief autobiography is presented, and Sousa reveals that he developed rapidly in his profession because his parents gently encouraged him to pursue his own first love.

"The Most Familiar Melody in the World" *Great Lakes Recruit,* March, 1918

This is a short treatise on the history of the song "God Save the King," or "My Country 'Tis of Thee," known in several countries as a national song. Lieutenant Sousa asks why a monument should not be erected to Henry Carey, whom he credits with its composition. At the conclusion of the article he answers readers' questions on musical subjects. The most revealing is his explanation of the background of his march, "Hands Across the Sea," which he says was inspired by an obscure quotation.

"Music, an Ideal Christmas Present" *Etude,* December, 1921

Sousa observes that music has changed greatly since the days of Beethoven; it now has commercial rewards for composers and performers. A gift of music would therefore be a practical Christmas present, especially for children. He states that gifts of music will outlast the usual Christmas presents. Among the musical gifts he suggests are lessons, instruments, sheet music, concert tickets, and phonograph records.

"Music and Labor" (See "From the Gardens of Paradise to the Great Industrial Plants")

"Music Becomes a Profession" 1926 Sousa Band souvenir program

The American public is liberal in its support of music, Sousa notes. It has not always been, however, as evidenced by the struggles of his own career. He points to progress on many levels of music participation and remarks that perhaps this has been the most gratifying development of his time.

"Music We Must Have" *Chicago Tribune,* November 23, 1890

The editors had asked Theodore Thomas, Walter Damrosch, Sousa, and several other prominent musicians for their comments on the nature of music which should be presented at the Chicago World's Fair (Columbian Exposition). Most important was the issue of whether or not new music should be written by American or foreign composers. Sousa weighs many factors and concludes that a competition should be open to composers of all nations but that American music should be given precedence on official days.

"Musical Instruments Like Men in Disposition"
Northward-Ho!, September(?), 1912
(Reprinted in *Musical America,*
September 28, 1912)

The theory advanced in this article is that people and instruments are sometimes alike in that they have similar dispositions. For example, a shrieking fife may be likened to a hysterical woman. Another example is the stolid man, thinking of nothing but breakfast, lunch, dinner; breakfast, lunch, dinner; ad infinitum, who may be likened to the bass drum with its thump, thump, thumping.

"Musicians of the Nineteenth Century"
(See "A Century of Music")

"My Contention"
Music Trades, Christmas issue, 1906

After studying the history of copyright law in the United States and other countries, Sousa reports on his findings. His conclusion is that the U.S. Constitution (namely, Article I, Section 8) clearly protects a composer's interest but that courts have not been consistent in their interpretations. This was the third of three articles written by Sousa in 1906 to gain support for composers in pending copyright legislation.

"My Dreadful Past"
Pearson's Weekly (London), September 3, 1911

In this short article Sousa presents anecdotes concerning his first music teacher, the elderly John Esputa.

"My Hobby — Trapshooting"
Country Life in America, June, 1914

Sousa tells of trapshooting's attributes and stresses the point that the sport is the apex of social democracy — like love, it levels all classes. He asserts that every man should have a hobby and explains why trapshooting is his. He discusses various aspects of the sport and accounts for its popularity in America. Three photographs showing him in action are included.

"Oh, Listen to the Band!"
Sousa Band souvenir program, 1920

Presented here is a concise history of military bands and a report on their current status. It is Sousa's dream that cities will some day form band leagues similar to baseball leagues. He summarizes his navy activities of 1917-18 and gives the instrumentation of his "Jackie" band. On the value of music in war and peace, he closes with this thought: "If the student of War and its means to a triumphant end places music as one of its first essentials, certainly Peace — nurturing the beautiful, replenishing the earth, bringing joy to mankind — should crown Music as its loveliest handmaiden."

"Parents of Patriotism Are Mother and Music"
Chicago Examiner, March 7, 1918

Sousa is of the opinion that a man's patriotism is brought out most effectively by two forces: music and motherhood. A man's patriotism may be aroused temporarily by patriotic music, but he has an eternal passion for his homeland if his mother sang native songs to him as a child. Much of this article had appeared in an earlier article, "Sidelights on Music."

"Playing 'The Star Spangled Banner' 'Round the World"
Ladies' Home Journal, December, 1917

The origin of "The Star Spangled Banner" is discussed. Sousa then presents anecdotes and interesting accounts of the piece as performed by his band in several foreign countries.

"Queer Instruments in the Modern
Military Band"
Wire service article, November, 1902

In discussing the history of various musical
instruments, Sousa reveals that several unusual instruments are presently being used
in the Sousa Band. One is the double-bell
euphonium. The other is the sarrusophone,
which he claims is used by no other band
in the United States. Pictures of both these
instruments are presented. [Note: Sousa
used the sarrusophone in his band only for
a short period, but the double-bell euphonium was a featured solo instrument for
many years.]

"Ready! Pull! Dead!"
New York Sun, June 14, 1914

Sousa gives the reasons for his great love
of trapshooting, the newest major sport in
the United States. He also explains some
of the lingo used by shooters. Two rare
photographs of Sousa on the firing line
are included.

"Sidelights on Music"
Pittsburgh Dispatch, September 18, 1907

A discourse on the antiquity of music, this
article declares that King David of biblical
times was the first bandmaster. Sousa
points out that the art of music is almost
as old as man-made laws.

"Songs of a Century That Never Grow
Old" (22 articles)
Wire service articles, 1924

In each of the articles comprising this
series Sousa presents the history of a well-
known song. The songs are: "Annie
Laurie," "Auld Lang Syne," "Battle Hymn
of the Republic," "Ben Bolt," "Comin'
Thru the Rye," "Dixie," "Drink to Me
Only with Thine Eyes," "From Green-
land's Icy Mountains," "John Brown's
Body," "The Last Rose of Summer," "The
Marseillaise," "Maryland, My Maryland,"
"Men of Harlech," "My Old Kentucky
Home," "Nearer, My God to Thee," "O,
Come, All Ye Faithful," "Old Black Joe,"

"Old Folks at Home," "The Old Oaken
Bucket," "Old Russian National Hymn,"
"The Star Spangled Banner," and "Yankee
Doodle."

"Songs of the Sea"
Great Lakes Recruit, December, 1917

Sousa always had a strong interest in sea
songs, as evidenced by this short article.
He traces their origin back to biblical
times, noting that England is an important
contributor and that the United States,
child of England, has done well in the tradition. He observes that nearly all sea
songs reflect the love of one's native land
and that sailors are preeminently patriotic
because of this.

"Sousa on the Influence of the Band
in Musical Education"
Metropolitan Magazine, July, 1900

One of the central points of Sousa's music
philosophy is brought out in this brief article. He defines classical music as "that
kind of music based upon natural laws
and finding an echo in the heart of the
universal world." In this broad sense, he
maintains that concert bands play a considerable amount of classical music and
therefore contribute greatly to the musical
education of the masses.

"Sousa — Who Has Made $1,000,000
with His Brass Band"
Farm and Fireside, January, 1924

This is the only Sousa article known to
have been ghost-written. It was pieced together from interviews by Earl C. Reeves,
who traveled with the Sousa Band to
gather material.

Sousa discusses the formula for his highly
successful concerts. According to this formula he uses a band rather than some
other kind of musical organization and
presents good music while still catering to
the public taste. He defines good music,
incidentally, as that which is demanded
the world over because it satisfies the longing for melody. Such music is the product
of inspiration, he adds.

"The Star Spangled Banner in Petrograd"
New York Telegram, circa 1916
(Reprinted in *Etude,* November, 1916)

This article was extracted almost word for word from Sousa's 1910 book *Through the Year with Sousa,* where it is found as the entry for May 28. He recounts the thrilling performance of the American and Russian national anthems by his band at a concert in Petrograd on the czar's birthday in 1903. He makes the statement that "No body of musicians ever played a piece with more fervor, dignity, and spirit than our boys did. . . ."

"Start with a Tune"
Evening Mail (New York),
October 14, 1921

While recovering from a fall from his horse near Willow Grove, Pennsylvania, Sousa penned this article for Charles D. Isaacson's column, "Our Family Music." He discusses the necessity of melody in music.

"Success in Music and How to Win It"
Published in an advertising booklet
of C. G. Conn, Ltd., 1926
(Reprinted in *Selmer Bulletin,*
October, 1926)

Sousa gives pointers to the young musician, stating that the first consideration in a music career is a respect for the public. One should compose or play up to the public, not down to it. He underscores the value of inspiration in both composition and performance and cites several classics as examples of compositions which are perennial favorites because they were inspired. He warns against slovenly workmanship and advises one not to enter the field of music with financial gain as the primary motivation.

Beneath a picture of the Sousa Band is Sousa's endorsement of Conn instruments, acquainting the reader with the fact that the entire band is equipped with them.

"The Symphony Orchestra and the
Concert Band"
Etude, May, 1917

In this article, which was reprinted in the Sousa Band souvenir program of 1920, Sousa outlines the history of music, commencing with biblical times. The emphasis is on instrumentation in general, but he also discusses the characteristics of individual band and orchestral instruments. Comparing the overall effects of both the band and the orchestra, he concludes there is a place for both. Several of the basic ideas of the article reappeared in a later *Etude* article, "What Every Music Lover Should Know about the Band" (February, 1927).

"Then and Now"
Etude, May, 1921

The editor of *Etude* asked several distinguished musicians to write articles comparing musical activities and opportunities of the past with those of the present. This article was the first of the series. Sousa explains that his ambitions were eventually realized because of his sincere efforts as a youth. He points out that an individual's success in nearly any endeavor depends upon his capacity for hard work.

"The Ultimate Musical Choice"
Etude, July, 1930

In this article famous Americans from many walks of life respond to the editor's question of what musical composition they would choose if they were told by their physicians that they had but twenty-four hours to live and could hear but one piece of music. In Sousa's brief but touching reply he states that he would choose "The Stars and Stripes Forever" and meet his Maker face to face with the inspiration that grows out of its melodies and the patriotism that gives it meaning.

"The Victrola and I"
Victor Talking Machine Magazine,
December, 1920

In telling of his visit to South Africa in 1911, Sousa leads up to one particular incident in which phonograph records of several of his marches were played for the benefit of natives. When he was introduced to the natives as the originator of the music they were hearing, their reaction bordered on idolatry.

"The Wave of Musical Creation Will Next Reach America"
Wire service article, October, 1913

It is Sousa's theory that musical genius is exotic and can spring up anywhere. He states that the United States will be the home of the next great school of music because its composers have few, if any, superiors abroad.

"We Must Have Standard Instrumentation"
Musical Observer, July, 1930

Whereas the instrumentation of the symphony orchestra is standardized, that of the military band is different in every country, Sousa observes. He is asking for standardization. This article was directed at band conductors, particularly those of the American Bandmasters Association, who had recently chosen him as their first honorary life president.

"What the Band Means to Your Home Community"
Etude, September 1931

The title of this article is misleading, because the band's value to a community is mentioned only briefly. From there Sousa goes on to discuss factors contributing to a band's excellence. In addition, he publicly airs three opinions which he had formerly entertained only privately. The first is that Theodore Thomas was the greatest conductor who ever lived and that Thomas had influenced his career more than any other man. Second, he asserts that Herbert L. Clarke, formerly of the Sousa Band, was the greatest cornetist of all time. Third, he suggests that the music student should be permitted to join school bands only if he excels in other subjects. At the end of the article the editor has added a section called "Sousaisms," which is a collection of quotes from the autobiography, *Marching Along.*

"What Constitutes True Beauty in a Woman"
Great Lakes Recruit, January, 1918

Rather than giving the reader a definition of beauty, Lieutenant Sousa stimulates his thinking. He notes that there is no universal agreement as to what constitutes beauty. Thus beauty is a relative thing, and ideals change with time.

"What Every Music Lover Should Know about the Band"
Etude, February, 1927

Sousa presents an interesting and informative history of instrumental music. He discusses the aesthetic and physical differences between the band and the orchestra and explains how modern instruments evolved. In his opinion, the stature of the band is as great as that of the orchestra. He points out that the development of the band is of extreme importance to the art of music and reminds the reader that every musical instrument added to the orchestra since Haydn's time has come by way of the band.

"What Our National Anthem Should Be"
New York Times, August 26, 1928

Noting that the adoption of "The Star Spangled Banner" as the national anthem of the United States has been under consideration several times in recent years, Sousa outlines the requirements he believes the eventual national anthem should meet. In his opinion it should be founded upon a strong emotional note, have a religious flavor, and emphasize liberty and courage. Musically, it should have a vigorous, inspiring melody and should have a comfortable range and register for singing. Above all, it should be the product of inspiration.

Lest the reader be given the mistaken impression that Sousa is promoting "The Stars and Stripes Forever" as a candidate, it must be noted that in many previous writings and interviews he disqualified it because its range and rhythm are too difficult for dignified singing. Unfortunately, he did not make this point clear in the article.

"What 'Rag Time' Means"
New York World, April 7, 1901

After briefly explaining how the term "ragtime" is commonly used, Sousa explains that the term probably grew from the expression "everybody rag," which is used in American country dances.

"When the Band Begins to Play"
American Legion Monthly, July, 1931

Sousa discusses such things as creativity and his early career, but the main topic is the programming of music. He explains that life is more strenuous in the United States than in most other countries and that audiences there are more restless and expectant of showmanship. He observes that American audiences accept music of all nationalities, whereas European audiences seem to prefer the music of their own countries.

"Where Is Jazz Leading America?"
Etude, August, 1924

Sousa was one of fifteen distinguished musicians or writers asked where jazz was leading America. Each responded with short replies, which were printed as one article. Sousa is almost noncommittal and refers to conflicting definitions of jazz. He passes judgment by quoting a nursery rhyme:
When she was good she was very, very good
And when she was bad she was horrid.

"Why Not Give Music This Christmas?"
Better Homes and Gardens,
December, 1930

Music is a necessary adjunct of boyhood, Sousa maintains, so music will make a splendid Christmas gift. Nearly anything musical — opera tickets, phonograph records, an instrument, lessons — will suffice. He tells of the importance of music in his own youth and gives a discourse on the virtues of music.

"Why the World Needs Bands"
Etude, September, 1930

The world needs bands, Sousa asserts, because it is hungry for the beauty and inspiration provided by music. People need the thrill of a band marching up and down the street. He suggests that if the reader questions the need for bands he should ask a Salvation Army musician who has seen music turn men to a better way of life. After discussing the benefit of bands and music in general, he presents a discourse on the history of band instruments, the finest of which he maintains are now made in America. Among other miscellaneous subjects which he touches on are the amazing status of school bands, the origins of some of his march titles, and the falsity of the "S.O., U.S.A." anagram.

"A Word as to Orchestration"
Music, March, 1897

In this short article Sousa stresses the importance of orchestration to both composer and orchestrator. He points out that the problem of achieving dramatic effects is more difficult than the public realizes and that several notable composers have been barren of ideas. He cites Wagner as the "wizard of the orchestra" in the matter of tone coloring and also names Saint Saëns and Massenet as masters of delicate scoring.

"The Year in Music"
Town Topics (New York),
December 6, 1906

Probably the cleverest of all Sousa's writings, this article was written at the time when he, Victor Herbert, and other composers were battling with the recording industry over pending copyright legislation. Sousa, at his satirical best, is lashing out at the manufacturers of phonographs, recordings, and piano rolls.

The article reviews a fictitious year of music in which nearly all concerts were presented not by live performers but by mechanical reproducers. Audiences listen in ecstacy to recordings played by persons ever so adept at cranking and placing the needle on the recordings. Phonograph orchestras and other such ensembles have replaced most live musicians in this year.

It is a banner year for prodigies, such as those who have earned music degrees overnight by enrolling in accelerated courses in how to pump the player piano.

"The Nineteenth Century in Music"
(See "A Century of Music")

Letters to the Editor

Augusta (Ga.) *Chronicle,* March 17, 1916

A critic of a Georgia newspaper had seen the *Hip Hip Hooray* extravaganza at the New York Hippodrome and had written a false report of Sousa's "March of the States." In one scene dancing girls had figures hanging from their dresses, and the critic interpreted this as a representation of Georgia lynchings. In Sousa's letter he explains that the state being represented in this scene is Nevada, not Georgia, and that the effigies are meant to represent divorced husbands. The music accompanying the scene is "I'm on My Way to Reno" and "Goodbye, Sweetheart, Goodbye," and Sousa suggests that the critic is "ear blind." The newspapers of several other southern cities carried Sousa's letter and editorial comments chastising the wayward critic.

Boston News, April 13, 1904

An earlier issue of this paper had caught Sousa's eye by posing the question, "Is It So or Sousa?" In this letter he states that his name is and always has been Sousa. He tells of his ancestry and adds that he was born "within the shadow of the Capitol" in Washington.

Daily Mail (London), April 22, 1905

This was the third of four letters to London newspapers written in 1903 and 1905 on the subject of piracy in music. Sousa had been following comments by London newspapers and was responding to one editorial in the *Daily Mail* in which the blame had been placed on music publishers be-

cause of their high prices. He is sharply critical of the paper's position and points out that in his own country the practice of selling pirated copies of music is akin to counterfeiting and is punishable by imprisonment. This letter, like an earlier one sent to the *Times,* was written at the request of Willie Boosey, general manager of Chappel and Company, a London music publisher.

Daily Telegraph (London), April 27, 1905

In this, the fourth and last letter to London newspapers regarding music piracy, Sousa lashes out at the irresponsibility of music hawkers. He reveals that recently he had had the music and descriptive materials for his operetta, *The Bride Elect,* shipped to London, but, after having been discouraged by the music pirates, he had declined to permit it to be produced. He makes the point that many professional people depend on a composer for music to be performed and that employment is affected when a composer is discouraged.

Etude, April, 1908

This humorous letter was written in response to a question the editors had raised regarding the origin of Sousa's name. He explains that one of his publicity agents had created the "S.O., U.S.A." anagram about ten years earlier and that the story had spread. Later this reply was used frequently. It was included in *Through the Year with Sousa, Marching Along,* several other articles, and in countless interviews.

Etude, May, 1921

In an earlier editorial, *Etude* had suggested the teaching of social ethics in schools. Their proposition was called "The Golden Hour" plan, and music was among the subjects to be emphasized. Sousa was one of many who enthusiastically endorsed the plan through letters to the editor.

Etude, January, 1926

Sousa is one of several dignitaries paying tribute to the late Theodore Presser, founder of *Etude.* Presser was also head of the firm which published Sousa's last few compositions.

Literary Digest, October 14, 1916

Sousa is again denying the "S.O., U.S.A." anagram.

New York Herald, June 25, 1922

One of the movements of Sousa's suite of 1922, *Leaves from My Notebook,* is called "The Lively Flapper." It depicts a ladies' dress style which was then receiving much criticism. In this letter Sousa refers to a rare book and points out that ladies' styles were the subject of similar scrutiny three centuries ago.

New York Herald, August 19, 1922

Satirically, Sousa is questioning the effectiveness of the Eighteenth Amendment. He suggests that fewer people are "on the water wagon" now than before the days of Prohibition.

New York Herald Tribune, July 16, 1925

After being ruffled by impolite pedestrians on New York's busy Forty-fifth Street, Sousa wrote this letter of protest. He remarks that the huge man who broke his glasses and the fat lady who nearly put his eye out with her parasol could not have descended from monkeys because monkeys are not uncouth.

New York Telegram, March 8, 1920

Noting the success of the American composer-conductor Henry Hadley, Sousa recalls an incident some twenty-five years back when he had predicted a great future for Hadley.

New York Times, November 7, 1915

A week previously, a *Times* reader had inquired if Sousa's name was really Sousa. He responds with this affirmative reply. Under the heading, "In Other Words, It Isn't So," he again discounts the "S.O., U.S.A." story of his name.

Paris Herald, June or July, 1900

While the Sousa Band was in Europe for the Paris Exposition of 1900, Sousa attended concerts by several leading French orchestras and bands. Hearing only one non-French composition in a total of nine concerts, he was prompted to write about the "evil" effects of governmental patronage of the arts. In rebuttal to a reader's reply, Sousa tactfully refutes his critic and leaves no doubt that his position is unaltered. The letters stimulated much editorial comment in French newspapers.

Presto, September 27, 1917

The question of whether or not "The Star Spangled Banner" is officially the national anthem of the United States is clarified. Sousa points out that although such a decision has never been made by Congress, the piece is recognized as the national air by the military services.

Times (London), January 16, 1903

Sousa expresses his astonishment at the sale of pirated editions of his music on the streets of London. This was the first of four letters to London newspapers in 1903 and 1905, and was reprinted in the *Daily Mail* and *Daily News,* as well as in several American newspapers.

Times (London), February 27, 1905

This was the second of four letters to London newspapers on the subject of music piracy in Britain and was written at the request of Willie Boosey of Chappell & Company, a London music publisher. Sousa states emphatically that Britain is the only participant in international copyright conferences who has failed to live up to the agreements. He appeals to Britain's national honor and pride and asks that the government take action to correct the matter.

Washington Post, circa 1890

This humorous letter was reprinted on pp. 96-97 of Sousa's autobiography, *Marching Along.* He is correcting an account printed by the newspaper that erroneously reported on a concert by the U.S. Marine Band which they did not perform.

Westminster (England) *Gazette,*
September 2, 1911

Regarding nationalism in music — one of Sousa's favorite subjects in interviews and conversation — he believes that there is no such thing. While certain types of compositions seem peculiar to one country, he maintains that they would instead be peculiar to other countries if the composers had been born elsewhere. It is not the music itself but the native instruments of a country which give music the flavor of that country.

Miscellaneous Writings

Sousa wrote a number of very short literary pieces which were probably never intended to be included in articles, books, or any collection. They are mostly humorous poems. For the most part, they appeared in columns written by newspaper reporters. A number of items are also found in *Through the Year with Sousa* with the sources not always given. Sousa wrote a number of other verses, none of which was published, for the amusement of friends and associates. Nonsensical rhymes for some of his marches are examples of this. Still other verses are found in Sousa Band programs, where they served as background information on his compositions, particularly the suites. These were seldom accredited to anyone, so it would be an almost impossible task to separate his writing from that of others. Some of his writings no doubt date back to his youth, when he wrote things for Washington's Vis-à-Vis literary club. None of these items has ever been positively identified.

Sousa's most significant unpublished work was an unfinished book which was apparently to be called *In Quest of the Quail* — a handbook for hunters. Fragments of ten chapters were discovered among other documents in 1969 by his granddaughter, Jane Abert.

BIBLIOGRAPHY

Books

Baldwin, Charles E., and Phillips, J. Harry. *History of Columbia Commandery No. 2 Knights Templar 1863-1963* (Washington, D.C.). Private publication, 1963.

Berger, Kenneth. *Band Encyclopedia.* Evanston, Ind.: Band Associates, 1960.

Berger, Kenneth. *The March King and His Band.* New York: Exposition Press, 1957.

Bridges, Glenn. *Pioneers in Brass.* Detroit: Sherwood Publications, 1965.

Burford, Cary Clive. *We're Loyal to You, Illinois.* Danville, Ill.: The Interstate, 1952.

Heney, John J. *The Correct Way to Drum.* St. Augustine, Fla.: Heney School of Percussion, 1934.

Schwartz, Harry W. *Bands of America.* Garden City, N.Y.: Doubleday and Company, 1957.

Smart, James R. *The Sousa Band: A Discography.* Washington, D.C.: Library of Congress, 1970.

Sousa, John Philip. *The Fifth String.* Indianapolis: Bowen-Merrill Company, 1902.

———. *Marching Along.* Boston: Hale, Cushman, and Flint, 1928.

———. *National, Patriotic and Typical Airs of All Lands.* Philadelphia: Harry Coleman, 1890.

———. *Pipetown Sandy.* Indianapolis: Bobbs-Merrill Company, 1905.

———. *Through the Year with Sousa.* New York: Thomas Y. Crowell and Company, 1910.

———. *The Transit of Venus.* Boston: Small, Maynard and Company, 1920.

———. *The Trumpet and Drum.* Publisher not known. 1886.

Sousa's Band. Promotional book published and distributed by the management of Sousa's Band in 1897. Contains reprints of several hundred press reviews of Sousa Band concerts.

Waters, Edward N. *Victor Herbert.* New York: Macmillan Company, 1955.

Articles

Ambrose, Joan. "John Philip Sousa." Publicity release. U.S. Marine Band, 1962.

Bierley, Paul E. "Sousa's Mystery March." *Instrumentalist,* February, 1966.

Dvorak, Raymond F. "Recollections of Sousa's March Performances." *School Musician Director and Teacher,* December, 1969.

Evenson, Orville. "The March Style of Sousa." *Instrumentalist,* November, 1954.

Helmecke, August. "Why the Accents Weren't Written In." *Instrumentalist,* March-April, 1951.

Larson, Cedric. "John Philip Sousa as an Author." *Etude,* August, 1941.

Mangrum, Mary Gailey, as told to Harold Geerdes. "Experiences as Violin Soloist with the Sousa Band." *Instrumentalist,* October, 1969.

———. "Sousa the Patriot." *Instrumentalist,* January, 1970.

Mayer, Francis N. "John Philip Sousa — His Instrumentation and Scoring." *Music Educators Journal,* January, 1960.

Sousa, John Philip. Articles and letters to the editor.

Stewart, G. Hollis. "The Royal Welch Fusiliers March." Publicity release. U.S. Marine Corps Historical Section, December 16, 1930.

Thompson, Harry H. "The Marine Band — The Washington Post." *Marine Corps Gazette,* August, 1932.

Miscellaneous

Copyright entry books (unpublished) and the *Catalogue of Copyright Entries* (published), all volumes, 1870-1969. The unpublished, handwritten copyright entry books are on file at the Copyright Division, Library of Congress.

"John Philip Sousa, 1854-1932." List of Sousa's copyrighted works. Library of Congress, Division of Music, July 23, 1935.

Sousa Band Fraternal Society News, all issues, 1944-1969. Published in Los Angeles, then Anderson, Ind., and then New York. Complete set at the Library of Congress.

Sousa Band press books. Set of eighty-five hardbound scrapbooks containing approximately 55,000 clippings and programs of the Sousa Band, 1892-1931. In custody of the U.S. Marine Corps Museum, Quantico, Virginia.

APPENDIX I

Chronology of John Philip Sousa's Compositions

1872
Waltz, "Moonlight on the Potomac Waltzes" (Opus 3)

1873
March, "Review" (Opus 5)
March, "Salutation"
Song, "Day and Night" (words by Emma M. Swallow)
Song, "Wilt Thou Be True" (poem by E. Cook)
Galop, "Cuckoo"

1874
Song, "O My Country" (words by B. Lowlaws)
Song (untitled) (words by Emma M. Swallow)
"Te Deum in B-Flat" (Opus 12)
Waltz, "La Reine d'Amour Valses" (Opus 9)

1875
March, "The Phoenix March"
Incidental music to *The Phoenix*

1876
March, "The Honored Dead"
March, "Revival March"
Song, "Ah Me!" (poem by Emma M. Swallow) (Opus 29)
Song, "Only a Dream" (words by Mary A. Denison) (Opus 25)
Song, "Only Thee" (poem by Charles Swain) (Opus 24)
Song, "The Song of the Sea" (words by Emma M. Swallow) (Opus 27)
Gavotte, "Myrrha Gavotte" (Opus 30)
Galop, "On Wings of Lightning" (Opus 26)
Fantasy, "Sounds from the Revivals"
Fantasy, "In the Sweet Bye and Bye"
Fantasy, "The International Congress"
Incidental music to *Matt Morgan's Living Pictures*

1877
March, "Across the Danube" (Opus 36)
Song, " 'Deed I Has to Laugh"
Song, "The Free Lunch Cadets"
Song, "Hoping" (poem by Jefferson H. Nones) (Opus 39)
Song, "Lonely" (poem by Jefferson H. Nones)
Song, "Love Me Little, Love Me Long" (Opus 37)
Song, "The Magic Glass" (poem by Charles Swain) (Opus 31)
Waltz, "Sardanapolis"
Fantasy, "Medley"
Overture, "The Rivals"

1878
March, "Esprit de Corps" (Opus 45)
Song, "Mavourneen Asthore" (words by Albert S. Nones)
Song, "Smick, Smack, Smuck"
Schottische, "Silver Spray Schottische"

1879
Operetta, *Katherine* (libretto by Wilson J. Vance)
March, "Globe and Eagle"
March, "On the Tramp"
March, "Resumption March"
Fantasy, "Adamsonia"
Fantasy, "Home, Sweet Home"
Cornet solo, "La Reine d'Amour"

1880
March, "Our Flirtation"
Song, "When He Is Near" (words by Mary A. Denison)
Waltz, "Paroles d'Amour Valses"
Fantasy, "In Parlor and Street"
Fantasy, "Out of Work"
Fantasy, "Under the Eaves"

Incidental music to *Our Flirtations*
Violin solo, "Nymphalin"

1881

Operetta, *Florine* (unfinished) (libretto by
Mary A. Denison)
March, "Guide Right"
March, "In Memoriam"
March, "President Garfield's Inauguration
March" (Opus 131)
March, "Right Forward"
March, "The Wolverine March"
March, "Yorktown Centennial"
Song, "Pretty Patty Honeywood" (poem by
Cuthbert Bede)
Song, "A Rare Old Fellow" (poem by Barry
Cornwall)

1882

Operetta, *The Smugglers* (libretto by
Wilson J. Vance)
March, "Congress Hall"
Song, "Star of Light" (poem by Bessie Beach)

1883

Operetta, *Desiree* (libretto by Edward M.
Taber)
March, "Bonnie Annie Laurie"
March, "Mother Goose"
March, "Pet of the Petticoats"
March, "Right — Left"
March, "Transit of Venus"

1884

March, "The White Plume"
Song, "We'll Follow Where the White Plume
Waves" (words by Edward M. Taber)
Waltz, "Intaglio Waltzes"
"Four Marches for Regimental Drums and
Trumpets"

1885

Operetta, *The Queen of Hearts* (libretto by
Edward M. Taber)
March, "Mikado March"
March, "Mother Hubbard March"
March, "Sound Off"
March, "Triumph of Time"
Song, "Tally-Ho!" (poem by Joaquin Miller)
Waltz, "Wissahickon Waltz"
Humoresque, "A Little Peach in an Orchard
Grew"
Saxophone solo, "Belle Mahone"

1886

March, "The Gladiator"
March, "The Rifle Regiment"
Waltz, "La Reine de la Mer Valses"
Waltz, "Sandalphon Waltzes"
Polonaise, "Presidential Polonaise"

Overture, "Tally-Ho!"
Overture, "Vautour"
Eight pieces for trumpets and drums

1887

March, "The Occidental"
Song, "My Own, My Geraldine" (poem by
Francis C. Long)
Song, "O Ye Lilies White" (poem by
Francis C. Long)
Song, "Sweet Miss Industry" (poem by
S. Conant Foster)
Song, "The Window Blind" (words by
Edward M. Taber)
Caprice, "The Coquette"
Fantasy, "The Blending of the Blue and the
Gray"

1888

Operetta, *The Wolf* (libretto by Sousa)
March, "Ben Bolt"
March, "The Crusader"
March, "National Fencibles"
March, "Semper Fidelis"
Song, "I Wonder" (words by Edward M.
Taber)

1889

March, "The Picador"
March, "The Quilting Party March"
March, "The Thunderer"
March, "The Washington Post"
Song, "Do We? We Do"
Song, "Love That Comes When May-Roses
Blow"
Song, "O'Reilly's Kettledrum" (words by
Edward M. Taber)
Song, "There's Something Mysterious" (words
by Hunter MacCulloch)
Song, "2:15" (words by Edward M. Taber)
Quadrille, "Queen of the Harvest"

1890

March, "Corcoran Cadets"
March, "The High School Cadets"
March, "The Loyal Legion"
Descriptive piece, "The Chariot Race"
Song, "Nail the Flag to the Mast" (poem by
William Russell Frisbie)
Song, "Reveille" (poem by Robert J.
Burdette)
Song, "You'll Miss Lots of Fun When You're
Married" (words by Edward M. Taber)

1891

Descriptive piece, "Sheridan's Ride"

1892

March, "The Belle of Chicago"
March, "March of the Royal Trumpets"

March, "On Parade"
March, "The Triton"
Humoresque, "Good-Bye"
Fantasy, "Songs of Grace and Songs of Glory"

1893

Operetta, *The Devil's Deputy* (unfinished)
  (libretto by J. Cheever Goodwin)
March, "The Beau Ideal"
March, "The Liberty Bell"
March, "Manhattan Beach"
Suite, *The Last Days of Pompeii*
Fantasy, "The Salute of the Nations"

1894

March, "The Directorate"
Song, "Stuffed Stork"

1895

Operetta, *El Capitan* (libretto by Charles
  Klein)
March, "King Cotton"
Suite, *Three Quotations*
Humoresque, "The Band Came Back"

1896

March, "El Capitan"
March, "The Stars and Stripes Forever"
Waltz, "The Colonial Dames Waltzes"

1897

Operetta, *The Bride Elect*
March, "The Bride Elect"
Song, "Maid of the Meadow"
Waltz, "The Lady of the White House"

1898

Operetta, *The Charlatan* (libretto by Charles
  Klein)
March, "The Charlatan"
Pageant, *The Trooping of the Colors*

1899

Operetta, *Chris and the Wonderful Lamp*
  (libretto by Glen MacDonough)
March, "Hands Across the Sea"
March, "The Man Behind the Gun"
Hymn, "Oh, Why Should the Spirit of Mortal
  Be Proud?" (poem by William Knox)

1900

March, "Hail to the Spirit of Liberty"

1901

March, "The Invincible Eagle"
March, "The Pride of Pittsburgh"
Fantasy, "Rose, Thistle and Shamrock"
Concert piece, "The Summer Girl"

1902

March, "Imperial Edward"

Suite, *Looking Upward*
Hymn, "The Messiah of Nations" (poem by
  James Whitcomb Riley)
Fantasy, "In the Realm of the Dance"

1903

March, "Jack Tar"

1904

March, "The Diplomat"
Suite, *At the King's Court*

1905

Operetta, *The Free Lance* (libretto by Harry
  Bache Smith)

1906

March, "The Free Lance"

1907

March, "Powhatan's Daughter"
Song, "I've Made My Plans for the Summer"

1908

March, "The Fairest of the Fair"

1909

Operetta, *The American Maid* (liberetto by
  Leonard Liebling)
March, "The Glory of the Yankee Navy"
Suite, *People Who Live in Glass Houses*

1910

March, "The Federal"
Suite, *Dwellers of the Western World*

1911

Suite, *Tales of a Traveler*
Song, "The Belle of Bayou Teche" (poem by
  O. E. Lynne)

1912

Tango, "The Gilding Girl"
Dance hilarious, "With Pleasure"

1913

March, "From Maine to Oregon"
Song, "It Was Really Very Fortunate for Me"
  (words by Charles Brown)

1914

March, "Columbia's Pride"
March, "The Lambs' March"
Song, "The Milkmaid" (poem by Austin
  Dobson)
Overture, "The Lambs' Gambol"
Processional hymn, "We March, We March to
  Victory" (words by Gerard Moultrie)

1915

Operetta, *The Irish Dragoon* (libretto by
  Joseph Herbert)
Operetta, *The Victory* (unfinished) (libretto
  by Ella Wheeler Wilcox)

March, "The New York Hippodrome"
March, "The Pathfinder of Panama"
Fantasy, "Tipperary"
Incidental music to *Hip Hip Hooray*

1916

March, "America First"
March, "Boy Scouts of America"
March, "March of the Pan-Americans"
Song, "Boots" (poem by Rudyard Kipling)
Song, "Come Laugh and Be Merry" (words by ?)
Song, "The Song of the Dagger"
Fantasy, "On the 5:15"
Incidental music to *Cheer Up*
Concert piece, "Willow Blossoms"

1917

March, "Liberty Loan"
March, "The Naval Reserve"
March, "U.S. Field Artillery"
March, "The White Rose"
March, "Wisconsin Forward Forever"
Song, "Blue Ridge, I'm Coming Back to You"
Song, "The Love That Lives Forever" (words by George P. Wallihan)
Fantasy, "In Pulpit and Pew"

1918

March, "Anchor and Star"
March, "Bullets and Bayonets"
March, "The Chantyman's March"
March, "Flags of Freedom"
March, "Sabre and Spurs"
March, "Solid Men to the Front"
March, "USAAC March"
March, "The Victory Chest"
March, "The Volunteers"
March, "Wedding March"
Song, "In Flanders Fields the Poppies Grow" (poem by John D. McCrae)
Song, "Lovely Mary Donnelly" (poem by William Allingham)
Song, "Pushing On" (words by Guy F. Lee)
Song, "The Toast" (words by R. H. Burnside)
Song, "We Are Coming" (words by Edith Willis Linn)
Song, "When the Boys Come Sailing Home!" (words by Helen Sousa Abert)
Incidental music to *Everything*

1919

March, "The Golden Star"
Song, "The Fighting Race" (poem by J. I. C. Clarke)
Humoresque, "Showing Off before Company"
Humoresque, "Smiles"

1920

March, "Comrades of the Legion"

March, "On the Campus"
March, "Who's Who in Navy Blue"
Suite, *Camera Studies*
Song, "Yale Marching Song" (words by Joseph Grant Ewing)
Ballad for chorus, "The Last Crusade" (poem by Anne Higginson Spicer)
Vocal trio, "Non-Committal Declarations"
Humoresque, "Swanee"
Fantasy, "A Study in Rhythms"

1921

March, "Keeping Step with the Union"
Fantasy, "The Fancy of the Town"

1922

March, "The Dauntless Battalion"
March, "The Gallant Seventh"
Suite, *Impressions at the Movies*
Suite, *Leaves from My Notebook*
Humoresque, "Look for the Silver Lining"
Fantasy, "Music of the Minute"
Fantasy, "An Old Fashioned Girl"

1923

March, "March of the Mitten Men"
March, "Nobles of the Mystic Shrine"
Song, "While Navy Ships Are Coaling" (poem by Wells Hawks)
Fox trot, "Love's But a Dance, Where Time Plays the Fiddle"
Humoresque, "Gallagher and Shean"
Fantasy, "The Merry-Merry Chorus"
Fantasy, "On with the Dance"

1924

March, "Ancient and Honorable Artillery Company"
March, "The Black Horse Troop"
March, "Marquette University March"
Song, "The Journal"
Song, "A Serenade in Seville" (words by James Francis Cooke)
Fox trot, "Peaches and Cream"
Humoresque, "What Do You Do Sunday, Mary?"

1925

March, "The National Game"
Suite, *Cubaland*
Waltz, "The Coeds of Michigan"
Fantasy, "Assembly of the Artisans"
Fantasy, "Jazz America"

1926

March, "The Gridiron Club"
March, "Old Ironsides"
March, "The Pride of the Wolverines"
March, "Sesquicentennial Exposition March"
Song, "Crossing the Bar" (poem by Alfred, Lord Tennyson)

Song, "There's a Merry Brown Thrush"
(poem by Lucy Larcom)
Humoresque, "Follow the Swallow"
Humoresque, "The Mingling of the Wets and
the Drys"
Humoresque, "Oh, How I've Waited for You"

1927
March, "The Atlantic City Pageant"
March, "Magna Charta"
March, "The Minnesota March"
March, "Riders for the Flag"
Song, "Forever and a Day" (words by Irving
Bibo)

1928
March, "Golden Jubilee"
March, "New Mexico"
March, "Prince Charming"
March, "University of Nebraska"
Addenda to suite (*Tales of a Traveler*),
"Easter Monday on the White House Lawn"
Song, "Love's Radiant Hour" (words by Helen
Boardman Knox)
Humoresque, "Among My Souvenirs"

1929
March, "Daughters of Texas"
March, "La Flor de Sevilla"
March, "Foshay Tower Washington Memorial"
March, "The Royal Welch Fusiliers" (No. 1)
March, "University of Illinois"
Fantasy, "When My Dreams Come True"

1930
March, "George Washington Bicentennial"
March, "Harmonica Wizard"
March, "The Legionnaires"

March, "The Royal Welch Fusiliers" (No. 2)
March, "The Salvation Army"
March (untitled)

1931
March, "The Aviators"
March, "A Century of Progress"
March, "The Circumnavigators Club"
March, "Kansas Wildcats"
March, "The Northern Pines"
Song, "Annabel Lee" (poem by Edgar Allan
Poe)

NO DATE
March, "Homeward Bound" (1891 or 1892)
March, "Recognition March" (circa 1880)
March, "Universal Peace" (probably 1925
or 1926)
March, "The Wildcats" (1930 or 1931)
Song, "Fall Tenderly, Roses" (probably late
1860's)
Song, "I Love Jim" (words by Helen Sousa
Abert) (circa 1916)
Song, "It's a Thing We Are Apt to Forget"
(1900 or after)
Song, "Mallie" (words by J. W. Heysinger)
Song, "My Sweet Sweetheart" (words by Jack
Nilpon)
Song, "Sea Nymph" (words by B. P. Wilmot)
Song, "Through Dolly Is Married" (words by
M. E. W.)
Song (untitled) (words by James Adams)
Gavotte, "Alexander" (1876 or 1877)
Humoresque, "The Stag Party" (circa 1885)
Fantasy, "Tyrolienne" (between 1880 and
1892)
Violin solo, "An Album Leaf" (circa 1863)

APPENDIX II

Publishers of John Philip Sousa's Compositions

Code used in this book	*Full name and city location*
Andre	G. Andre & Co., Philadelphia
Balmer & Weber	Balmer & Weber, St. Louis
Barnes	B. F. Barnes & Co., Philadelphia
Bibo	Bibo, Bloedan & Lang, Inc., New York
Chappell	Chappell & Co., Ltd., London
Church	John Church Co., Cincinnati
Coleman	Harry Coleman, Philadelphia
Ditson	J. F. Ditson, Philadelphia, and Oliver Ditson, Boston, New York, and London
Eberbach	Henry Eberbach, Washington, D.C.
Ellis	John F. Ellis & Co., Washington, D.C.
Fischer	Carl Fischer, Inc., New York
Fisk	Fisk, Achenbach & Co. (Stopper and Fisk), Williamsport, Pa.
Flammer	Harold Flammer, Inc., New York
Fox	Sam Fox Publishing Co., Cleveland, New York
Grasmuk & Schott	Grasmuk & Schott, New York
Harms	T. B. Harms & Francis, Day & Hunter, New York
Hitchcock	B. W. Hitchcock (Hitchcock & McCargo), New York
Lee & Walker	Lee & Walker, Philadelphia
Meyer	Louis Meyer, Philadelphia
National	National Music Co., Chicago
North	F. A. North & Co., Philadelphia
Pepper	J. W. Pepper, Philadelphia
Pond	William A. Pond & Co., New York
Presser	Theodore Presser Co., Philadelphia
Schirmer	G. Schirmer, Inc., New York
Shaw	W. F. Shaw, Philadelphia
Stoddart	J. M. Stoddart & Co., Philadelphia
Strawbridge & Clothier	Strawbridge & Clothier, Philadelphia (department store)
Vandersloot	Vandersloot Music Co., Williamsport, Pa.
Witmark	M. Witmark & Sons, New York